PRAISE FOR *STRA~~T~~*
DECISION MAKING

'The timing of this book could not have been better! In a world that is uncertain, with political, economic and social disruption the norm, the insight provided is invaluable. The balance between academic rigour and, crucially, real-life practice, makes it a must-read for any senior executive tasked with the privilege and challenge of making decisions that affect the future of their organization. It is refreshing to read a book about strategy that focuses on the importance of situational factors and, especially, on the impact we have as leaders on strategy and its execution.'
Louise Gulliver, Managing Director, Institute of Directors

'This book presents fresh insights and a contemporary perspective based on an iterative, non-linear approach to strategic decision making. It offers a holistic framework for organizations seeking to adapt to the chaotic and challenging times of the 21st century.'
Stephan Thoma, Executive Advisor, formerly Learning and Development Director, Google

'Most executives struggle with strategy and as the nature and pace of change has accelerated, the challenges have become intractable. This book presents a useful critique of the strategic planning methods we have become used to before going on to set out an approach that is altogether more suited to the digital era. It is an important read for anybody involved in developing strategy.'
Simon Murray, Co-founder of the acumen7 network, former Chairman of Osborne and Non-Executive Director of Highways England

'As an organization operating in a multinational environment, with a fast-changing environmental backdrop coupled with not insignificant internal change programmes, this book delivers pragmatic insights into the realities of modern strategy formulation and execution.'
Russell Higginbotham, Global Head of Life and Health, Swiss Re

'Simon Haslam and Ben Shenoy have the ability to demystify and weave the multitude of theories and models on business strategy into relevant applications for today's complex environment. As an organization that is constantly challenged by global complexity, our leadership team benefited greatly from the ideas in this book and its thought-provoking questions to enable clear strategic pathways and options to be developed. *Strategic Decision Making* is for managers and senior executives trying to navigate complexity in customer, product or service offerings, where a dynamic marketplace demands constant strategic model development.'
Alistair Macdonald, CEO, INC inVentiv

'*Strategic Decision Making* represents a refreshing and challenging view on how leaders and managers make decisions and need to make them in the current era of unprecedented disruption. Bringing to bear ideas of "wicked problems" which challenge the traditional strategic analysis techniques, and expanding on the implications of volatile, uncertain, complex and ambiguous (VUCA) times, the authors introduce, explain and evidence an approach for this century. With due evaluation of classic strategy tools, and both "top-down" and "middle-out" approaches to strategic decision making, an alternative conceptualization is developed around "discovery-led" strategy. This is built around three ideas: framing, experimenting and scaling, which are brought to life with contemporary examples of companies and decisions which have started from big decisions, with small test implementations, which when successful are expanded into businesses we recognize in the 21st century. A recommended alternative take for managers and students alike.'
Professor Susan Hart, Dean, Durham University Business School

Strategic Decision Making

A discovery-led approach to critical choices in turbulent times

Simon Haslam and Ben Shenoy

KoganPage

First published in Great Britain and the United States in 2018 by Kogan Page Limited

2nd Floor, 45 Gee Street	c/o Martin P Hill Consulting	4737/23 Ansari Road
London	122 W 27th St, 10th Floor	Daryaganj
EC1V 3RS	New York, NY 10001	New Delhi 110002
United Kingdom	USA	India

www.koganpage.com

© Simon Haslam and Ben Shenoy, 2018

The right of Simon Haslam and Ben Shenoy to be identified as the authors of this work has been asserted by them in accordance with the Copyright, Designs and Patents Act 1988.

ISBN   978 0 7494 7260 3
E-ISBN 978 0 7494 7261 0

British Library Cataloguing-in-Publication Data

A CIP record for this book is available from the British Library.

Library of Congress Cataloging-in-Publication Data

Names: Haslam, Simon, author. | Shenoy, Ben, author.
Title: Strategic decision making : a discovery-led approach to critical choices in turbulent times / Simon Haslam and Ben Shenoy.
Description: London ; New York : Kogan Page, [2018] | Includes index.
Identifiers: LCCN 2017035212 (print) | LCCN 2017036510 (ebook) | ISBN 9780749472610 (ebook) | ISBN 9780749472603 (pbk.)
Subjects: LCSH: Strategic planning. | Decision making. | Uncertainty.
Classification: LCC HD30.28 (ebook) | LCC HD30.28 .H3823 2018 (print) | DDC 658.4/0301–dc23
LC record available at https://lccn.loc.gov/2017035212

Typeset by Integra Software Services, Pondicherry
Print production managed by Jellyfish
Printed and bound by Page Bros, Norwich

References to websites (URLs) were accurate at the time of writing. Neither the author nor Kogan Page is responsible for URLs that may have expired or changed since the manuscript was prepared.

CONTENTS

ABOUT THE AUTHORS

Simon Haslam

Simon Haslam is a Chartered Director and strategy consultant. He is a two-time UK 'Consultant of the Year' finalist and co-owns the research and consulting firm FMR Research, whose work has been cited in the Scottish and Westminster Parliaments.

Simon is Chair of the Academic Fellows in management consulting for the International Council of Management Consulting Institutes and is a member of the advisory committee for the UK Institute of Consulting.

He is Programme Lead for strategy at the Institute of Directors and works with boards and senior leadership teams around the world on strategy development projects, with recent clients in Chile, Croatia, Denmark, Germany, Guernsey, Hong Kong, Ireland, Jersey, Kazakhstan, Peru, Rwanda, Saudi Arabia, Switzerland, UK and the USA. He is a Visiting Fellow at Durham University Business School, where he heads programmes on strategic management and leadership. He contributes guest lectures on strategic decision making to other business and management schools.

Simon's PhD, from Strathclyde Business School, explored the grounded theory method in the context of management consulting, and his MBA from Durham University focused on learning organization approaches. He lives in Scotland with his family and can be contacted through his personal website simonhaslam.com or by email on simon@consult.co.uk.

Ben Shenoy

Ben Shenoy explores, decodes and narrates how behavioural science can diagnose dilemmas relating to strategy, organization and leadership in perplexing times. He is a hybrid, having been an electronic engineer and a management consultant before retraining as a social psychologist. His experience spans academia and practice, as well as both the natural and social sciences.

Ben is a Visiting Professor at the London School of Economics (LSE) and Director of the Business Insights Lab at the University of Surrey's Centre for the Digital Economy. He has taught executive courses on leadership, organizational change, senior teams, decision making and innovation at Harvard University, the LSE and Duke Corporate Education. Organizations Ben has advised at the executive level include ArcelorMittal, the BBC, BP, Cisco, Daimler, E.ON, General Dynamics, NATO, McCann-Erickson, Pearson, Unilever and Virgin Media.

Ben holds a PhD in Organizational Behaviour from Harvard Business School. He also holds master's degrees from Cambridge University, London Business School and Harvard University in systems engineering, business administration and social psychology.

He lives with his wife, daughters and an ever-growing menagerie of animals outside London. He can be found online at BenShenoy.com and @BenShenoy.

ACKNOWLEDGEMENTS

Thanks to Liz Barlow, formerly of Kogan Page, for initiating the discussion which led to this book, and to the team at Kogan Page for their support and continuing contribution as the project evolved.

Simon Haslam

To Alistair Russell for introducing me to Ben, and providing the opportunity for those first discussions about leaders and strategy several years ago. Also to my clients and colleagues (past and present) for helping me shape my thinking and for providing inspiration. Finally, thanks to those most dear to me – my wonderful partner, Nikki Bell, daughters, Olivia and Rowan, and son, Lucas, to my mum and the memory of my dad.

Ben Shenoy

To my father, mother and big brother Ram, who taught me the transformative power of learning. To my dear friend Susie Lunt, who helped me give voice to my ideas. And not least, to my darling wife, Charlotte, and beloved daughters, Cara and Anya, who continually remind me of the joy of discovery.

Introduction

Why strategic decision making
needs to become discovery-led

Why did we write this book?

Good decision making is at the heart of effective strategy. It's therefore not surprising that plenty of books have been written on the topic of strategic decision making. Why the need for yet another one?

We've written this book to help senior leaders with one of their most important responsibilities – making good strategic decisions. While leaders might be willing to make decisions, we're not going to pretend that this is easy. Strategy is sometimes described as the route from point A to point B: herein lies one of the main difficulties. While leaders *might* understand the point of departure (point A), the world is increasingly not ready to lay down its cards about what might be an appropriate point B (Hoverstadt and Loh, 2017). Making sense of a shifting landscape and navigating without a clear road map conspire to make strategy tricky.

Our approach to this topic is coloured by who we are and what we've done. We both work on the boundary that spans academia and practice. We're schooled in academic research, and we work and teach in business schools. However, we've also both spent years holding executive office and advising the top tier of client organizations across a range of sectors and geographies. The catalyst for our writing this book is the growing disjunct we've observed between a) conventional strategic decision making practice and b) the messiness of the contemporary challenges confronting organizations – combined with the possibility that relevant academic research might be able to close this gap.

We began this book project two years ago. Our initial focus was decision making biases and the way that leaders' personal perspectives and predilections further distort an already complicated situation. Over two years of sharing our evolving insights with clients, we've discovered that decision making biases are not the only quandary that leaders face. Guided by what we've seen and experienced, we've broadened the scope of the book to include additional challenges to effective strategic decision making confronting today's leaders. We're privileged in that we're experiencing this shift in the nature of this topic in real time. Practically every month, our clients are wrestling with dilemmas and scenarios that are in effect narrow perspectives on incomplete information, to which, nonetheless, they need to respond. We're lucky to be engaging with some enlightened organizations sailing their ships on the high seas of value creation during stormy times.

Strategic problems are increasingly 'wicked'

Nearly a decade ago, strategy professor John Camillus concluded that executives increasingly face strategic 'wicked problems' for which they are ill equipped (Camillus, 2008). The term 'wicked problem' was coined in the 1970s by Horst Rittel and Melvin Webber, professors of design and urban planning at the University of California at Berkeley, to categorize problems that have multiple causes, are tough to define and don't have a right answer (Rittel and Webber, 1973). Jon Kolko, Founder and Director of the Austin Center for Design, reckons that four factors contribute to the emergence of a wicked problem (Kolko, 2012):

- incomplete – or contradictory – knowledge;
- the number of people – and opinions – involved;
- the actual or potential economic burden associated with the problem; and
- the way in which the problem is interwoven with other problems to form a tangled mess.

Given these characteristics, it's not surprising that an organization wrestling with wicked problems suffers from discord, confusion, lack of progress, and angst amongst stakeholders. These stakeholders typically have different values and perspectives on the situation, and the issues they're trying to comprehend are complex and tangled. A satisfactory resolution may well not exist, and because of its interconnected nature the wicked problem may well keep changing as the organization attempts to address it.

Camillus (2008) discovered that, while organizations have moved on from the annual ritual of top-down planning, the more sophisticated techniques now in use still are not capable of coping with the big challenges presenting themselves. He recounts several chief executive officers (CEOs) admitting that they're facing issues that cannot be resolved merely by gathering additional data, defining issues more clearly, or decomposing them into smaller problems. He concludes that a growing number of strategy issues aren't just tough or persistent – instead they're 'wicked'.

Designer and strategist Marty Neumeier conducted a survey in 2008 of 1,500 executives, sponsored by Stanford University and his firm Neutron Group, asking them to name the wickedest problems facing their companies (Neumeier, 2009). The results were as follows:

1 balancing long-term goals with short-term demands;

2 predicting the return on innovative concepts;

3 innovating at the increasing speed of change;

4 winning the war for world-class talent;

5 combining profitability with social responsibility;

6 protecting margins in a commoditizing industry;

7 multiplying success by collaborating across silos;

8 finding unclaimed yet profitable market space;

9 addressing the challenge of eco-sustainability; and

10 aligning strategy with customer experience.

For us, two points stand out from a list that's nearly 10 years old. First, while some of the problems have a timeless quality about them (eg items 1, 6, 10), the majority of them (eg items 2, 3, 5, 8, 9) have come to the fore in the new millennium – and are not easily addressed using 20th-century management techniques. Second, we would predict that, if we were to rerun the survey today, the results would reflect an even greater degree of 'wickedness' that organizations are having to handle.

Our interactions with clients tally with Camillus's observations and Neumeier's data: enterprises are struggling to make sound decisions in a world that's ever more confusing and unpredictable. Much of the strategic toolkit in use today was created in the last century, when the prevailing rules were that you could imagine what you're aiming for, and have a reasonably good idea of how to get there. However, forces arising from technology, globalization, economics and society are conspiring to create a complex, changing and confusing environment in which this conventional wisdom increasingly falls short.

Nowadays, competitors may appear from outside your sector. The confluence of globalization and its consequences, emerging physical and biological technologies, and the constraints imposed by the planet and its people are combining to mutate possible recipes for success. The convergence of industries and lack of available knowledge are conspiring to create wicked problems. As a highly visible example, information technology and the internet have transformed the postal mail, music, sports entertainment, film, television, radio, telephone and intellectual property industries radically. They have also profoundly shaped the biomedical, bioinformatic and biometric industries, and will continue to do so over the coming years. To illustrate how profoundly this is altering enterprises' environments, and therefore the strategic wicked problems that are confronting them, let us look at a couple of organizations with which we've worked.

Global medicines research

The medicines research market is big and growing. In some respects, it's a conservative sector with well-embedded methods for the verification of new pharmaceutical formulations underpinned by regulatory hurdles.

Our client, positioned in the world's top 10 research firms, senses the simultaneous threat and opportunity of technology rewriting the rules of how the testing of new drug and medicine formulae can be verified, especially as advances in diagnosis lead to a future of highly customized treatments.

The challenge our client faces relates to the most appropriate strategic response to these trends. The 'do-nothing' option implies a continuation of playing to strengths in medical research (our client is operationally extremely capable and financially successful), betting either on the long time it might take for drug regulators to change their approvals process, or on finding a place in a new technology-oriented ecosystem as domain experts. The more adventurous immediate options involve either developing the technological competence to become a first-tier player in a world of electronic sensors, microchip implants and real-time physiological data, or making a significant acquisition of a digital specialist that gives our client a step-change in research capability. And, while these options are considered, the medicines research world moves ever forward, with the likelihood of fewer seats around the table as the clock ticks.

Construction in healthcare

A British construction services company won a contract from a UK National Health Service (NHS) trust to build a large specialist accident and emergency (ie emergency room) hospital, and operate it for 30 years. When we first spoke with them, they had to break ground in six weeks' time in order to complete the hospital on schedule. However, they had no idea how technology would alter the provision of emergency health services during the course of 30 years, and therefore what the best design of the building would be.

For example, 5G mobile telecommunications will most likely be able to carry ultra-high definition (UHD) video signals over mobile broadband in the next three to five years. One potential implication of this would be that accident and emergency doctors and nurses would be able to see a high-quality video of a patient – and therefore make appropriate remote interventions – while *he or she is still in the ambulance*. The survival and recovery rates of emergency patients (eg heart attack and stroke victims) are greatly improved if interventions are carried out within the first few minutes of the onset of symptoms. But, if the majority of interventions *might* be conducted in ambulances before they arrive at the hospital, how should the accident and emergency treatment facilities and wards be designed? And remember: our client wanted to break ground in six weeks to meet the construction deadline!

The planning dilemma

The above examples illustrate patterns in how the environment is changing. In particular, the world seems to be changing faster, and in ways that are harder to predict and interpret. However, classic approaches to strategic decision making that have evolved over the preceding decades are founded on the assumption that we know what we're aiming for – as well as how to get there – when we begin any individual initiative. In the turbulent times in which we live this assumption increasingly isn't necessarily true. We start by knowing very little about a new situation and – hopefully! – we learn more about it over time. Applying classic decision making techniques to such confusing situations leads to what has been termed 'the planning dilemma': namely, we make the biggest decisions about an endeavour when we know the least, and then we're surprised when things don't turn out as we'd anticipated (see Figure 0.1)! So how can enterprises respond appropriately to such wicked problems?

Figure 0.1   The planning dilemma

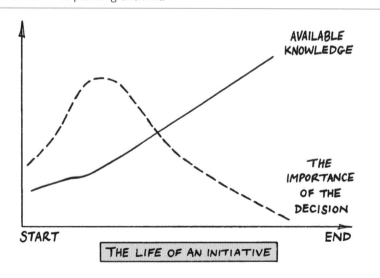

Discovery-led decision making

Looking at the shape of the curve in Figure 0.1, we need to spread the importance of decisions we make more evenly over the life of an initiative, and to speed up our acquisition of available knowledge by emphasizing the importance of *learning* in our decision making. In this book we'll advocate a more *discovery-led* approach to strategic decision making designed to address the planning dilemma and tackle strategic wicked problems.

By 'discovery-led', we mean that the way in which we make decisions depends on the balance between what we know, what we *don't* know and what we *think* we know (ie our *assumptions*). We believe that enterprises need to shift from the ritual of strategic planning to a more fluid, dynamic and iterative approach suited to contemporary contexts. We advocate three modes of strategic decision making (see Figure 0.2):

- When our unknowns and our assumptions dominate our knowns, we should *experiment. Experimenting* helps us learn by converting unknowns and assumptions into knowns. We can do this by generating *just enough* insight, testing assumptions and trialling approaches. When the world is harder to predict, it pays to move from analysis to active *problem solving* faster.

- When we've figured out what works and have reduced our unknowns and assumptions to a level we can tolerate, we should *scale. Scaling* recognizes the distinction between a *business model* (how the enterprise will create value) and a *management model* (a particular way of working, with an associated mindset, habits and behaviours). *Scaling* helps us *spread solutions* that work more widely.

- Finally, in fast-changing environments we need to be wary of solving the *wrong* problem precisely. To minimize this risk, we need to *frame. Framing* cautions against an over-reliance on existing knowledge – dangerous in a fast-changing environment – by encouraging us to focus on *problem finding* by considering a situation through a variety of perspectives.

Figure 0.2 Discovery-led decision making

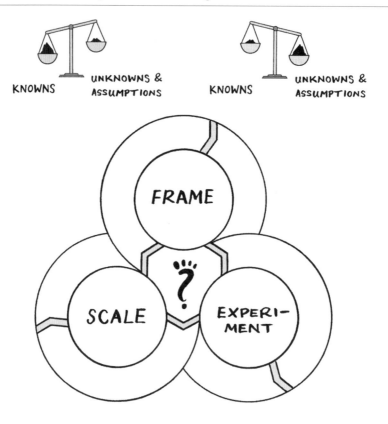

Frame, experiment and *scale* together form the discovery-led decision making framework at the heart of this book (Shenoy, 2017).

Implications for enterprises

This discovery-led approach is iterative and non-linear, which has profound implications for incumbent enterprises that are used to operating under orderly Industrial Age guidelines that have evolved over decades. Enterprises need to overcome the organizational inertia that makes change difficult for businesses. They need to question whether the conventional, 'top-down' approach to strategic decision making is most appropriate in a turbulent, fast-moving world.

Frame, *experiment* and *scale* decisions need to be managed in contrasting – even conflicting – ways: they differ in terms of pace, time horizon, bias to action, tolerance for taking risks and attitude to failure. This way of managing decision making is often better allied to a 'middle-out' approach to management, where different parts of the organization operate in different modes with more local discretion, rather than the 'top-down' expectation that senior levels control all strategic decisions.

We explore how enterprises can create the appropriate contexts so that they can operate in these different modes simultaneously, and figure out how to coordinate smoothly across disparate activities.

Implications for individual decision makers

The different modes *frame*, *experiment* and *scale* also pose challenges for executive decision makers who have developed their careers in Industrial Age organizations. Being aware of where in the landscape of *frame*, *experiment* and *scale* your activities fit is key to success in this environment, as is the recognition that the pace of decision making is not necessarily constant.

Managers will need to develop the flexibility to think and act effectively across *frame*, *experiment* and *scale*. This will require that they cultivate an awareness of which mode is most appropriate for a particular activity, as well as cultivating a repertoire of suitable behaviours that they adapt to particular situations. The challenge of becoming *tridextrous* leaders (ie skilful in shifting between the three modes of *framing*, *experimenting* and *scaling*) is not trivial, demanding that executives overhaul their ingrained managerial habits learned over many years of work experience.

Making critical choices in turbulent times

This book outlines an approach that helps us, as decision makers, apply a cycle of *framing*, *experimentation* and *scaling* to make productive progress when confronted with a perplexing environment. This cycle enables us to interpret available information, design appropriate choices and convert chosen ideas into reality by exercising control and coordination appropriately – and letting go of them, if necessary.

An overview of the rest of the book

The following chapters explain how the discovery-led decision making framework can help leaders construct a meaningful strategy in a contemporary world of wicked problems and the planning dilemma. In such turbulent times, merely having good intentions and bright people at the helm is insufficient to ensuring enduring success.

The earlier chapters explore the core ingredients of strategic decision making and the associated particular challenges, and the mechanisms by which strategy evolves. Chapter 1 considers the changing nature of the world and the difficulties facing leaders in making sense of it, especially when using the strategy theories in common use today. Chapter 2 explores organizational inertia and individual decision making biases, as well as the particular paths on which many organizations find themselves trapped, which can collectively constrain strategic choice. Chapter 3 discusses the idea of 'top-down' decisions, which for many enterprises represents the conventional style by which strategic choices are made in practice. Chapter 4 introduces the idea of 'middle-out' decision making as an alternative avenue by which organizational direction is realized.

Having looked at the challenges that organizations and their leaders face in respect of strategic decision making, and the mechanisms by which decisions are made, Chapter 5 explains the rationale behind the discovery-led decision making framework (see Figure 0.2). Chapters 6, 7 and 8 explore the different modes of the framework in greater detail: *frame* (what's the *right* problem to solve?), *experiment* (how do we *learn* what need to know?) and *scale* (how do we do *more* of what works?).

We conclude with two chapters looking at the implications of a discovery-led approach to strategic decision making for organizations (Chapter 9) and their leaders (Chapter 10).

Summary

We've written this book because we've noticed a growing gap between conventional strategic decision making practice and the messiness of the contemporary challenges confronting organizations. We believe that insights from relevant academic research can shape how strategic decisions are made so as to close this gap.

This disjunct has appeared because strategy is increasingly composed of 'wicked problems' – intractable challenges that have multiple causes, are tough to define and don't have a right answer. Conventional strategic decision making techniques are ill equipped to address wicked problems, resulting in the planning dilemma: namely, we make the biggest decisions about an endeavour when we know the least, and we're then surprised when things don't turn out as we'd anticipated.

Our approach to tackling the growing incidence of wicked problems is to make strategic decision making more discovery-led, so that the way in which we make decisions depends on the balance between what we know, what we *don't* know and what we *think* we know (ie our *assumptions*). This discovery-led decision making framework is composed of three modes:

- *Frame*: what's the *right* problem to solve?
- *Experiment*: how do we *learn* what we need to know?
- *Scale*: how do we do *more* of what works?

The following chapters explain how this discovery-led decision-making framework can help leaders construct meaningful strategy in a contemporary world of wicked problems and the planning dilemma.

References

Camillus, J C (2008) Strategy as a wicked problem, *Harvard Business Review*, **86** (5), 98–106

Hoverstadt, P and Loh, L (2017) *Patterns of Strategy*, Gower, London

Kolko, J (2012) Wicked problems: problems worth solving, *Stanford Social Innovation Review*, 6 March, https://ssir.org/articles/entry/wicked_problems_problems_worth_solving

Neumeier, M (2009) *The Designful Company: How to build a culture of nonstop innovation*, New Riders, Berkeley, CA

Rittel, H W J and Webber, M M (1973) Dilemmas in a general theory of planning, *Policy Science*, **4**, 155–69

Shenoy, B (2017) Discovery-led decision-making, 1 April, http://benshenoy.com/index.php/dilemmas/discovery-led

The world is changing, but we don't always see it   01

In the Introduction, we mentioned challenges that are conspiring to make strategic decision making difficult. This chapter begins to shine a light on these – starting with 'The world is changing, but we don't always see it.'

Being able to use change to advantage is core to strategic success. With change comes opportunity, and much of strategy relates to the risks that come with uncertainty and how these can best be handled in the pursuit of value. However, we see organizations struggling to recognize change, with the consequence their resultant strategic options are partially developed and strategic decisions compromised. There are two factors that contribute to this state of affairs. These are: 1) the changing nature of change, which is reshaping how organizations need to respond; 2) the use of what we term 'classical' strategy models in situations for which they are no longer well suited. We will explore each in turn, starting with the changing nature of change.

The changing nature of change

Explanations of strategy typically acknowledge that environments change and effective strategies should accommodate this. As strategic success is normally associated with the longer term, the importance of remaining connected with the flow of markets becomes more important. The Greek philosopher Heraclitus wrote about the constancy of change five centuries before the birth of Christ. It is not so much the presence of change in our lives that complicates strategic decision making; it's that change itself is changing.

There currently seem to be more variables at play, for example the nature of technological change, the speed at which new enterprises can be created and scaled, and influences that are more globally than locally rooted. This means the type of change is less predictable than it might once have been and the time taken for change to take effect has shortened. When things happen, they happen more quickly. It took 75 years for the telephone to reach 50 million users, whereas 40 times this number of smartphones have been shifted in just seven years. As the pace of change has increased, we can see this in other areas too. Research into new technology ventures by Play Bigger, a Silicon Valley consultancy, observed that today's start-ups are growing at twice the rate of those a decade ago (Ramadan et al, 2015). If companies are growing more quickly, they are also dying earlier. Of the original companies listed on Standard & Poor's 500 (S&P 500), 82 per cent are no more (*PR Newswire*, 2007), and the average lifespan of an S&P company has dropped from 67 years in the 1920s to 15 years in 2013 (Williams, 2013).

A different style of language has crept into management. This illuminates the changing nature of change and draws attention to the different thinking that's now required for strategic decision making. Kevin Roberts, the former CEO of the creative organization Saatchi & Saatchi, helped popularize the military acronym VUCA in business circles. The notion that the world is volatile, uncertain, complex and ambiguous (VUCA) epitomizes a view that 'Hey, it's crazy out there' (Bennett and Lemoine, 2014). We are becoming more acquainted with terms like 'agile', 'disruptive innovation', 'fail fast/fail forward' and 'servitization'. We are increasingly needing to manage when we're unsure of our objectives. In *Second Curve*, Charles Handy (2015) writes that the recipes that have worked in the past for business and broader society will almost certainly not work in an uncertain future. We are living in different times.

Different business climate

In *No Ordinary Disruption*, Richard Dodds, James Manyika and Jonathan Woetzel (2015) from consulting firm McKinsey & Company cite four forces of disruption in the world. These are the rise of emerging markets, the accelerating impact of technology on the natural forces of market competition, an ageing world population, and accelerating flows of trade, capital and people. While all are disruptive, some are more predictable than others. Of particular interest to today's leaders should be the force of digital technology: from big data to driverless cars to smart buildings. It's true that change is nothing new: what is different is the rate of technological change that we are currently witnessing. As Mario Angelastro, former head of Accenture in Latin America, points out, the pace of technology is now quicker than the pace of business thinking. According to digital economy experts Erik Brynjolfsson and Andrew McAfee (2014), the world stands on the cusp of a new era of progress, which they label the 'second machine age'. They argue that the impact of this new age will be as fundamental to the way we live and work as the Industrial Revolution was nearly 250 years ago.

One key factor that has led us to this launching point for metamorphic change is the application of Moore's law – the power of constant doubling – to so many elements of electronic components (price, processing speed, energy efficiency and storage capacity). To illustrate this phenomenon, consider batteries. Over the past few decades, few breakthrough advances have been made in battery technology. As battery life is often the limiting factor for the usefulness of many electronic devices, researchers have been wrestling with ways to address this issue. Recently, Huawei Technologies revealed a new type of lithium-ion battery that allows superfast charging, giving up to 10 hours of talk time on a mobile phone after only five minutes' charge. Such advances will add further fuel to propel the rocket of change. Experiments are being conducted to prototype a much wider range of fuel cell technologies, which might lead to batteries containing sugars, enzymes and even viruses.

The perceptions of value of consumers are shifting too. Less and less depends on physical material and more on services and knowledge. For example, between 1997 and 2001, the amount of material required to meet all the needs of people in the United States fell from 0.54 trillion kilograms to 0.49 trillion kilograms, despite a population increase of 55 million over that time. Buckminster Fuller coined the term 'ephemeralization' to describe the ability of technological advancement to do more and more with less and less, until you can do everything with nothing (Fuller, 1938). Business is dematerializing.

But it is not just technologies and products that are transforming. The markets in which businesses and consumers operate have also undergone profound changes and continue to mutate. In the past, companies that produced a successful product or process could generally rely on a sustained period of competitive advantage. Rapid expansion to allow economies of scale to develop were the order of the day. Furthermore, companies could use their size and scale to deter competitors from entering the market.

Different businesses

In a post-industrial age, advances in the understanding and the application of technology have opened up commercial opportunity in unforeseen ways. For example, we have a situation where the world's largest hotel business doesn't own bedrooms (Airbnb) and the world's biggest taxi company doesn't own cars (Uber). These enterprises have grown quickly. Airbnb grew from inception in 2008 to 10 million nights booked by 2012. Uber launched in 2010, and within its first six months it had around 5,000 users who had between them travelled about 20,000 journeys. The value of Uber's global bookings in 2016 exceeded $20 billion. We should note not only the scale of these businesses, but the speed at which this scale was achieved. Whereas both of their value propositions will have to some degree stimulated their markets, both hotel accommodation and taxi services are established business sectors. Both Uber and Airbnb have been eating someone else's lunch. A decade previously, it was the turn of eBay to re-create the rules of the sector. Its rapid growth was no less impressive between 1999 and 2003, and its impact on retailing no less dramatic.

Strategic management scholar Rita McGrath (2013) argues that an existing competitive advantage is now most likely to be disrupted by the emergence of something totally different, not from current competitors but from a new entrant to the sector. Digital technology – in the form of processing power and connectivity – is now starting to shift the structure of professional services firms because of the ease with which markets can match projects with independent contractors on demand. Eden McCallum, founded in the UK in 2000, can access a network of 500 freelance consultants to provide consultancy at a fraction of the cost of big firms like McKinsey, Accenture or Deloitte. This allows it to provide advice to small companies as well as to behemoths like GSK or Ford. Axiom employs 650 lawyers, claims half the *Fortune* 100 as clients, and earned revenues in excess of $100 million in 2012. Medicast is applying a similar model to doctors on the Eastern and Western seaboards of the United States. Patients use a location-based app to request a doctor. Medicast guarantees that a doctor will arrive within two hours, already briefed on the symptoms. This model is even being applied in the interim executive market. The Business Talent Group, based in Los Angeles, provides companies with temporary managers to tackle specific problems without adding extra senior executives to the payroll.

In a prescient book, Swedish management consultant and researcher Richard Normann (2001) explored in great depth how digital technologies could change the way in which organizations could innovate new services. He argued that digital technology 'dematerialized' products and services, effectively by increasing the proportion of value of these products and services arising purely from 'intangible' information. He predicted that organizations would create value not by offering a static output (what he labelled 'frozen knowledge') but by using the 'liquid' nature of information to let customers get involved in creating what they wanted on the fly. Eden McCallum, together with enterprises like European intercity bus service Flixbus and EPL (the men's association football English Premier League), is an exemplar of organizations – some new, some older – that are exploiting this shift towards dynamic, dematerialized services.

In order to exploit the opportunities offered by dematerialization, Normann suggests that firms need to 'reframe business' by thinking about how to create and capture value in fundamentally different ways. He points to a world in which innovation is less likely to occur linearly through value chains. Instead, it emerges dynamically from clusters of companies and customers combining information and services in novel ways. According to Normann, reframing business is an imperative: firms must 'obey the call of business today: reconfigure or be reconfigured' (Normann, 2001).

Normann contends that reframing businesses requires what he terms 'upframing': in other words, consideration of the overall system of which the firm is a part. This upframing prevents myopia (Levitt, 1960). Creating new frames or, in Normann's terms, 'maps that change the landscape' enables businesses to redefine their roles. As an example, IKEA has reframed the home furnishings arena by outsourcing assembly to customers in exchange for flexibility of delivery, customization and choice.

This goes beyond organizations having resilience to cope with unforeseen change. It looks more towards the idea of 'antifragile' enterprises (Taleb, 2013) where the reaction to change is not debilitating or draining but instead the organization becomes stronger as a result of the experience.

We are also seeing moves in the way businesses and organizations are viewed and, perhaps as a consequence, changes in corporate governance. The realm of public services and the not-for-distributed-profit sector, founded upon principles of inclusion and social justice, are now encouraged towards financial efficiency and have 'customers'. The private sector, traditionally oriented towards shareholder wealth, is experiencing a shift in the other direction. The lexicon now includes 'enlightened' shareholder value, accompanied by a broadening of focus on a wider stakeholder map, for example employees, communities and environmental sustainability. In this age of citizenship, social media and 24/7 news, no organization seems able to 'get away' with things to the degree that was possible just a couple of decades earlier. Branding has transformed from a construct that could have been employed as an external façade into an extrapolation of the organization's values and internal behaviour. VW Group (with the US engine emissions scandal) and United Airlines (with the eviction of a passenger from a flight) are living testaments to this.

Classical strategy models only partially helpful

Classical strategy is the version of strategy that emerged around the 1960s, when the term began its rise in popularity in the business world (Freedman, 2013), and has been continually developed since. The ascent of business schools as an educational phenomenon has fanned the flames of classical strategy, with researchers, academics, business practitioners and leaders building on the array of tools and concepts available. This was paralleled by a growing appetite in the business sector for the application of the ideas in the pursuit of competitive advantage. Although strategic thinking has evolved, it was the first movers in this field who put the markers down. Early theories formed the foundation upon which strategy began to be understood and communicated, and the anchor for the further development of thought. These original concepts continue to be taught, written about and used. For example, a Google search for the Ansoff matrix (recognized as the first strategy model) scores over 700,000 hits, PEST analysis over 1,000,000 hits and Porter's five forces (which is the world's most cited strategy model) over 13,000,000 hits. This illustrates the degree to which the earlier ideas in strategy endure. In addition, strategy models emerge from this digestion of practice. Strategy theory follows the reality upon which the theory is based, meaning that, by the time a strategic concept or theory is published and promoted, the contemporary practice on which it is based is no longer contemporary.

We are not saying that these earlier strategy models are redundant, but we are pointing out they were largely created when the business world was a different place to what we are experiencing today. These models still have a role in strategy deliberations, but only if we have our eyes wide open to their limits. We explore some of these below.

PESTLE analysis

Many leaders will recognize the sentiment in the Danish proverb 'It is difficult to make predictions, especially about the future.' The

PESTLE analysis has been strategy's go-to framework to help leaders look outward and forward. In the attempt to understand environmental dynamics, PESTLE analysis is well used. The hypothesis is that the changes to markets can be understood by recognizing the main macro trends at play and considering their impact. Originally portrayed as four drivers of change, political, economic, social, technological (Aguilar, 1967), the model was extended to include legal and environmental considerations to create a six-component model. The legal and environmental factors grew out of the original four because they became big enough in their own right to merit headlining.

PESTLE analysis is based on the assumption that the forces of change are identifiable. In some situations, the implications of trends can be extrapolated to quantified risks and opportunities, for example with population demographics. In other situations the force at play might be indefinable and its effect uncertain in advance, for example political referenda and elections (a risk can be quantified in terms of scale and probability, whereas an uncertainty cannot be described as precisely).

Our experience with PESTLE analysis is that, although it helps stimulate thinking about possible futures, it does so from the perspective of the present, ie what people currently experience. As a result, the current situation becomes the reference point, and thought gravitates to linear extension rather than radical futures. In some situations this works perfectly well. Where the phenomenon is strong and highly predictable, a PESTLE analysis can help shed a bright light on commercial opportunity. For example, Ryanair, on its way to becoming Europe's biggest airline, capitalized on the deregulation of the European airlines industry, the so-called 'open skies' policy. Legislative factors tend to have a distinct role in PESTLE analysis, as they carry with them a high degree of predictability and clarity. Ryanair was able to follow the growing debate around open skies and, when it became sufficiently confident around the outcome, orientate itself to take advantage of the opportunity. Ryanair's flotation in 1997 realized funds to invest in opening new routes, and by the turn of the millennium the step-change in Ryanair's growth in passengers carried per year was evident. The issue is whether, in current times, the direction of travel in the world is sufficiently predictable (as it was in the Ryanair example) for a PESTLE analysis to be as valuable.

The uncertainties resulting from PESTLE analyses provided the stimulus for scenario planning, where the implications of different possibilities can be examined and business responses designed and tested (van der Heijden et al, 2002) using scenario thinking (Wright and Cairns, 2011). These developments have succeeded in extending the utility of the PESTLE approach. However, there remain three significant challenges with this form of analysis.

First, the model presumes that the data employed are valid – the term 'garbage in, garbage out' applies. A leadership team needs to take responsibility for the quality of information around which any decision is to be made.

Second is the 'perfect storm'. The factors emerging from PESTLE analyses need to be considered alongside each other, as it's the combination that's important. It can be hard to meld together the implications of different factors, and if we're able to do this at all the effect the factors have on each other is less easy to predict. We're increasingly referring to this phenomenon as a 'perfect storm'. The term was made popular by the 2000 film starring George Clooney and Mark Wahlberg, based on Sebastian Junger's book about the *Andrea Gail* fishing vessel, which was lost at sea with all on board in a perfect storm (Junger, 1997). A perfect storm is a concatenation of factors that, while individually predictable, combine and amplify their mutual effect such that their impact is greater than the sum of the parts. This interpretation of the term has meteorological origins (as demonstrated by Junger's book). When strategists talk about perfect storms, they do so typically retrospectively, as perfect storms are easier to unpick after the event than to predict ahead. Here is an example.

The global economic crisis saw a step-change in the behaviour of UK banks towards the small business community. Within a very short period of time, starting in 2008, small businesses found it significantly harder to gain financial support from banks. The perfect storm that happened was as follows:

- Banks usually require security on lending. Real estate is popular (often the business owner-manager's house), but the value of real estate fell heavily during the recession.

- Up until the global economic crisis, the economy in the UK was consistently benevolent. Many small businesses succeeded not by being good but by being there. With the economic crisis came the implosion of many markets and tougher competition. Small businesses found themselves talking to banks not for funding around specific development projects (with an expected rate of return) but simply to shore up cash flow and meet operational expenses.

- The term 'zombie business' (see Pym, 2012) became popular around this time for the reason above, and the stigma carried by the term impacted adversely on the lending activity of banks.

- Following banks' speculation and risk-taking behaviour in certain areas (other than lending to small firms) the behaviour of banks was brought into line. Banks were expected to become less financially frail enterprises in their own right and to be more conservative in their behaviour, which made them more risk averse in their lending to small businesses.

The factors were linked, with no single item working in isolation. The combination of factors created the amplification, and the impact was dramatic. It is easier to understand the perfect storm looking backward than it would have been to predict it forward. Although 20/20 hindsight is interesting, it is rarely as valuable as foresight.

Finally there are the 'unknown unknowns'. If a factor isn't on the organization's radar, it lacks a voice in the analysis. It can be hard for the analysis to be comprehensive and expansive, especially as its starting point is constrained by familiarity with the present. In the arena of politics Donald Rumsfeld, the former US Secretary of State for Defense, explained the presence of unknown unknowns: important considerations for decision making that we don't know we don't know. This is what he said:

> Reports that say that something hasn't happened are always interesting to me, because as we know, there are known knowns; there are things we know we know. We also know there are known unknowns; that is to say we know there are some things we do not know. But there are also unknown unknowns – the ones we don't know we don't know. And if one looks throughout the history of our country and other free countries, it is the latter category that tend to be the difficult ones.
>
> (Rumsfeld, 2002)

The relevance of Rumsfeld's contribution was its timeliness and its authority. The notion of unknown unknowns had been part of the organizational development landscape for several years, with ideas like the Johari window (Luft and Ingham, 1955). But Rumsfeld's words resonated with leaders presiding over organizations in what they viewed as an increasingly harder-to-predict world. In 2007, Nassim Nicholas Taleb introduced black swan theory. It was named after an old saying that black swans didn't exist, which had to be revised upon the discovery of black swans in the wild. Taleb's focus was unexpected events with significant impact. Taleb felt these extreme occurrences had a disproportionately higher disruptive effect than regular ones (Taleb, 2007).

Sensemaking and situational intelligence in strategy are more a problem of induction than deduction (Ricks, 2011). In inductive study, one makes a series of observations and infers a new claim based on them. There are no bounds to the data upon which observations are based, no equation into which to drop the data, and no irrefutable answer. It is more artistic than scientific. Leaders are encouraged to scan for weak signals (Harrysson, Métayer and Sarrazin, 2014). Weak signals might herald important changes or opportunities, but it is a difficult task to determine what is a useful weak signal and what is noise: where and when to focus the antennae. With the changing tone of the world and the implications of a VUCA context, trusting the predictable path of identifiable and independent variables is seeming less relevant to strategic decision making.

Five forces analysis

Since its creation in 1979 (Porter, 1979), organizations across the planet have derived benefit from the consideration of Michael Porter's five competitive forces. The model helps them to appreciate the structure of the industry sector under examination and provide a framework for considering the potential impact of trends, changes and avenues of commercial opportunity. Such has been the impact of the five forces on strategic thought that it has been spoken about as the most extensively used strategy framework of all time (Stewart, 2008).

Five forces analysis can add great value to the understanding of the strategic landscape, but it comes with two increasingly prominent characteristics that have hampered leaders' abilities to think strategically and make good strategic decisions. First, the five forces analysis is very much a 'micro external' model, meaning its functionality depends on being clear about the industry sector you're looking at. This thinking has typically worked better in the product sector than it has with services, as the intangibility of the latter leads to softening of the hard edges associated with a bounded industry sector with a linear value chain. When working with service-dominated value propositions and/or with a reorientation on a different 'industry', the five forces approach requires a little more dexterity in its application. This is countered by the recognition that the more embedded an organization becomes within its supply chain, the more restricted its strategic movement. We look further into this in Chapter 2.

With the growth of global competition, the 'level playing field' that added to the logic of looking within an industry, is disappearing. Players within a sector are now less likely to be subject to the same operating conditions as each other. For example, one of our clients in the mobile telecoms sector was seeking to replace its network infrastructure. A few years ago, our client would have chosen from products made by similar types of competitor. These were typically from organizations based in developed economies and operated under a joint-stock, private sector model. Recently, our client was offered a technically proficient network infrastructure from an Asian-based enterprise, at a price 80 per cent lower than for the established competition. The Asian enterprise was also prepared to lend our client the many millions of dollars to buy the system at a 1.5 per cent rate. This provider wasn't desperate for business and giving its products away. It was simply that it had a longer-term strategic focus, and substantially different economic structure, than the traditional players in this sector.

Despite the challenges, industry shift is possible, as demonstrated by BMW, one of Europe's leading car brands, when it announced that it was moving to becoming a mobility business (Branman, 2016). The industry structure pertaining to the manufacturing and distribution of cars looks very different to that for personal mobility. This business was able to loosen the shackles of an established industry position and well-discussed opportunities for incremental advantage, and move towards something that, for it, was fresh and uncharted. This factor is further hampered by the recognition that, increasingly, competition takes place not between individual companies but between the supply chains or supply networks of which the company is a part (Rice and Hoppe, 2001). Much of Amazon's success, for example, is based on its excellence in supply chain management, a point emphasized by the technology consulting firm Gartner, which saw Amazon as third best in the world in its 2016 supply chain management rankings (Aronow, 2016).

Second, what we interpret as a substitute has shifted in emphasis over the past few decades. Originally, the term focused on the alternative prevailing technology that tempered the commercial freedom of the central part of the value chain (the established players). If people in the hat-making business started charging too much for their products, they might drive the market to umbrellas as a substitute product. We've noticed that the nature of substitutes is moving towards new and embryonic technologies. This means that a company can conduct a five forces analysis and not notice the very business model that will eventually account for the current industry's demise. We've seen with Uber, eBay and Airbnb how quickly these technological solutions can expand, rendering entire supply chains redundant and reshaping industry structures. There are, for example, digital fireworks becoming available. These are not direct replacements for traditional fireworks but offer a totally different and interactive user experience, perhaps capable of revolutionizing the sector.

Strategist Don Sull's paper 'Why good companies go bad' (Sull, 1999) points out that rarely do our businesses suffer terminally through the actions of direct competitors. They are too similar to us and on our radar, and none of us in the sector can make a move out of the sightline of the rest. What the research points out is that the harshest blows to companies are dealt by businesses and business models outside of the sector.

In 1997, consumer behaviour specialist Morris Holebrook addressed the UK Academy of Marketing conference, and in his keynote session (in which the audience were invited to wear 3-D glasses) illustrated that in the future the most interesting developments were less likely to occur within functions or sectors as we have bounded them but in those areas where there are overlaps or undefined spaces. There is a tendency for organizations to be sensitive to competition from within their own sector and also to be mindful of established players from other sectors making a move into their market. Holebrook encouraged his audience to look neither at the 'land' nor at the 'sea' but to the littoral area where land meets sea. The threat and the opportunity lie at the intersection. Some years on, we are considering the implications of the 'fourth age' and the confluence between biology, electronics and digital technology.

Ansoff matrix

Created in 1957, the Ansoff matrix is regarded as the first business strategy model (Ansoff, 1957). Similar to Porter's five forces, the model has proven a capable lens through which organizations can view their strategies, and it continues to have a role. Igor Ansoff's original proposition that, in strategy, there are two main variables (what you do and where you do it) feels as true now as it did over five decades ago. For example, while Hans Vestberg was its CEO, the Swedish communications technology giant Ericsson (2013) explained its strategic direction in an Ansoff manner:

- Excel in networks.

- Expand in services.

- Extend in support solutions.

- Establish a leading position in Networked Society enablers.

In its application, the main strength of the Ansoff matrix is probably also its main vulnerability. The logical starting place is top left, the area encompassing an organization's existing footprint; organizations have an existing market and an existing product or service offer. After exploring possibilities to maximize the current position, a senior leadership team usually finds it a straightforward move to questions such as 'What should the next product be for us?' (the 'product development' box) or 'If we were to extend our products into another market, where would we go first?' (the 'market development' box). People talk about 'adjacency' to describe the logical extension of a current enterprise into related areas. These are natural steps from the organization's present place in the world, and for many businesses represent well-charted territory in their strategy discussions. It is in the area of novel and discontinuous strategic options that the Ansoff matrix serves leaders less well. The bottom-right 'new/new' option (labelled 'diversification') draws attention to a broad commercial space but offers little more help than pointing to it.

Executive leaders find themselves imbued with the organization's current reality, the presence of which can serve to blinker people to more expansive possibilities. The Ansoff matrix probably amplifies this owing to the greater tangibility around the data in the top-left box. Conversely, the bottom-right box affords the greatest scope for change but typically is the most difficult to discuss, as it involves a higher degree of speculation and assumptions. We have one client whose organization has particular difficulty with the relatively unbounded conversations in the bottom-right area and refers to the 'new/new' space on the matrix as the 'daft box'. Yet, as we've seen in our examples and glean from terms like 'disruptive innovation' and 'dematerialization', the ability of leaders to think outside of the conventional box looks increasingly important.

SAFe

The final strategy framework to consider in this chapter is SAFe. Particularly relevant to decision making in strategy, SAFe (suitability, acceptability and feasibility evaluation) has helped many leadership teams weigh up the merits of various strategic options and move to a decision (Johnson et al, 2014). SAFe has its foundations in the rational school of decision making, whereby an option can be objectively scrutinized through relevant lenses. This has its roots over 250 years ago, as demonstrated in a letter from Benjamin Franklin to Joseph Priestley, in which Franklin describes his approach to decision making through goal clarification, listing influences, weighting and ascertaining the balance.

In strategy decisions using the SAFe approach, the lens of suitability is about whether the option aligns with the organization's purpose and helps move it towards its vision. The acceptability lens is about stakeholder buy-in, including whether the option is within the risk appetite of the organization, whether the organization can live with the consequences of adoption or non-adoption and whether the main stakeholder groups will support the initiative. Feasibility is about whether the option is executable by the organization, and whether it has the capability to put whatever it is into practice successfully.

The main quality of SAFe, and the reason it remains a framework valued by many organizations, is that it provides a way of focusing and structuring a discussion around strategic decisions when there's a group of people involved and, because every option needs to be interrogated from at least three perspectives, the use of SAFe usually entails a more rigorous conversation. A subtle further benefit is that, as a framework provides a way of handling a large array of data, it encourages teams to extend their list of strategic options beyond what would have otherwise been the case. As we'll discuss later, a more expansive list of strategic possibilities to consider is usually a good thing.

Our preferred approach with SAFe analysis is to build a matrix where the options are cross-linked to screening criteria that are either the three SAFe terms or rooted in them. The merits of each strategic option are considered in relation to each of the screening criteria, usually using a rating scale. Often, as in the example in Figure 1.1, a total column is used. The example looks at the possible strategy for the legendary character Robin Hood. Robin and his Merry Men lived in Sherwood Forest, where they robbed from the rich to give to the poor, a social justice crusade of railing against a harsh monarchy and an adversary in local administration in the form of the Sheriff of Nottingham. The Robin Hood strategy session was stimulated by the dual recognition that Sherwood Forest was becoming too congested and Robin's enterprise unsustainable, as more sought to join the Merry Men. Rich people had also started to give Sherwood Forest a wide berth as the stories about the robberies spread. With less income and an unwieldy organization, it was time to make some changes.

Figure 1.1 SAFe grid example

STRATEGIC OPTION	ACHIEVE MAIN OBJECTIVES	ACCEPTABLE TIMESCALE	FEASIBLE WITHIN RESOURCES	'BUY IN' AND SUPPORT	ACCEPTABLE CONSEQUENCES	TOTAL
FRANCHISE THE SHERWOOD MODEL TO OTHER FORESTS	3	4	4	4	4	19
KILL THE SHERIFF OF NOTTINGHAM	5	5	2	3	2	17
REDUCE SIZE OF CURRENT SHERWOOD ENTERPRISE TO PRESERVE THE BUSINESS MODEL	3	4	4	3	4	18
ALIGN WITH THE BARONS AND BECOME AN 'OVERT' TAX RAISING OPERATION	5	4	4	2	3	18

The basic form of SAFe analysis can be augmented by weighting the screening factors to reflect relative importance or having hurdles (eg yes/no) where screening factors are about thresholds. Rating scales can also be calibrated against levels of performance, with top of the scales and mid-points defined to make judgement easier, but the framework remains a route to harnessing subjectivity. Herein lie its three main vulnerabilities. First, for some it introduces what they see as science to decision making and with that a tendency to believe the scores. However, even if the technique wears the clothes of mathematics, it is still based on subjectivity and qualitative data. Psychologist Professor Jonathan Haidt referred to this illusion of logic as 'scientism' (Haidt, 2013).

Second, people tend to favour comparing things that are directly comparable (Ariely, 2008) and avoid comparing things that can't be easily compared. Hence SAFe resonates most where strategic options are more variations on a theme rather than diverse and radical departures in direction.

Third, SAFe analysis can discriminate against novel ideas, especially around the feasibility criterion. Departures from current business models, the jumping of curves and the shifting of horizons typically expose an organization to a capability deficit. To do something fundamentally different to what's currently happening usually necessitates new capabilities. While the organization might already possess some useful capabilities for step-change thinking, it is unlikely to possess the full suite. A consequence is that more radical ideas get scored low on feasibility, while those options closer to the current business model get stronger feasibility marks. Also, options that represent a departure from a current business model tend to score low on acceptability. Discontinuous change tends to demand high levels of effort in respect of stakeholders. Given the implications of the nature of change and disruption reported above, a leadership team should be mindful of SAFe's inherent leaning in the direction of the status quo.

The effects of these vulnerabilities can be minimized by skilled facilitation, but this depends upon the group of people who've come together having the required insight to use SAFe appropriately. As with many strategy frameworks, SAFe's role is not to give answers but to help leaders have better conversations.

Yes, we struggle to join the dots

Strategic decision making is difficult because the world is changing, but we don't always see it. We are uncertain whether the application of classical strategy models provides the best help to leaders in this context. Classical strategy models are pretty much hard-wired into the way that strategy is presented in the literature and in management education.

The understanding of business strategy is changing and, with that, classic strategy approaches are being increasingly used out of context. David Snowden, while working at IBM, led the development of the Cynefin decision making framework (Kurtz and Snowden, 2003). 'Cynefin' is a Welsh word that means 'habitat' or 'accustomed'. What Snowden sought to do was offer a habitat for executives' decision making that was relevant to the particular situation under investigation, appreciating that different situations had different habitat defining characteristics. Snowden identified four main habitats, together with an additional central one of disorder.

The 'simple' or 'obvious' habitat is about known knowns. In this habitat, the relationship between cause and effect are sufficiently clear and it is possible to apply what Snowden called 'best practice'. The 'complicated' habitat involves known unknowns, and the approach to solving challenges in this area is to appreciate that the relationship between cause and effect has several possible solutions, expertise is required, and scenarios can be built and tested. Snowden referred to this area as requiring 'good practice'. The 'complex' habitat deals with unknown unknowns. Here, cause and effect can only be determined retrospectively, as the interrelatedness and dynamism of the many factors involved make the complex habitat impervious to reductionist approaches (Stewart, 2002). The complex habitat favours 'emergent practice'. The fourth habitat is 'chaos'. Here the relationship between cause and effect is unclear and too confusing to wait for a knowledge-based response (Lambe, 2007: 136). The recipe here is to act first, being quick and decisive, then retrospectively reflective. Snowden sees the chaos habitat as being the domain of 'novel practice'. The central 'disorder' habitat serves to represent situations where it is unclear which of the habitats prevails in a situation, hence which approach to decision making will serve best. Within the Cynefin framework, classic strategy is most relevant to decisions in the 'simple' habitat and, when techniques around scenario planning are involved, in the 'complicated' one. Outside of these domains, other ways of approaching strategic decision making will serve better.

In their article 'Your strategy needs a strategy', Martin Reeves and colleagues from Boston Consulting Group suggested two main variables that govern the best approach to strategic management for a given context (Reeves, Love and Tillmanns, 2012). The two variables are 'predictability', which is about how accurately into the future one can forecast, and 'malleability', which is about the degree to which the shape, size and nature of the sector can be influenced by the actions of any of the competitors within it. Placing those two variables as axes of a matrix leads to four broad strategy styles. One is labelled 'classical'. This is where the prevailing sector characteristics are high predictability and low malleability. This is the domain served well by the well-known, established strategy frameworks and concepts. The other three areas on the matrix lend themselves to other approaches to strategy. In 'visionary' strategy, predictability is high, as is malleability. Here, a company has the power to shape the future and also the ability to predict the pathway by which that future can be realized. This approach to strategy can draw capably on classical strategy concepts, as companies can take deliberate steps without the need to keep too many options open. The combination of low predictability and low malleability leads to an 'adaptive' approach. A successful strategy here is likely to be based around the flexibility of a constant refocusing of goals, resources and tactics, with the organization in tune with the nature of change the sector is subject to. In contexts that are not predictable but are malleable, a 'shaping' style of strategic practice is suggested. As with adaptive strategy, shapers typically will employ shorter planning cycles, but unlike in the adaptive style the focus of shapers is beyond the current ecosystem. This requires skills in collaboration and marketing especially, as new capabilities are assembled, networks formed and sectors redefined.

In the book that followed the original paper, Reeves and colleagues introduced a fifth approach to strategic practice (Reeves, Haanæs and Sinha, 2015). In keeping with the original four, the fifth approach, 'renewal', suggested a recommended strategic style somewhat removed from classical strategy. Renewal is about preserving resources in the revitalization of the organization when it faces external circumstances so challenging that prevailing business approaches can't be sustained.

A further codification of the strategy practice landscape comes from the authors of the UK's best-selling strategy text. In *Exploring Strategy*, Gerry Johnson and colleagues relate the degree of certainty around the sector in question and the degree of complexity (Johnson et al, 2014). This is also the representation of strategy used by the Institute of Directors when it helps boards of directors and senior leaders determine the most effective way to approach strategic decision making in their organizations (see Figure 1.2). In contexts of high certainty and low complexity, classic strategy approaches can be very useful for analysis as a precursor to execution. In situations where certainty is low but complexity is low (meaning there are few variables in play), different scenarios can

Figure 1.2   Certainty–complexity grid

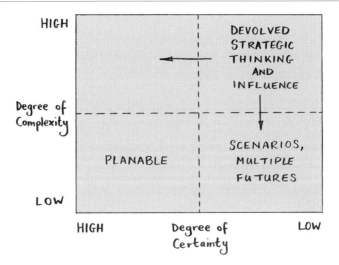

be built and tested. We know of one strategy consulting firm based in Glasgow that took the precaution of registering a new company under English law and setting up a London office in the run-up to the Scottish independence referendum of 2014. In other situations, where uncertainty is high and complexity also high, the recommended approach to the development of strategy involves devolution of strategic thinking and influence, with more power given lower down the organization and more expected in terms of connections and strategic capability.

While there are differences between the three approaches above – Cynefin, 'predictability/malleability', 'certainty/complexity' – they are unified on one key point. Classic strategy concepts are useful, but not universally so. Indeed, advances in computing technology are suggesting that, as algorithms can forecast linear relationships better than the human brain, letting a computer make decisions in a stable environment where predictions are based on historical data becomes a possible route to stronger performance. However, the further the context in question moves from a simple predictable one, the more strategic decision making needs to look beyond traditional frameworks and the more it needs to draw upon a human ability to make the calls.

Summary

In this chapter we have looked at why businesses find it increasingly difficult to grasp the shifts going on in the world, and how this makes strategic decision making difficult:

- The pace of change seems faster and the nature of change is more complex in the 21st century. The popular classical strategy models, while useful for more linear contexts, are appearing less valuable in contemporary strategy.

- Technological advances are facilitating opportunities for novel approaches and rendering many current business models vulnerable – exposing businesses to competition from outside of their sectors.

- Shifting socioeconomic boundaries are seeing a broadening of success criteria for organizations, for example the private sector's embrace of corporate responsibility, and are altering the terms of reference around which strategic decisions are made.

Chapter 2 explores the second of the two main challenges that organizations need to address – the internal climate, with its organizational inertia and individual biases.

References

Aguilar, F (1967) *Scanning the Business Environment*, Macmillan, New York

Ansoff, I (1957) Strategies for diversification, *Harvard Business Review*, 35 (5), 113–24

Ariely, D (2008) *Predictable Irrational: The hidden forces that shape our decisions*, HarperCollins, London

Aronow, S (2016) Gartner Supply Chain Top 25, www.gartner.com/technology/supply-chain/top25.jsp

Bennett, N and Lemoine, G J (2014) What VUCA really means for you, *Harvard Business Review*, January–February

Branman, M (2016) Place your bets: BMW is running one heck of an innovation race, *Digital Trends*, 24 October

Brynjolfsson, E and McAfee, A (2014) *The Second Machine Age: Work, progress and prosperity in a time of brilliant technologies*, W W Norton & Company, New York

Dodds, R, Manyika, J and Woetzel, J (2015) *No Ordinary Disruption: The four global forces breaking all trends*, PublicAffairs, New York

Ericsson (2013) *Annual Report 2013*, Ericsson, Stockholm

Freedman, L (2013) *Strategy: A history*, Oxford University Press, Oxford

Fuller, R B (1938) *Nine Chains to the Moon*, Anchor Books, New York

Haidt, J (2013) *The Righteous Mind: Why good people are divided by politics and religion*, Penguin, London

Handy, C (2015) *Second Curve: Thoughts on reinventing society*, Random House Business, London

Harrysson, M, Métayer, S and Sarrazin, H (2014) The strength of weak signals, *McKinsey Quarterly*, February

Johnson, G et al (2014) *Exploring Strategy: Texts and cases*, 10th edn, Pearson, London

Junger, S (1997) *The Perfect Storm: A true story of men against the sea*, W W Norton & Company, New York

Kurtz, C F and Snowden, D J (2003) The new dynamics of strategy: sense-making in a complex and complicated world, *IBM Systems Journal*, **42** (3), 462–83

Lambe, Patrick (2007) *Organising Knowledge: Taxonomies, knowledge and organisational effectiveness*, Chandos Publishing, Oxford

Levitt, T (1960) Marketing myopia, *Harvard Business Review*, July–August

Luft, J and Ingham, H (1955) The Johari window, a graphic model of interpersonal awareness, *Proceedings of the Western Training Laboratory in Group Development*, University of California, Los Angeles

McGrath, R G (2013) *The End of Competitive Advantage: How to keep your strategy moving as fast as your business*, Harvard Business Review Press, Cambridge, MA

Normann, R A (2001) *Reframing Business: When the map changes the landscape*, John Wiley & Sons, Chichester

Porter, M E (1979) How competitive forces shape strategy, *Harvard Business Review*, March–April

PR Newswire (2007) S&P releases list of 86 companies in the S&P 500 since 1957, 2 March

Pym, H (2012) Zombie companies eating away at economic growth, *BBC News Online*, 13 November

Ramadan, A et al (2015) *Time to Market Cap: The new metric that matters*, A Category Design Research Report, Play Bigger Advisors

Reeves, M, Haanæs, K and Sinha, S (2015) *Your Strategy Needs a Strategy: How to choose and execute the right approach*, Harvard Business Review Press, Boston, MA

Reeves, M, Love, C and Tillmanns, P (2012) Your strategy needs a strategy, *Harvard Business Review*, September

Rice, J B and Hoppe, R M (2001) Supply chain versus supply chain: the hype and the reality, *Supply Chain Management*, September–October

Ricks, T E (2011) Rumelt on strategy (VI): A real strategy is made more by induction than deduction, *Foreign Policy: The Global Magazine for News and Ideas*, 25 October

Rumsfeld, D (2002) USA Defense Department Briefing, 12 February

Stewart, T (2002) How to think with your gut, *Business 2.0*, November

Stewart, T (2008) The five competitive forces that shape strategy: Interview with Professor Michael E Porter, *Harvard Business Review*, https://www.youtube.com/watch?v=mYF2_FBCvXw

Sull, D (1999) Why good companies go bad, *Harvard Business Review*, July–August

Taleb, N N (2007) *The Black Swan: The impact of the highly improbable*, Penguin, London

Taleb, N N (2013) *Antifragile: Things that gain from disorder*, Penguin, London

van der Heijden, K et al (2002) *The Sixth Sense: Accelerating organizational learning with scenarios*, Wiley, Chichester

Williams, D K (2013) Staying in business forever: how to create a 100 year company, *Forbes*, 10 April

Wright, G and Cairns, G (2011) *Scenario Thinking: Practical approaches to the future*, Palgrave Macmillan, Basingstoke

Organizational inertia 02

Why enterprises find it difficult to change

If you do what you always do, you'll get what you've always got.
HENRY FORD

In Chapter 1 we explored the challenge that leaders face in making sense of the world. This chapter looks internally, at organizational inertia, which is the second of the two challenges that organizations face in making effective strategic decisions. Central to the idea of organizational inertia is the notion of the 'incumbent's curse' – a term relating to the apparent lack of radical innovation demonstrated by organizations within their current market space (Chandy and Tellis, 2000).

Yes, you have a strategy

'We don't have a strategy.' This is one of the comments we sometimes face at the start of strategy workshops with senior executives. Any existing organization has momentum and has a strategy. It is deploying resources, generating value and doing this with a degree of intent. Whether or not the strategy is understood, debated or even optimized is another thing. Strategy is that sequence of actions or events unfolding in real time, as realized even if not planned. If organizations are unclear about what their strategy is, the lines of enquiry posed in Osterwalder and Pigneur's *Business Model Generation* (2010) can help shine a light.

An organization's current trajectory is its default position, and becomes the reference point for the decisions it takes about strategy. Newton's second law of motion states that any change in momentum for a body will require the application of force. Without such force, prior momentum prevails.

Organizations and 'becoming'

The word 'becoming' describes the evolution of an organization as it seeks to remain relevant in a shifting world. 'Becoming' can involve periods of incremental change where approaches are tweaked and modified. It can also include more intense periods of change where the business is effectively remodelled. The result is that the organization changes form over its life and becomes something different to how it started out.

Netflix was established in 1997 with an original business model that involved serving the US market with DVDs by mail order. Its competitors at the time were the video and DVD rental stores, such as Blockbuster. Netflix started with the 'pay per rental' model of the well-established rivals, with an initial offering of under 1,000 titles. It altered its approach quickly and introduced a monthly subscription concept in 1999. In the following year it extended this to unlimited rentals for a flat fee and without late fees for returns, thus offering a very different value proposition to that of its bricks-and-mortar competitors. By 2005, Netflix offered 35,000 film titles and was shipping 1 million DVDs every day. As technology progressed, Netflix reoriented the business towards streamed content. This took the emphasis away from putting DVDs into packages and then into the post, and oriented it towards the digital access of video content. In 2011, Netflix began its next move, which was into original content for on-demand television. It became the creator of content, and not just the conduit for it. Netflix has enjoyed success, with critical acclaim and an audience appetite for its productions like *House of Cards*, *Arrested Development* and *Orange Is the New Black*. Comments have been made that what Netflix has achieved will accelerate the demise of conventional television programming. With the strategic acumen demonstrated thus far by this relatively young company, few believe that Netflix's current shape will be its final one.

Netflix's success in remaining relevant in a changing world needed decisions and actions to alter its momentum. The process of 'becoming' is unlikely to happen without intervention. As reported in *Harvard Business Review*, Shane Tedjarati, President and CEO of high-growth regions at Honeywell, painted a picture of the approach he took to shock the organization's top team about opportunities within China. He recognized he had to be unconventional in his approach and not rely on a set of 'pretty slides'. Instead he crafted presentations that chimed with the business and culture. In one, titled 'The hungry Chinese entrepreneur', he told a story about five people who grew multimillion-dollar businesses in China by developing products in direct competition with Honeywell's. The combined impact of their effect, he said, 'was like the Red Army march'. The dramatic impact of the presentation moved the top tier of Honeywell, including its four business group leaders, to invite Shane to work with their senior staff. 'The globalization conversation had begun', he reflected (Minguet et al, 2014: 82).

Not every organization demonstrates the same strategic dexterity as Netflix, as the fortunes of Blockbuster show. Blockbuster was set up in 1985 and grew strongly by rolling out its model of video rental via locally sited stores. One of Netflix's founders, Reed Hastings, reputedly came up with the idea for Netflix when he had to pay a $40 late return fine for *Apollo 13* at a local rental store, although this story is contested (Keating, 2014). Having tightly managed rental periods with penalties for late returns was very much the prevailing model in the video rental sector at the time, and was indeed the Blockbuster approach. Starting with a relatively clean sheet of paper, Netflix was more able to pursue the idea of a subscription model without overdue fines. Blockbuster was imbued with the established approach and stayed with late payment fees as part of its economic model until 2005, when it dropped them with 'The end of late fees' advertising campaign. Blockbuster never perhaps felt comfortable with this move; it effectively reintroduced them in 2010 as 'additional daily rentals' at a time it was struggling to make money. Blockbuster, still functioning as a bricks-and-mortar service provider, filed for bankruptcy protection in September 2010. Ten years earlier, Blockbuster had the opportunity to buy Netflix. The asking price was $50 million. Blockbuster declined. While people have, with the benefit of hindsight, criticized Blockbuster for lack of enterprise, at that time it had a turnover of nearly $5 billion and effectively owned the sector. Netflix's revenue was $36 million, and it also had yet to show a profit. Blockbuster had already put in place a response to the very thing that the acquisition of Netflix could have offered – a solution to online opportunities. In July 2000 Blockbuster announced a 20-year deal with Enron Broadband Services (a subsidiary of Enron) to sell movie-on-demand services on its broadband network by the end of the year. Two Enron executives were arrested for fraud for allegedly reporting $111 million of fictitious revenue from the venture with Blockbuster, and this scandal, revealed in October 2001, contributed to Enron's demise. Throughout its short life the Blockbuster–Enron Broadband Services relationship was beset by difficulties. Blockbuster lost pace, and probably also lost some heart. It wasn't until 2008, two years before its own demise, that Blockbuster re-energized its ambitions in streamed content when it announced a venture with Californian-based broadband company 2Wire (*PR Newswire*, 2008).

Blockbuster's own response to a changing world can be viewed as a consequence of the type of organization it had become as a result of the decisions it had made in previous years. History matters. It demonstrated a path dependency whereby its history was shaping its future. Organizational momentum is as hard to change as the momentum of the physical objects to which Sir Isaac Newton originally referred. Consultants often ask clients a question designed to surface issues of path dependency and the legacy of previous decisions. That question is: 'If you were to set this organization up from scratch, would it look like it does now?'

Emergent strategy meets path dependency

The idea of emergent strategy, as promoted by Henry Mintzberg, is well represented in the strategy literature (Mintzberg, 1978). It describes the situation where an organization's strategy evolves over time, based on decisions taken by its managers and their consequences in a changing world, rather than a grand plan that is crafted at the beginning and then faithfully implemented. The following example from the fireworks sector illustrates the concept in practice.

The UK's leading firework business is Black Cat, a wholly owned subsidiary of Chinese manufacturing and trading business Li & Fung. In the UK, Black Cat's strategy focuses on multiple retailers. While few in number, they accounted for around 80 per cent of fireworks sales to the general public. In 2009, Black Cat introduced an e-commerce platform to sell fireworks direct to the public. By having multiple brands, being mindful of price parity and being able to offer different products, Black Cat worked out a way to bring to life this new route to market without upsetting its core business via the multiples. This enabled Black Cat to sell fireworks on a 365-day and 24/7 basis, whereas the multiples had a sales window restricted by retailing regulations to just a few weeks a year, and also to claw back the retailers' part of the margin in the value chain. In parallel with this, Black Cat continued to develop its relationship with the UK multiples sector and extended its share of the market via this channel by focusing on service, logistics and back-office support for multiples that stocked fireworks. In 2013, as more of the multiples moved into providing online platforms in addition to their stores networks, Black Cat was invited by two of the UK's leading multiples to work with them on the online retailing of fireworks under the retailers' own brands. The 2013 opportunity was probably off the radar four years earlier and was probably only possible as a result of the actions Black Cat took in 2009 onwards. Working with multiples on the online retailing of fireworks was not part of Black Cat's original plan, but an opportunity that emerged from decisions Black Cat had made previously and actions it took accordingly.

Strategic decisions can be viewed as logically incremental (Johnson et al, 2014). Behind the idea of logical incrementalism is recognition by leaders that the uncertainty present in markets can't be managed using forecasts and predictions based on historic data. In logically incremental approaches, organizations can avoid going for precise goals that might be too restrictive and favour more liberally crafted aspirations that act as guiding principles or beacons on the horizon for the organization to aim towards. The organization may also deliberately experiment with new ideas and initiatives around the edges of its core business such that it stimulates its learning and seeks to future-proof itself, mitigating its dependency on a single recipe.

Many businesses have a tacit understanding of logical incremental-ism, even if they are not familiar with the label. Several of our clients have turned this into practice by having strategies reaching forward three or five years. But these businesses understand the need to keep their finger on the pulse of their strategy, knowing that change will be necessary within its life. Typically every year, the organization takes stock and reappraises itself with respect to its environment and finesses elements of its strategy accordingly. The present fash-ion for the annual strategy 'away day' is often part of this recipe for leadership teams (Hill, 2016), to the point this has become parodied (Vincent, 2016).

The magnitude of the changes depends on what the organization learns, with fundamental changes often predicated on seismic shifts in the world and more moderate changes linked to a more gradual evolution of markets. In this way, strategic decisions have a logical foundation and strategies move forward incrementally. Figure 2.1 shows this dynamic, where the business's strategy is annually refreshed to take account of the way its world unfolds.

'Strategic drift' occurs when an organization's strategy develops in a way that's progressively out of step with the world, despite the intents of its leadership. It drifts away from a strategy that was highly appropriate and fitting to one that appears increasingly disconnected

Figure 2.1   Stage 1: logical incrementalism

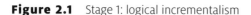
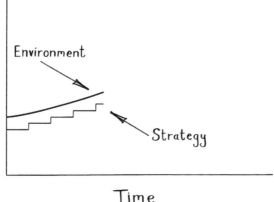

with the flow of markets. This can be a slow burn. The strategy becomes less relevant over time, and the organization seems to preside over its own potential demise as a consequence. This is not to say leaders deliberately sabotage their organizations. It is a reflection that, despite the intention of keeping the strategy tuned, the freedom to be properly 'logically incremental' is constrained. One of our favourite client insights came from the head of strategy in a public sector body. She said it never failed to surprise her how little changes in the environment over 18 months but over a decade, how much. Companies typically overestimate external shifts over the short term, but substantially underestimate them over the longer period.

The roots of HMV can be traced back to the start of the recorded music industry. In the mid-part of last century, this UK-based business was active in the areas of record production, the manufacturing of television sets and radios, and retailing music via high street music stores. It was this retail element of the business that became the core enterprise. There were over 300 HMV stores by the end of last century, including the world's largest record store at the time in Oxford Street, London. In its 2002 annual report, the HMV Group posted the following statement, which effectively heralded HMV's intent to stay away from online channels: 'Contrary to some forecasts in recent years, the internet has settled down to become a worthwhile but minority channel to market. For example, internet book sales have plateaued at just over 5 per cent of the market, and it seems unlikely that there will be sufficient demand to enable multiple operators to develop profitably.'

The statement was made in support of HMV's bricks-and-mortar approach to retailing in the face of embryonic competition. In January 2013, the HMV Group entered administration. There are many factors that contributed to the demise of a highly respected brand. Path dependency implies that, once an organization is progressing along a certain course of action, it has a momentum that serves to guide its future decisions along that same path. And each strategic decision potentially reinforces the organization's wiring and impact on its future mobility – it is difficult to 'un-build' an organization that has been assembled for a specific purpose. In so many cases, strategic decisions are not fully reversible. What are known as 'hard wiring' and 'soft wiring' factors can result in an organization's path dependency. Hard wiring relates to the enterprise's tangible aspects such as structure, systems and processes, staff and strategy. Soft wiring is about the organization's skillset and competences, prevailing culture, values and leadership style. Visually, path dependency in the context of an emergent strategy can be represented as in Figure 2.2. As the environment changes over time, the enterprise's leadership annually tunes the strategy to keep it relevant in a changing world, but in so doing conditions the organization down a specific path.

HMV's 2002 dismissal of the threat of online retailing in its space was made in the wake of the dot.com crash, which saw many investors lose significant sums in tech ventures. But HMV's challenges went beyond external factors. The organization's hard and soft wiring conspired against it. HMV's path dependency was oriented along the route of conventional retail. It had become highly proficient in the sourcing and management of suitable real estate. It progressively mastered upstream logistics and knew how to recruit, train and support front-of-house staff to provide the necessary customer experience in store. It presided over an operating profit in excess

Figure 2.2   Stage 2: emergent strategy and strategic drift

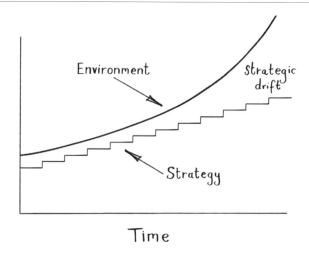

of £100 million, which numbed the appetite to change its recipe, especially in light of the failure of many e-commerce enterprises at this time.

Path dependency resulting from hard and soft wiring can be seen at the core of many of the strategic impasses that beset the commercial sector. Organizations are intentional. It's not that they become stupid. Instead, they were set up for a specific purpose and tend to be at their most high-functioning when focused on their original purpose. Once an organization has put in place a particular type of management system, it focuses its attention on the data that the system generates. And, while it might respond to the messages in the data, it becomes more blinkered in its approach. For example, the falling fortunes of the major UK-based retailer Tesco have been partly explained as a consequence of its Clubcard data, gathered electronically at the point of sale, which shows the spending behaviour of its customers on Tesco products and services. It was this system that had helped make Tesco the market leader a decade or so previously and generated a strategic advantage that was the envy of the sector. But any management information is only capable, at best, of answering the questions asked of it. The changing behaviour patterns in consumer markets, stimulated in no small way by the 2008 global economic crisis, were not sensed and acted upon quickly by Tesco, as it was too busy looking in other directions. Organizations become the product of their previous investments, commitments and decisions.

We've referred to the impact of strategic drift and shown the progressive gap that can occur between the organization's strategic decisions and its environment, as played out in its strategy. There comes a time when strategic drift makes the organization too disconnected from what the world is looking for and incapable of being valuable. Such redundancy often leads to a crisis point. The crisis point is visible at the moment it occurs. But, from the point of view of strategic decision making, the issue is less to do with any decisions immediately prior to the point of crisis and more to do with those taken (or not taken) further back in time. Blockbuster's own crisis towards the end in 2010 was less attributable to the actions of its main competitors Netflix and Redbox around the time in 2009/10 and more attributable to the dynamics of the Blockbuster machine in earlier years.

Why organizational momentum is unchallenged

There are several reasons why organizations behave more like Blockbuster than Netflix, perpetuate existing trajectories and don't challenge their momentum.

First, as we have seen, organizations have their own strategic DNA that sets the tone for how they approach future possibilities. This is the 'soft wiring' that subtly but strongly guides the organization forward. Soft wiring has been considered to be a major factor that hampered British Airways' (BA's) attempt to participate in the European low-cost short-haul market, with its creation of Go. Go was BA's venture into low-cost short-haul air travel. It was established in 1998 following the success of firms like EasyJet and the growth of the low-cost sector. Go didn't fulfil its commercial aspirations in what was becoming an increasingly competitive low-cost air travel market. It was also felt that it was beginning to cannibalize BA's own short-haul service by capturing customers who would otherwise have travelled on BA branded planes (the Go value proposition was not seen as distinct from that of BA's). In 2006, Go was put up for sale by BA and eventually bought by its management team led by Go's chief executive Barbara Cassani. Go had the benefit of its own chief executive, administrative headquarters separate from the rest of BA, and its own distinctive branding, but under its BA custodianship it was infused with the 'deep pile dark blue carpet' sense of conservative establishment that its parent, one of the strongest operators in global premium long haul, had at its core. Ryanair's reflection on Go at the time of sale was 'expensive aircraft, flying to expensive, congested airports' (Cope, 2000). Culture, as we know, trumps strategy. The term 'strategic essence' is sometimes used in a similar vein. In the opinion of strategy consultant James Robertson (2015), an organization's strategic essence 'virtually never changes'. Colloquially the expression of culture as 'the way we do things around here' resonates with many, but Edgar Schein's view that an organization's culture is a 'residue of success' (Schein, 1999) reminds us that culture is a legacy issue. It is the past projecting itself on to the future.

Second, the development trajectory of organizations can also be limited through isomorphism. Institutional isomorphism was first described by Paul DiMaggio and Walter Powell (1983). With isomorphism, organizations grow up similarly to those they compete directly with. This is for two main reasons: 1) organizations in the same sector tend to be subject to the same environmental conditions, which means the organizational design solutions that each of them figure out look similar; and 2) there is a tendency for organizations in the same sector to imitate each other by importing what each sees as good practice and salving anxieties about missing out on what competitors might achieve. This means that, with multiple players all developing in the same general way, the ecosystem in which they participate becomes constrained, making it harder for independent action by any one firm.

Third is investment. Research by McKinsey & Co looked at the capital allocation decisions of 1,600 US companies over a 20-year period. The findings showed that for one-third of businesses in the sample 'the amount of capital they received was almost exactly that received the year before'. The energy devoted to strategic planning in corporations seems to result in only modest shifts in where resources are focused. Consequently, these businesses 'moved forward at a lower gear' than those in the sample that were more fluid in their allocation of resources across business units from one year to the next (Hall, Lovallo and Musters, 2012).

Fourth is the human element in relation to how information is interpreted and used in decision making. It is estimated that a person's day-on-day behaviour is 40 per cent habit (Rubin, 2015), an unquestioned and automatic replay of what the person has become accustomed to doing.

In this context human decision making is dominated by a 'satisficing' approach. 'Satisficing' is the amalgamation of 'satisfying' and 'sufficing', a concept introduced by American social and political scientist Herbert Simon (1947) that illustrates how people limit their search for information to 'just enough' for the matter in hand. Rather than having exhaustive insight and a complete picture, we seek a satisfactory solution rather than an optimal one. The bounds of our search are influenced by what we've seen before, and we end up extrapolating from the past. We exhibit the tendency to see the problem, or solution, from our own experiential vantage point (Wright, 2001). As leadership coach Dr Mike Comer, President of Hayes Group International, expressed it, 'We view things autobiographically.' Within decision making there is a phenomenon called 'projection bias', which is the tendency of individuals to overplay how much their future preferences will be like today's. Projection bias helps explain why people are more likely to buy a convertible car when it's warm and sunny and a four-wheel drive after a fall of snow. Projection is also played through in the way that innovative changes are initially framed. The automobile was first developed in the late 1800s. The first automobiles were called 'horseless carriages' and did indeed look like carriages without horses. For most businesses, their first websites amounted to little more than electronic brochures, just as the first online newspapers closely resembled their print forebears in style. In 1942, psychologist Abraham Luchins identified the Einstellung effect in decision making. Einstellung refers to a predisposition to solve a given problem in a specific manner even though better or more appropriate methods of approaching it may exist.

The familiar patterns or characteristics a problem presents usually reinforce prevailing decision making biases and hence the outcome of the deliberations. When we're under pressure and subjected to information overload, we are less likely to think laterally and more likely to exhibit a dominant response that amounts to an extension of the current situation – we'll pedal harder, rather than think perhaps we should get off this bike. In an easy task the dominant response is usually correct, while in a more difficult one (for example a strategic decision) the dominant response is usually sub-optimal. As Andrew Campbell and colleagues explain in their paper 'Why good leaders make bad decisions', our brains assess what's going on using pattern recognition, which integrates information from many different parts of the brain. Faced with a new situation, we make assumptions based on our prior experience and judgement. This can lead us to think we understand what we don't, and make the incorrect call (Campbell et al, 2013).

The personal element in decision making

There are additional complications in strategic decision making that are rooted in human factors, especially in the way people process information and the way that is affected by people's subconscious. These are typically labelled as biases and heuristics. A 'bias' suggests an inclination, preference or prejudice. A 'heuristic' is a rule of thumb, a practical approach to problem resolution that while not perfect is sufficient for the matter in hand. Jonathan Haidt (2006) presented a helpful metaphor when he described the human mind as 'elephant and rider'. The emotional side of the brain is the elephant and the rational side the rider. Sitting on top of the elephant, the rider holds the reins and looks to be the leader. However, the rider's control is precarious, as the elephant is significantly stronger. The elephant's hunger for instant gratification is the opposite of the rider's quality, which is the ability to think long-term, to plan, to think beyond the moment.

Much about biases and heuristics is about the instinctive, subconscious elephantine reaction – the autopilot to decision making. This is not to say that heuristics, as fast and frugal short cuts, in decision making are bad things. We depend on them greatly to handle the vast quantity of decisions we have to make on a day-to-day basis, and to do so reasonably effortlessly – rational, conscious decision making is harder work (Gigerenzer and Todd, 1998). There's a good reason we have emotion – it's quick and efficient. However, we can be enlightened by understanding more about how biases and heuristics can impact on decision making, so we're in a better position to manage them. As Einstein said, 'The intuitive mind is a sacred gift and the rational mind is a faithful servant. We have created a society that honours the servant and has forgotten the gift' (Gigerenzer, 2014).

We tend to overplay the role of the rider (logical, rational decision making) in our lives and underplay the contribution of the instinctive and automatic reaction. As Haidt (2012) points out, the issue is not that people don't reason; it's that people reason to support conclusions they have already made. It is post hoc rationalization. We judge based on intuition and rationalize this decision after the fact. Our reasoning works more like a public relations executive or lawyer in justifying our opinions to others than it does like a researcher or judge weighing up evidence en route to insight. If challenges around reasoning were not big enough, our memories play tricks too. Our brains piece together fragments of information that make sense to us and hence feel like real memories. This is not a conscious act, but an automatic process based on the confabulation of information and our unwitting confusion of the actual sources of each of these snippets of information (Shaw, 2016). Just because we see clear pictures in our memories doesn't mean our recall is accurate.

Hindsight bias

Related to this is 'hindsight bias'. Hindsight bias is the inclination to see an event retrospectively as predictable, despite an absence of any objective basis for predicting it at the time. Once we learn something, it is hard for us to suspend our awareness of it. This is sometimes referred to as the 'curse of knowledge' – when people look back it is difficult not to be influenced by what is now known but wasn't known at the time. In hindsight bias, people looking back create tidy explanations for the outcomes of complex situations – a desire driven by a natural aversion to ambiguity. This leads to what Phil Rosenzweig (2007) refers to as the delusion of single explanations. Insight is misplaced and learning possibly delusional.

Thinking fast – instinctive reactions

When we work with groups of executives around strategic decision making, we often use the 'bat and ball' question as a lead into the topic of personal biases (Kahneman, 2013). Here's the question: 'The bat and ball together cost £11. The bat costs £10 more than the ball. How much does the ball cost?'

We ask the group this question and ask people to shout out the answer as soon as they're able. We push people for a quick answer and typically seek a response in a matter of seconds. The different answers we hear help illustrate the difference between the two systems of thinking in decision making – instinctive thinking and more deliberate thought.

The correct answer is £0.50. People who approached the question using deliberate thought, building a formula in their heads and slotting in the data tend to get the question right. However, people making a quick connection between the numbers 11 and 10 and the word 'more' can conclude that the answer is £1. The question is structured to lead the more casual down this path, especially when encouraged to answer quickly. In talking about the difference between the two answers, we draw attention to the difference between thinking fast and thinking slow, referencing the work of Daniel Kahneman (2013). Fast, or system one, thinking is the intuitive or instinctive reaction. It is a subconscious reaction – automatic and presenting itself readily. Slow, or system two, thinking is specific, deliberate consideration of the data. It is conscious thought, it feels harder to do, and the instinctive voice needs to be quelled to create the space for slow thinking.

Both forms of thinking are useful to people. Fast thinking does the vast majority of the heavy lifting in our lives, handling around 99 per cent of the thousands of decisions we make a day. Dealing with many choices probably necessitates automatic responses, as this volume of conscious deliberation might see people grind to a neural halt. Indeed, the capacity for fast thinking is a key factor in our being alive today. It was fast thinking that enabled our forebears to escape from danger, and the Darwinian process of natural selection has done the rest. The challenge is that the thought processes that enable us to avoid death by a sabre-toothed tiger are not necessarily the optimum for strategic decision making.

There are other biases that can affect decision making. Here are some of the more prominent ones.

Mere familiarity

We have in our nature a heuristic that psychologists refer to as 'mere exposure'. People tend to be more comfortable with what they regard as familiar rather than new territory. 'Familiarity breeds content' replaces 'Familiarity breeds contempt.' Mere exposure helps us understand why, in change situations, people have special regard for what they might lose, as that is their familiar ground. It also illuminates how branding works – subjecting people to a consistent message over time builds the foundation of awareness, easing the selling process.

In terms of decision making, it emphasizes the value of socializing ideas beforehand rather than introducing surprises at decision time. As one of our clients expressed it, nobody ponies up to the board meeting and drops the board agenda on to the table – or, at least, not more than once. Similarly, we met one chief executive who has instilled the mantra in her organization that surprises are just for birthdays and Christmas.

The psychological value of certainty over uncertainty is well understood in the change management arena, where the danger of the unknown might be a more important factor than the promise of a better future. As the sentiment attributed to psychotherapist Virginia Satir goes, 'The certainty of misery is better than the misery of uncertainty.' In strategic decision making this can translate to leadership teams homing in on the first plausible option suggested, as it reintroduces certainty where ambiguity existed. The will to go for closure quickly on options characteristically leads to a quick decision rather than the best decision.

Wilful blindness

Judges in English courts of law are supposed to have referred to 'Nelsonian knowledge'. This means a wilful ignorance of the facts and is named after the naval commander Lord Nelson, who raised his telescope to his blind eye and reported that he could see no ships. In wilful blindness there is a lack of ability to make the connections between the pieces of evidence. In some cases, as in Nelsonian knowledge, this can be a deliberate act. In other situations it could be an unwillingness to face the facts for fear of the picture they might paint. In decision making, wilful blindness can cover the failure to 'join the dots' and pick up on the implications of the signals received.

Margaret Heffernan was first sensitized to the idea of wilful blindness when reading about the trial of the disgraced CEO and Chairman of Enron: 'In his summing-up, Judge Simeon Lake gave this instruction to the jury: "You may find that a defendant had knowledge of a fact if you find that the defendant deliberately closed his eyes to what would otherwise have been obvious to him. Knowledge can be inferred if the defendant deliberately blinded himself to the existence of a fact"' (Heffernan, 2011). It's not necessarily a rational reaction – it's an emotional one – not wanting to know.

Anchoring

Anchoring describes the tendency to rely too heavily on the first piece of information offered (the anchor) when making decisions. In decision making, anchoring occurs when an initial piece of data has a subconscious effect on subsequent judgements. In trade union negotiations, for example, the trade union will set the anchor by declaring what pay rise it wishes for its members. Management rejects this claim, and this is the prelude to protracted negotiations before a management offer close to the anchor is accepted by the union. Anchoring was first identified in experiments conducted by Amos Tversky and Daniel Kahneman (1974).

Halo effect

Beyond being anchored by numbers, people are also anchored by first impressions. These resonate over a long stream of decisions. Once formed, first impressions are relatively hard to change. First impressions are a manifestation of the 'halo effect'. It is so called because psychologist Edward Thorndike likened it to a person having a halo. The halo effect describes the situation where (usually positive) impressions are extrapolated without justification, for example the assumption that a person who is successful in one area will be just as effective elsewhere (Kahneman, Lovallo and Sibony, 2013). Professor John Kay, quoted in the *Financial Times*, described its influence: 'when things are going well praise spills over on every aspect of the performance, but also when the wheel of fortune spins, the re-appraisal is equally extensive. Our search for excessively simple calculations, our desire to find great men and excellent companies gets in the way of the truth' (Rosenzweig, 2007).

Variations on these include the 'hot hand fallacy'. This is the belief that a person who has experienced success with a seemingly random event has a greater chance of further success in additional attempts. The concept has been applied primarily to sports, such as basketball (hence the name 'hot hand'), testing whether previous success at a skill-based athletic task, such as making a shot in basketball, can change the psychological behaviour and subsequent success rate of a player. Gamblers will be familiar with the idea of the 'lucky streak', and investors with the term 'Midas touch'. Some leaders are referred to as 'talismanic'. While the existence of the hot hand fallacy in different contexts is contended (Cohen, 2015), researchers have recognized it in business decision making. Working with Christina Fang at the Stern School of Business, Warwick Business School's Jerker Denrell analysed years of experts' quarterly forecasts for interest rates and inflation, reported in the *Wall Street Journal*. People whose predictions were most in line with conventional thinking proved the most accurate overall. But those who made contrarian big predictions that paid off big once or twice were viewed as the real market sages – even though their forecasts were incorrect more often than not. Follow-up lab studies confirmed that people who made wild but successful bets are remembered for those hits – but on average are the worst predictors (Denrell, 2013).

Representativeness bias

Representativeness bias is where we make generalizations based on small samples of data. We extrapolate beyond the bounds of probability and over-represent narrow experience. The extrapolation can create bias, which makes an objective view of data difficult.

In one conversation we had with a director from a Michelin-starred London restaurant, she wistfully expressed a desire to return to work in her native Scotland. She also said her Italian husband, who was the chef at the same restaurant, wasn't keen to make the move because it 'always rains there'. His view wasn't based on a study of Scotland's meteorological data but an opinion formed from three short trips to Scotland from London.

What colours our judgement is the emotional richness that is woven into our small sample of experience. As Rolf Dobelli (2013) states, people suffer from base-rate neglect. They let the story cloud a more objective analysis of the situation using baseline data and probability. What strategic decision making should benefit from is a more balanced consideration of the data, where subjectivity based on limited but personal experience can be handled appropriately without it having too loud a voice.

Confirmation bias

Confirmation bias can be demonstrated by the 'four-card challenge'. Each card features a number on one side and a letter on the other. People are invited to turn over the minimum number of cards to confirm or refute a particular hypothesis. The hypothesis relates to a particular letter-and-number combination. The task is solvable with two cards. In our experience, nearly everyone selects the same first card to turn over. This card is the most powerful card out of the four in terms of confirming or refuting the hypothesis. But very few people turn the correct second card, which is the only card in the set of four capable of also refuting the hypothesis.

This question sensitizes people to 'confirmation bias'. This is the characteristic that we're inclined to seek information that supports our beliefs and less inclined to be open to information that contradicts them. For example, in the Italian chef's next trip to Scotland, one brief shower of rain, or rain being featured on the local weather forecast, is likely to reinforce his picture.

In the context of strategic decision making, confirmation bias can lead to leaders being selective in their consideration of data and information. People can draw on information that supports their own views and, in so doing, galvanize backing for ideas that would otherwise struggle to gain momentum.

Overconfidence bias

Another one of the questions we use with groups of leaders relates to gold medals won by Greek competitors in the summer Olympic

Games over the past century. The question asks each person for three numbers. The first number is the person's estimate of the number of medals won by Greek competitors in the summer Olympic Games over this period. The second and third figures are the lower- and upper-limit number of medals within which the person is 90 per cent confident that his or her estimate for the number of gold medals rests.

The estimate of the number of Greek golds at summer Olympic Games can be worked out on the basis of the number of Olympic Games in this time period and the likely number of gold medals that Greek competitors win at each games. But what we consistently see is that, irrespective of where each estimate of the actual number of golds lies, the upper and lower limits are placed too narrowly. People have a far greater belief in their ability to estimate data than is warranted. We are overconfident.

For strategic decision making this means that, even when we're given the scope to put confidence estimates to our forecasts, we are too precise and largely incapable of embracing the breadth of confidence that more accurately represents the situation. It is as though the process of estimating, including all the assumptions we make in order to arrive at the estimate, raises the status of the estimate to something more robust than it actually is. Strategies can be founded on assumptions about market dynamics that are too narrow and about aspirations in which leaders' confidence is unwarranted.

Sunk-cost fallacy

In the context of strategic decisions there remains a real threat to leaders around continuing to support opportunities, mainly because they've already sunk resources into them and there's a psychological drive to recoup the investment by continuing to support them. This can be amplified by a view that the venture is starting to achieve results albeit not at the rate or of the scale envisaged, so there is a tendency to approve additional support as a means of helping redeem the investment already made. Sometimes this can work, but often it doesn't. The phrase that springs to mind here is 'throwing good money after bad'.

Risk aversion

Extending beyond the fallacy of sunk costs clouding the assessment of strategic opportunity comes the default human reaction to risk and investment. Risk aversion is linked to what Daniel Kahneman and Amos Tversky (1979) labelled as 'prospect theory'. People are more likely to choose things based on their need to avoid negative experiences than their desire to get positive experiences.

The experiments that shed light on this usually involve people being faced with two scenarios. In each scenario there are two options. One option is a fixed consequence of 100 per cent probability; the other option involves a gamble with the probability of success and potential scale of reward defined. The value of the fixed option is the same as the potential reward in the gamble multiplied by the probability of the gamble succeeding. For example, the fixed option is £100, and the variable option is a 25 per cent chance of winning £400. That is, both the fixed and gamble options have the same overall numerical value on a probability basis. The experiment is based on the scenario being framed in two different ways. In one way, the scenario is one of desperation, with the two options (fixed and gamble) presented as deficits. In the other way the scenario is one of relative strength, with two options (fixed and gamble) being offered as potential gains.

Researchers consistently find that people have a greater disposition to gamble when faced with positions of potential loss and a lower disposition to gamble when the context is one of potential gain. We witnessed the unintentional and unfortunate application of this bias by one independent director on a board contemplating an acquisition opportunity. The executive directors had brought this opportunity to the board with enthusiasm and, whereas the price tag on the business for sale was £80 million, the decision for that board meeting was purely about whether the organization should proceed to due diligence with this opportunity and learn more than was already known (the due diligence costs were estimated at £50,000). The independent director effectively killed the appetite to go further when she asked the executive directors whether they would bet their pensions on this deal. Not only did this change the frame of reference, as a decision to spend north of £80 million on completing and embedding an acquisition is more substantial than investing £50,000 on focused research, but she exposed the executive directors to a sense of loss in respect of their healthy pension pots. The result was a board decision not to proceed to due diligence.

A-rational decision making

We're using the term 'a-rational decision making' to describe nuanced and quirky aspects in the way that people make decisions, as distinct from the logical and rational approach. Care is needed in translating the results of psychological experiments to the domain of making strategic decisions in the real world, but what the psychologists highlight has been demonstrated in practice. Leaders are more inclined to attempt to gamble their way out of a difficult situation than they are to speculate when in a position of relative strength. As we've seen, the logic for speculation from positions of strength is strong. Without the appetite for this, a business will find it very difficult to operate any other business model than the one it's currently using. Understanding the heuristic of sunk-cost fallacy, the inclination to 'throw good money after bad' should be more readily challenged.

The overriding message is that the very people central to making strategic decisions within organizations bring into the mix a range of biases and heuristics, which add an additional layer of complication to the way information is perceived and processed. The biases and heuristics we've mentioned above are not the only ones with which the strategic decision making process has to contend. We'll return to this topic in Chapters 9 and 10 and talk about how, in our experience, their effects can be mitigated in decision making processes.

Summary

In this chapter we've looked at organizational inertia and its implications for strategic decision making. These are the key points:

- Organizations are inertial: once they invest in a certain direction and gather momentum along that trajectory, their strategic direction becomes harder to change.

- The effects of 'hard' and 'soft' wiring are further exacerbated by current success, creating a path dependency.

- Quirks in human behaviour, or biases and heuristics in the way people assimilate and process information, can lead to certain ways of acting that we are not fully aware of at the time. These also contribute to inertia at the collective or organizational level.

The result is that we're badly equipped to deal with the situations described in Chapter 1. The next two chapters look at the two types of strategic decisions organizations make – top-down and middle-out.

References

Campbell, A, Whitehead, J and Finkelstein, S (2013) Why good leaders make bad decisions, in *On Making Smart Decisions*, *HBR's 10 Must Reads*, 145–56, Harvard Business Review Press, Boston, MA

Chandy, R K and Tellis, G J (2000) The incumbent's curse? Incumbency, size and radical product innovation, *Journal of Marketing*, **64** (July), 1–17

Cohen, B (2015) The 'hot hand' debate gets flipped on its head, *Wall Street Journal*, 30 September

Cope, N (2000) BA puts its budget airline Go up for sale, *Independent*, 7 November

Denrell, J (2013) 'Experts' who beat the odds are probably just lucky, *Harvard Business Review*, April

DiMaggio, P J and Powell, W (1983) The iron cage revisited: institutional isomorphism and collective rationality in organizational fields, *American Sociological Review*, **48**, 147–60

Dobelli, R (2013) *The Art of Thinking Clearly*, Sceptre, London

Gigerenzer, G (2014) *Risk Savvy: How to make good decisions*, Allen Lane, New York

Gigerenzer, G and Todd, M P (1998) *Simple Heuristics That Make Us Smart*, Oxford University Press, Oxford

Haidt, J (2006) *The Happiness Hypothesis: Finding modern truth in ancient wisdom*, Basic Books, New York

Haidt, J (2012) *The Righteous Mind: Why good people are divided by politics and religion*, Random House, New York

Hall, S, Lovallo, D and Musters, R (2012) How to put your money where your strategy is, *McKinsey Quarterly*, March

Heffernan, M (2011) *Wilful Blindness: Why we ignore the obvious at our peril*, Simon & Schuster, London

Hill, A (2016) Strategy away days are an absurd but useful ritual, *Financial Times*, 29 August

Johnson, G et al (2014) *Exploring Strategy: Texts and cases*, 10th edn, Pearson, Harlow

Kahneman, D (2013) *Thinking Fast and Slow*, Farrar, Straus and Giroux, New York

Kahneman, Daniel and Tversky, Amos (1979) Prospect theory: an analysis of decision under risk, *Econometrica*, **47** (2), 263–92

Kahneman, D, Lovallo, D and Sibony, O (2013) Before you make that big decision…, in *On Making Smart Decisions*, HBR's 10 Must Reads, 21–40, Harvard Business Review Press, Boston, MA

Keating, G (2014) Five myths about Netflix, *Washington Post*, 21 February

Minguet, L et al (2014) Voices from the front lines, *Harvard Business Review*, September

Mintzberg, H (1978) Patterns in strategy formation, *Management Science*, **24** (9), 934–48

Osterwalder, A and Pigneur, Y (2010) *Business Model Generation: A handbook for visionaries, game changers and challengers*, John Wiley & Sons, Hoboken, NJ

PR Newswire (2008) Blockbuster and 2Wire introduce new digital media player, 25 November, http://www.prnewswire.com/news-releases/ blockbuster-and-2wire-introduce-new-digital-media-player-65519032. html

Robertson, J (2015) Strategic essence: the missing link in business improvement, 18 October, https://www.linkedin.com/pulse/ strategic-essence-missing-link-business-improvement-james-robertson

Rosenzweig, P (2007) *The Halo Effect… and the Eight Other Business Delusions That Deceive Managers*, Free Press, New York

Rubin, G (2015) *Better than Before: Mastering the habits of our everyday lives*, Crown, New York

Schein, E H (1999) *Corporate Culture Survival Guide*, Jossey-Bass, San Francisco, CA

Shaw, J (2016) *The Memory Illusion: Remembering, forgetting and the science of false memory*, Random House, London

Simon, H A (1947) *Administrative Behavior*, Macmillan, New York

Tversky, A and Kahneman, D (1974) Judgment under uncertainty: Heuristics and biases, *Science*, **185** (4157), 1124–31

Vincent, B (2016) *Five Go on a Strategy Away Day*, Quercus, London

Wright, G (2001) *Strategic Decision Making: A best practice blueprint*, John Wiley & Sons, Chichester

Top-down decisions

03

Whenever you see a successful business, someone once made a courageous decision. PETER F DRUCKER

Not making a decision means forgoing an opportunity. AULIQ ICE

The next two chapters look at two categories of strategic decisions for organizations. This chapter examines the characteristics of 'top-down' decisions and their implications for the strategy process. The next chapter (Chapter 4) looks at what we've labelled 'middle-out' decisions and explores their impact on strategy.

'Top-down decision making' is the label given to strategic decisions that are made at the senior level of the organization and then cascaded down and throughout the organization for execution. When leaders talk about strategic decision making, it is top-down decision making that is the mechanism typically implied. These strategic decisions are usually clear and substantial, and sometimes dramatic. This was illustrated by the chief executive of a sport clothing firm in the UK that was formed over 100 years ago. The chief executive said her firm had only made four strategic decisions in its history, and two of them were made on her watch (these were shifting to designing and making clothes in fabrics other than the one upon which the firm's reputation was founded and moving manufacturing offshore). Top-down strategy decisions can be game changers.

This chapter outlines the role of top-down decision making and examines its efficacy.

We expect leaders to lead

There are many definitions of leadership, but the common elements are that it's about one person's influence over a group of others. The term 'follower' suggests that people in that group respond to the leader's steer. Most organizations follow a pyramid structure with fewer people at the top than at the bottom, with those at the top in the main positions of leadership.

The prevailing culture in many organizations is we expect that, the more senior people become, the more responsibility they take for the organization. As a consequence we expect senior people to make the bigger decisions. Terms like 'boss', 'gaffer', 'head honcho' and 'big enchilada' epitomize the seniority and responsibility gap between organizational tiers. Idioms that denote responsibility, such as 'the buck stops with me' and 'carry the can', are well known. We have one client, a chief operating officer tasked with the delivery of a strategic partnership in the healthcare field, who talks about knowing 'whose neck is in the noose'.

Reward structures also infer responsibility. As senior people are usually paid substantially more than junior people, those appointing senior people, such as shareholders or investment companies, expect more from them. People assume senior office with the understanding that the responsibility sits with them and their like.

In many cases the people at the helm of the business are also its owners. This is especially the case with smaller businesses, which account for the majority of enterprises on the planet. The higher level of commitment by owner-managers to their businesses is reciprocated by affording them the freedom of action and also the inclination to make the bigger decisions.

The result of this is that, in many organizations, strategy is a top-down activity. An enterprise's strategy is influenced from top to bottom and delivered from bottom to top.

Leadership responsibility, legal ramifications

Senior-level responsibility for an organization can extend to a legal duty. For example, the UK Companies Act 2006 provides a comprehensive code of company law for companies and their directors. The title 'director' may imply seniority (many people have that term in their job title to convey only that), but in several regions of the world the most senior people in an organization also carry a responsibility in law for the conduct of the organization. There is a fiduciary duty, and most corporate governance legal codes stress two core aspects: loyalty (placing the company's interest ahead of one's own) and prudence (applying proper care, skill and diligence to business decisions). The UK's Institute of Directors, for example, helps equip thousands of senior leaders with an understanding of not only their legal duties but also the broader ramifications of corporate governance and strategic leadership.

As well as presiding over the performance of their organizations, directors have responsibilities around the conformance of their organizations with the prevailing legislation (Webster, 2010). It is easy to figure out that, if someone is put in the position of carrying the can, we can expect them to be more active and involved, so they exert a greater influence over the behaviour of their subordinates and avoid exposing themselves to situations where they become liable for the consequences of other people's decisions. In 2012, two directors from the sub-prime lending firm Cattles and its subsidiary Welcome Financial Services were fined for publishing misleading information to investors about the credit quality of Welcome's loan book and acting without integrity in discharging their responsibilities (Jones, 2012). In other cases, two former directors of Northern Rock were given six-figure fines for misrepresenting mortgage arrears data and failing to ensure the accuracy of financial information (Barrow and Sims, 2010), and four directors from two different road haulage firms were disqualified from being directors when they failed to comply with their legal duties while trying to keep their businesses afloat in difficult economic conditions (Jennings and Jones, 2015). Company officers are a potential target for litigation. According to research by professional services firm Willis Towers Watson, regulatory and other investigations top the list of director liability concerns. There are also claims made against directors and officers by private shareholders and employees, plus the growing threat of directors' liability due to cyber-security issues (Kean, 2016). Such possible legal consequences help reinforce the senior locus for decision making.

The power of vision, purpose and guiding lights

Napoleon Hill famously said the starting point of all achievement is desire (Hill, 1928), intimating that both will and direction are necessary precursors to accomplishment. Strategy is a purposive activity in that it seeks to serve or perform a useful function, and Hill's view is a central premise to how many organizations approach it. The organizational direction and will are expressed in terms like 'vision', 'mission', 'goals', 'purpose', 'mission', 'principles', 'values' and 'the why'. Whatever the terminology, this encapsulation of purpose seeks to meld direction and meaning as a route to orienting effort and galvanizing support.

Organizational purpose provides the statement of reference with which strategic decisions can be made. This element of strategic decision making recognizes that, for any organization to capitalize on the flow of the external world and make judgements on how to apply resources, an explicit or implicit understanding of purpose becomes the touchstone for interpretation. We recognize that in some strategic decision making processes the part played by vision will be greater than in others; strategy writers Donald MacLean and Robert MacIntosh refer to strategic leadership in such situations as 'inspiration givers' (MacLean and MacIntosh, 2014). The following examples from Amazon show popular forms by which organizations present their purpose. In this case, the vision is used to describe what the organization is seeking to achieve – it's a future-focused, aspirational construct. The mission outlines the value proposition or rationale behind the enterprise (Gregory, 2016):

Vision: 'To be the earth's most customer-centric company; to build a place where people can come to find and discover anything they might want to buy online.'

Mission: 'To strive to offer our customers the lowest possible prices, the best available selection, and the utmost convenience.'

Memorability around organizational purpose is also enhanced if it relates to people on an emotional level as well as a rational one. This technique is well known to marketing communications specialists, who often refer to such messages as 'sticky'. Here is how Japanese plant and equipment company Komatsu used brevity and emotion to help make its organizational purpose come alive in the late 1970s and 1980s. Komatsu had agreed its purpose as 'surround and then kill Cat' (Brown et al, 2013). Cat refers to Caterpillar Inc, the US-based global leader in the earthmoving equipment sector. To reinforce the message to its workers, Komatsu put Caterpillar's largest bulldozer on the roof of its headquarters in Tokyo, and it created the internal slogan 'Maru-C', which means 'Surround Cat.' This focus was key to Komatsu's intent to move from being a relatively small player to challenge the sector's global leader. The strategy involved building strong positions in markets outside of Cat's main areas of focus and then gradually moving into Cat's domain with a pincer movement.

Being the communicator and even the originator of the vision, mission or however the organization's purpose is articulated is considered part of the top-down approach. Here, strategic leadership becomes prominent in part of the overall strategy process. Jim Collins and Jerry Porras's (1994) study of US firms with long-term high performance concluded that this role of being the strategic catalyst by clarifying and promoting the organization's vision or purpose is a centrally important role of the strategic leader, adding weight to the efficacy of top-down decision making.

Does step-change necessitate top-down decision making?

In Chapter 1, we spoke about the need for organizations to think beyond the current horizon of an enterprise. Although timelines vary, business models are transient recipes rather than permanent solutions. The focus and energy needed to guide an organization from one horizon or business model to another usually need to come from the top. This is perhaps the most compelling argument for top-down decision making from the perspective of strategic management.

Alibaba founder Jack Ma has spoken about the need for him to keep resetting the vision. Alibaba's initial focus was to be 'an e-commerce company serving China's small exporting companies'. 'From the outset', according to the firm's website, 'the company's founders shared a belief that the Internet would level the playing field by enabling small enterprises to leverage innovation and technology to grow and compete more effectively in the domestic and global economies.' But, as the market changed and Chinese domestic consumption escalated, Alibaba launched its consumer-focused online marketplace Taobao in 2003. The focus of the enterprise moved away from its B2B origins. This was followed by the creation of Alipay, an online payment service, in 2004. By the time 2008 arrived, Alibaba's focus had broadened out to 'the development of an ecommerce system for China'. With the launch of Ali Express, the focus stepped away from just e-commerce, for example the launch of Cainiao (a logistics venture). In 2011 Alibaba announced that it was reorganizing Taobao (China's biggest online shopping site, hosting 30,000 online stores) into three separate units.

Former IBM boss Lou Gerstner points out that 'the willingness to tackle outmoded orthodoxies decisively is crucial to sustained value creation. In anything other than a protected industry, longevity is the capacity to change, not to stay with what you've got. Companies that last 100 years are never truly the same company: they've changed four or five times over that 100 years' (Barton and Wiseman, 2015). Prevailing cultures, working practices and structures tend to support the continuity of existing recipes. While this might be helpful in relation to an existing business model, established patterns of work tend not to encourage transformation to new recipes. In situations where the focus of resources needs to shift, top-down decision making can provide clarity of intent to the organization and the signal of commitment that helps declutter ambiguity.

It is difficult to conceive that organizations that have made successful strategic transitions of significant magnitude would have done so without a strong senior leadership steer. Examples here include IBM's move from being a computer business to being a services business, Netflix's shift from a mail order model to streaming technology, CBS's departure from the musical instruments business and into broadcasting and entertainment, and John Menzies's change from being a high street retailer of newspapers to a logistics and aviation service. It is hard to conceive how they would have been successful without clear guidance from the top and the preparedness of leaders to make decisions that would have been very unpopular for some.

Challenges with top-down decision making

So far, this chapter has looked at the characteristics and benefits of top-down decision making. However, its effectiveness is to a high degree dependent upon the top-down process not falling foul of any one of a series of potential pitfalls. It's important however to recognize that, along with the merits of a clear articulation of organizational purpose that comes with top-down decision making, there are shortcomings to accept.

Top-down decisions provide both focus and blinkers

The very act of focusing attention and galvanizing a business along a certain path places the object of focus under the spotlight and leaves everything in the periphery in the dark. The articulation of a clear vision generates business blinkers. Richard Wiseman, the author of *The Luck Factor* (2004), points out that people who focus too much on one issue or task tend to miss out on other opportunities. Clarity of vision, while being both a beacon and a magnet for achievement, becomes a barrier to possibilities.

Komatsu, for example, benefited from the clear sense of purpose that its 'Maru-C' slogan engendered but recognized that this focus was also restrictive. In 1989 Komatsu's new president, Tetsuya Katada, realized that Komatsu had been hampered to a degree by its unrelenting goal of eclipsing Caterpillar. Changes in the nature of the markets for construction equipment raised the vulnerability that Komatsu lacked the ability to adapt. Katada believed that focusing on Caterpillar had dampened the creativity of Komatsu's middle managers to the point that they had become afraid to question the direction of the company. Katada's solution was to recalibrate Komatsu's purpose and stop the organization comparing itself to Cat. In so doing, he deliberately moved the organization away from its crisp, clear statement of intent.

As we discussed in the Introduction, strategy is a wicked problem (Camillus, 2008). The challenges of satisfying the conflicting needs of different stakeholders lead to a situation where there is no 'correct' answer on the way to proceed. The ability of the senior team to reconcile competing agendas, and to make the call capably, is key to top-down decision making. We don't pretend this is easy. Michael Porter (1996) reminded us that selecting strategy required 'trade-offs', where a focus in one direction involved the acceptance of the shift of focus away from other directions. The reason for Michael Dell's purchase of his company's shares for $24.9 billion in 2013 was to provide Dell's founder with the opportunity to transform Dell into a supplier of services to business (Patterson, 2013), a shift whose magnitude was unlikely to have found favour with Dell's previous external investors and their appetite for quarter-by-quarter performance. The move inflated Dell's valuation by just over 25 per cent, with the share price agreed for delisting being $13.65 per share, compared to $10.88 per share immediately before the rumours of the intended delisting started to emerge some months previously. This represented a premium of just under $5 billion to bring the firm private, before the costs of any radical change to its strategy have been considered. Having the clarity and confidence to make the call, plus the ability to live with the consequences, is difficult. Frameworks such as SAFe (as covered in Chapter 1), if used well, can help a leadership team with challenging dilemmas. The increasing complexity of today's world and the upward shift in pace brought about by technology are upping the ante in this respect.

Top team strategic competence and capacity

In a top-down approach, strategic decisions rest in the hands of the few. Successful top-down decision making rests on the ability of those at the top to make appropriate strategic choices. Sir David Walker, the chairman of the board at Barclays and a noted authority on corporate governance in the UK, opined in *Harvard Business Review* that most boards don't spend enough time and effort assessing the organization's long-term strategy (Barton and Wiseman, 2015). This implies both a level of competence and capacity at the top of the organization in relation to strategic thinking.

In her work on strategic thinking, Jeanne Liedtka (1998) talks about the need for leaders to have a 'systems perspective', which implies a grasp of the big picture. She also mentions the need for leadership teams to 'think in time', which is to know enough about the mechanics of the organization for decisions to be made on the basis of the fruits of learning from experience and a dose of pragmatism. Indeed, Henry Mintzberg points out that, if one takes the 'helicopter view' (the big picture) and looks down on a forest, all that's seen is a carpet of green. How different the forest looks from ground level (Mintzberg, 2011). Both perspectives are necessary in top-down decision making. In the field of complex change this is referred to as the ability of people to 'jump up and down'. We have a client in the medical research field whose chief executive encourages all board members – irrespective of their executive or non-executive responsibilities – to 'spend more time in the macro' so they have a sense of the fundamental trends shifting the company's sector. This is direct encouragement to all members of the senior leadership team to be sufficiently engaged with the organization's markets and its external world so they can contribute big-picture perspectives to strategy discussions. Conversely, in November 2015, Andrew Green QC's enquiry into the failure of HBOS (the UK-based bank that collapsed in 2008) drew attention to the fact that not enough of the directors on the board knew enough about banking to make appropriate strategic decisions for a bank (Green, 2015). HBOS's leaders were bright people. They were just the wrong bright people. They collectively lacked the ability to understand the business from the forest floor.

McKinsey & Company's survey of 772 directors demonstrated an apparent disconnect between top-tier responsibility and a grasp of the issues – only 34 per cent of the sample said the boards on which they served fully understood their companies' strategies, and just 6 per cent felt their boards had a strong understanding of the dynamics of their firms' industries (Barton and Wiseman, 2015).

Jeanne Liedtka's work also suggests a vital quality of strategic thinking is the ability to be hypothesis-driven (Liedtka, 1998). This means the ability to bring challenge and creativity to a discussion by encouraging the subject to be considered from different perspectives. These perspectives can be organizational (for example the chief financial officer's view compared to that of the executive vice-president of

Asia Pacific operations), demographic (for example embracing gender and age distinctions) and cultural. We regularly see in our strategy consulting work that executive leaders are typically less challenging of their organization's business models than non-executive or independent voices, a factor that can limit the quality of strategic debate.

Personality issues also have a bearing. Some organizations have found personality profiles using tools such as MBTI, DISC, Belbin and Six Thinking Hats helpful for mutual awareness. There may also be variance in the top team in respect of where they choose to focus their strategic thoughts. In her exploration of critical thinking, Holly Green described five critical thinking types (Green, 2012). These are: critical thinking (objective analysis); implementation thinking (ability to organize ideas, plans and resources); conceptual thinking (seeing connections between abstract ideas); innovative thinking (generating new ideas and possibilities); and intuitive thinking (the ability to take what you sense to be true and, in the absence of evidence and knowledge, appropriately factor it into the decision).

Leon Mann and colleagues developed a research instrument to help leaders learn more about their decision making style. Called the Melbourne Decision Making Questionnaire, it distinguishes between vigilant decision making and three other default approaches. Vigilance involves a careful, unbiased and thorough evaluation of alternatives and rational decision making. Hypervigilance involves a hurried, anxious approach, epitomized by the phrase 'Whenever I face a difficult decision I feel pessimistic about finding a good solution.' Procrastination involves delaying decisions: 'Even after I have made a decision I delay acting upon it.' Buck passing involves leaving decisions to others and avoiding responsibility: 'I prefer to leave decisions to others.'

We have a colleague at the Institute of Directors who is an expert in corporate governance. He quotes the phrase 'That's another pig in the python' when talking about the capacity of a board of directors to deal with issues. The pig in this context is the issue, and the python represents the senior leadership team's limited capacity to digest. Our colleague claims this phrase is of Irish origin, but we have our doubts. However, it provides a useful reminder about the limited bandwidth that exists within any leadership team to cope with 'stuff'. With many of today's organizational models with their permeable boundaries and collaborative approaches, enterprises aren't subject to the same fixed resources and capacity as those with more traditional structures. But the fact remains, the capacity of senior leadership teams is finite and the quality of top-down decision making is dependent upon the ability of the top team to devote the necessary attention to it. Having too much to consider tends not to serve people well in decision making. If capacity is limited and people experience information overload, the tendency is for their dominant responses to prevail – that means whatever a person is naturally inclined to do becomes even more likely when the person is under pressure. This limits creative thought and fresh perspectives. People revert to type – as we've mentioned earlier, people will 'bike harder' instead of thinking 'I should get off this bike.'

At an individual level, top-down decision making also depends on the ability and disposition of the individuals contributing to the discussions and making the decisions. We touched on the area of decision making biases in Chapter 2, and linked with these is the importance of decision makers being physiologically prepared for the task. We witnessed a director of a prominent media corporation giving the instruction to his senior team that he hoped they would enjoy themselves at that evening's festivities but they were to be sure to turn up to tomorrow's strategic leadership meeting on their 'A-game'. Difficult discussions are better served by those around the table all being on their A-game. Decisions around the location for the discussions, the day of the week and the time of the day can help, as can the space given to the discussion. Cluttered and badly prioritized agendas don't help, nor does the pressure to make a decision. Having the mental space to reflect can be useful – we know one company chairman whose approach to airing ideas and exploring possibilities with the board of directors was a two-hour walk in the country for him and the other three board members. The phrase 'Sleep on it' is well known. Professor Rebecca Spencer points out that, 'when we sleep, the brain is doing some processing that gives us a clean slate', as information is shifted from short-term memory into longer-term memory (Berinato, 2016). In addition there are capabilities around tailoring, timing, emotions management, contextual sensitivity and buy-in that make some people more effective and influential in a decision making context (Ashford and Detert, 2015: 73).

The dangers of unfettered power

Typically, the number of people breathing the rarefied air at the top tier of organizations is small. The digits on two hands are normally sufficient to count them. Organizations with larger senior teams often bemoan more pedestrian board processes and ponderous decision making, while organizations with fewer people at the strategic decision making level talk of the benefits of more straightforward conversations with people they're able to know better. The term given to the latter, which involves very few, in some cases just one person, is strategic leadership as command. Here, the strategy of the organization might be directed by an individual. Canadian scholars Danny Miller and Isabelle Le Breton suggest there are advantages and disadvantages here – on the positive side it can mean speed of strategy adoption and 'sharp, innovative, unorthodox strategies that are difficult for others to imitate' (Johnson et al, 2014: 404). However, power in the hands of the few is not without its dangers. The downside is there can be 'hubris, excessive risk taking, quirky, irrelevant strategies'. Also, there is a greater exposure to the vested interests of those people – despite what is written in governance codes about putting the interests of the organization above those of the individual, conflict of interest bias, in which people are drawn to ideas that favour them, is a recognized and real issue (Banaji, Bazerman and Chugh, 2013).

When the few effectively become one, alarm bells ring. The UK Corporate Governance Code warns of any single director having 'unfettered' freedom on decision making and guides enterprises to a shared agreement on organizational purpose and a collective ownership of the strategy. In terms of forthright and focused strategic leadership in the hands of a single individual there are some exceptional successes, which include the contribution the late Steve Jobs made to the fortunes of Apple Inc. But for every Steve Jobs, whose impact on Apple was talismanic, there is also a Fred Goodwin (former CEO of the bank RBS) where unchallenged power can lead to ultimately catastrophic strategic decisions. Goodwin drove RBS's acquisition of ABN AMRO, an acquisition target greater in size than RBS, with such single-minded zeal that RBS didn't even carry out due diligence in the process, despite the near $100 billion price tag.

Defence against the risks of unfettered power is made all the more difficult by the reputation a leader might build and the impact of that reputation down the line. It is suggested that success has many fathers. An over-narrow interpretation of what has led to prior triumphs does little to diminish overconfidence in top-down decision making. We have in our behaviour a heuristic that overvalues outcomes (what we achieve) more than process. Nassim Nicholas Taleb, the author of *The Black Swan* (2007), explains this as being fooled by randomness. Achievements can lure us into thinking we have more control than we do. We may delude ourselves into believing we have a higher sense of control over the situation than external scrutiny would suggest.

The same 'halo effect' that we mentioned in Chapter 2 (Thorndike, 1920) can be experienced by leaders, to the possible detriment of effective top-down decision making. An example from UK retailer Tesco illustrates this phenomenon. In June 2010, Sir Terry Leahy announced his departure from Tesco, marking the end of a career of over 30 years, with the final 14 of those as CEO. In a brutally competitive market he presided over Tesco's substantial growth. During his time as CEO, Tesco increased its market share from 20 per cent to 30 per cent, and his reputation saw him being named *Fortune*'s European Business Leader of the Year in 2004 and, in 2005, receive the accolade of *Management Today*'s most admired business leader. The tributes poured in upon the announcement of his retirement: 'Leahy is an outstanding executive who has intellect and vision that are second to none', said Shore Capital analyst Darren Shirley. 'He must surely be written up as one of Britain's greatest businessmen' (Lynn, 2015). As time progressed, another picture started to build: the picture of a weak board and an enterprise that was caught up in its own ambition, overstretching itself burning millions on overseas ventures on its self-proclaimed growth trajectory. Documenting the story of Tesco's decline following its setbacks in the United States, scandals with horsemeat in burgers and the investigation by the Financial Conduct Authority, *Management Today* writer Matthew Lynn reports the views of a board member who sat at the top table with Leahy: 'It was an autocratic company where no-one was able to challenge Leahy and where bad news started to be ignored… and that is always a signal that a company is going to run into trouble' (Lynn, 2015). 'Success', as Bill Gates said, 'is a lousy teacher. It seduces smart people into thinking they can't lose' (Gates, Myhrvold and Rinearson, 1995). The Tesco board appeared delinquent in its duty, perhaps awed. It had ceded too much power to the hot hand of Terry Leahy and lacked the ability to contribute challenge and perspective to the decision making (Gilovich, Tversky and Vallone, 1985).

Unfettered power is just as much to do with the tone of conversations around the board table as it is with dominance of shareholding. The presence of unfettered decision making can be more subtle, as illustrated by the example below from the house-building sector.

One of the UK's major house builders suffered in this respect when it brought in a new CEO, recruited from a main competitor. The house builder in question had spent the previous decade strengthening its capability in social housing, developing a strong reputation and learning how to work with public sector and community organizations along the way. The incoming CEO, whose brief was to grow the house builder into a truly national enterprise, declared to the rest of the board of directors: 'We won't be doing any more social housing.' When challenged by the other board members, he repeated his assertion, with a little more force. There was no discussion of the rationale behind this view, and the other directors were left to hypothesize around their new CEO's commercial upbringing in a successful builder of high-volume private sector housing. This is not to say that the decision was right or wrong; hindsight is apt to distort. It was, however, one man's decision in a business that had fostered good governance and strategic decision making arrangements, involving a group of capable directors and seemingly sound board processes. The majority of the other board members sought other employment as a direct result of their experience of the new CEO, leaving others to fill the void (as selected by the CEO). The house builder subsequently moved away from social housing, focused on the more commodity-oriented sector of high-volume private sector houses, and surrendered its one area of relative advantage at around the time the UK government increased its commitment to the social housing agenda. The house builder's shareholders removed the CEO two years later.

Obstacles to small groups making good decisions

Choosing how to choose is a main theme of this book. In Chapter 1, we spoke about SAFe as a framework for helping leadership groups make decisions, and in Chapter 2 we looked at some of the biases and heuristics that beset people's decision making. There are additional challenges that can impact on the effectiveness of group decision making. These challenges extend beyond the determination of the decision making protocol (for example majority votes, unanimity, consensus, endorsement prior to further debate) that has been agreed:

- Research has shown that harmonious teams are not as effective as teams that confront, and learn through, conflict. Harmonious teams will often avoid unpleasant situations; problems will be ignored. The term 'groupthink' (Janis, 1971) refers to a situation where a discussion between people of similar disposition can fall short of its potential because all involved see things the same way. The discussion may be convivial, but the matter on hand remains under-scrutinized. Diversity of viewpoint is potentially rewarding in top-down decision making. The challenge for senior leaders in top-down decision making is to be able to harness the value that diversity brings, rather than be stifled by it.

- We spoke about the rhythm of annual strategy discussions in Chapter 2. Michael Mankins and Richard Steele call it the 'calendar effect'. In their research, Mankins and Steele found out that, for 66 per cent of the companies in their survey, planning is a periodic event, often conducted as a precursor to the yearly budgeting and capital approval process. This makes presumptions about when strategic decisions should be made, and also about the depth of effort necessary to make one (Mankins and Steele, 2013).

- The affect heuristic links with the halo effect and confirmation bias, but the impact is amplified, as it relates to a group of people rather than an individual. With the affect heuristic, the team behind a strategic proposal develops a-rational support for the idea. The more work the team puts into the idea, the more owner-ship the team feels for it. We overvalue that which is ours (Ariely, 2008). Whereas this can be helpful in respect of change leadership, the potential downside is that the team loses a grasp on objectiv-ity around the idea, closing its mind to critique and to alternative opportunities.

- The Einstellung effect (which we introduced in Chapter 2), or the 'law of the instrument', refers to a person's predisposition to solve a given problem in a specific manner even though better or more appropriate methods of solving the problem exist (Luchins, 1942). This usually reinforces existing decision making biases, is seized upon and prevents a better solution being found. The danger here is that individuals and weak teams will usually prefer to look for solutions that are 'good enough' rather than spending their energy looking for the difficult-to-achieve best solution. We worked with one director who was surprised that some boards used a method for strategic decisions other than board members giving their views on the matter before the chair summarized the position and sought consensus. While this approach may well be a sound way to proceed for some decisions, it is unlikely to be the most efficacious in every case. Top-down decision making should avail itself of the different methods by which decisions can be made. As Abraham Maslow (1966: 15) said, 'I suppose it is tempting, if the only tool you have is a hammer, to treat everything as if it were a nail.'

- Group conversations have a habit of focusing on common ground shared by group members, with topics where only some group members have experience or insight feeling more awkward. This is called the 'common information effect' (Stasser and Titus, 1985). It means the constituency of the group subtly shapes the agenda in practice and the tone of the discussion, irrespective of what the formal agenda might say.

- Group-based decision making can be affected by negativity bias (Baumeister et al, 2001). Leaders may have witnessed for them-selves the situation where they have facilitated SWOT analyses with groups and are confronted with a much longer list of weak-nesses than strengths. It is tacitly understood that bad news is stronger than good news. There are several possible reasons for this, including its alignment with threat and danger, which was key to the survival of the species. Learning tends to be richer from 'bad' experiences, as the information presented tends to be processed more thoroughly, and the general perception is that we think of people who see the downside and are more critical as more intelligent than 'glass half-full' individuals. But this bias towards negativity might not reflect the characteristics of the landscape under scrutiny.

- Evaluation apprehension is a psychological theory that predicts that, when we work in the presence of others, our concern over what they will think can either enhance or impair our performance. In poorly performing teams the group dynamic may create a 'negative evaluation apprehension', meaning that individuals hold back from making contributions for fear of being judged negatively. On the other hand, well-managed evaluation apprehension (by the chair or task owner) can lead to improved performance by creating positive pressure to perform well for your peer group, which means a higher motivation focus of effort (Cottrell et al, 1968).

- Social loafing is the tendency for people to exert less effort when working within a group than working as individuals, and it can have a negative effect on team performance and productivity. When social loafing occurs, other team members may decide to stand in for those 'slacking off', expending extra effort in order to try to overcome the potential loss of performance. The danger of this 'social compensation' is that it creates two debilitating effects. First, some people get drawn into extraordinary input – for example 25 per cent of the value-added collaboration within the group comes from 3–5 per cent of employees. Second, tension and friction increase within teams where there is high social loafing (and hence high social compensation). It causes eventual erosion of team trust and commitment, reduction of motivation and so on in performance, and even outright team failure. In high-performance teams where there is high trust, the effort and contribution are more evenly spread (Karau and Williams, 1993).

- There could be an inability to manage agreement. In the Abilene paradox, a group of people collectively decide on a course of action that is counter to the preferences of many (or all) of the individuals in the group. It involves a common breakdown of group communication in which each member mistakenly believes that his or her own preferences are counter to the group's and, therefore, does not raise objections. A common phrase relating to the Abilene paradox is a desire not to 'rock the boat'. The idea was introduced by management expert Jerry Harvey in his 1974 article 'The Abilene paradox: the management of agreement'.

While these challenges are not insurmountable, they place greater emphasis on issues like group membership, process design and chairing skills, even when decision making protocols are in place.

Can top-down decisions truly engage people?

If, and perhaps only if, top-down strategic decisions can cross the bridge to personal engagement and desire, can organizations derive the benefit? We've drawn attention to the central facet of top-down decision making being clarity of intent. We're also familiar with the levers by which top-down decisions are translated into strategic execution, for example by the allocation of resources, by changes to organizational structures and processes and by targets and measures. There is another factor to be explored, namely the degree to which the psychology of intent works as effectively with a collective as it can do at an individual level. Conversations with people about their careers, interests and accomplishments usually reinforce the picture that we attract information in line with our dominant thoughts. People often cite significant events on their own life journeys that could be dismissed as random occurrences or good fortune but under greater scrutiny became real and valuable because the person's own radar had become sensitized to them. The typical example used to illustrate this selective sensitivity to people is how many cars like the one we own we notice on the road.

The key enabler here is our personal choice about what's important to us. The radar is only activated if we are sufficiently clear on what we're looking for. There is a difference between individuals and organizations when it comes to motivation and desire. Much of the thinking around vision draws on the understanding of individual psychology. The clarity and appeal of our personal visions illuminate the pathway to us achieving them. But much of the appeal (and hence the effectiveness) from personal visions stems from the fact we worked them out for ourselves. We, individually, determine what is important to us. The challenge when translating this concept to organizations, as collections of individuals, is around whether people genuinely engage with a vision that they didn't create themselves and it is not for themselves. For example, we have one client in the higher education sector that has an ambitious vision set against a 20-year time horizon. With teams at this university, this vision has little traction, with many senior academics and managers pointing out that it means little to them as they don't expect still to be at this establishment in 20 years' time. Leaders talk about the importance of 'buy-in' and use expressions like 'skin in the game' to exemplify the importance of commitment. In the world of management thought, Simon Sinek has led the charge for leaders to engage first along the axis of personal relevance and purpose, ahead of destination (Sinek, 2011). Down at the point of strategic implementation, where decision meets practice, pragmatic consultants like Robin Speculand (2005) urge leaders to make clear why the strategy is important and what it means for everyone in the team, if the implementation is to be successful.

Can top-down decisions control organizational hydraulics?

Organizational hydraulics are the mechanisms used by business leaders to translate corporate ambition and strategy into the workings of the organization and the individuals therein. This covers the process to set priorities, cascade objectives and sense progress. They cover both hard and soft wiring. If an organization has good hydraulics, it is capable of aligning all its actions to the direction set from above – effective strategy being the application of multiple resources on a single objective. The metaphor was introduced to strategic decision making by Don Sull (2010) and has its roots in aeronautics. When a plane's pilot moves the controls, every relay, circuit and actuator responds faithfully and the plane changes course accordingly.

Contemporary strategy might question whether top-down mechanisms with faithful hydraulics are the most appropriate approach in a turbulent world. While there are attractions in cascading a central instruction through strategic objectives down to the performance management of local teams and individuals, differences between flying a plane and making strategic decisions in an organization should be appreciated. The pilot is likely to be working with information that is close to perfect, meaning it's comprehensive, robust and objective. She or he is also working in a context where the variables and the choice set are known and the terrain for the most part is predictable. This is different to most business strategy situations, where the appropriate signal from the board of directors is one that involves not just internal complexity but also external complications. Not only may the variables around which strategies are to be crafted change, but also the field of play in which the organization competes may not have a static boundary.

Summary

This chapter has explored the nature of top-down strategic decisions. It has sought to explain why this form of decision making exists and examine its efficacy with reference to the strengths and vulnerabilities associated with the approach. The key points are as follows:

- Top-down organizations evolved to sort out a particular set of problems or circumstances, for example how to manage limited liability and industrial-age values (volumes) of product or service.

- Over time, this has become the way we expect companies to work (capital structures, owner-managers etc).

- Top-down decision making, although beset by issues around conflicting priorities and limited bandwidth, has helped organizations make step-changes.

However, we are beginning to question whether, on balance, this is the best way of managing change in a VUCA world beset with wicked problems.

References

Ariely, D (2008) *Predictable Irrational: The hidden forces that shape our decisions*, HarperCollins, London

Ashford, S J and Detert, J R (2015) Get the boss to buy in, *Harvard Business Review*, January–February

Banaji, M R, Bazerman, M H and Chugh, D (2013) How (un)ethical are you?, in *On Making Smart Decisions*, HBR's 10 Must Reads, 115–32, Harvard Business Review Press, Boston, MA

Barrow, B and Sims, P (2010) Ex-Northern Rock chiefs fined for misreporting mortgage arrears figures, *Mail Online*, 14 April

Barton, D and Wiseman, M (2015) Where boards fall short, *Harvard Business Review*, January–February

Baumeister, R F et al (2001), Bad is stronger than good, *Review of General Psychology*, **5**, 323–70

Berinato, S (2016) Sleeping on it doesn't lead to better decisions, *Harvard Business Review*, May

Brown, S et al (2013) *Operations Management: Policy, practice and performance*, Routledge, Abingdon

Camillus, J (2008) Strategy as a wicked problem, *Harvard Business Review*, May

Collins, J and Porras, I J (1994) *Built to Last: Successful habits of visionary companies*, Harper Business Essentials, New York

Cottrell, N B et al (1968) Social facilitation of dominant responses by the presence of an audience and the mere presence of others, *Journal of Personality and Social Psychology*, **9** (3), 245–50

Gates, B, Myhrvold, N and Rinearson, P (1995) *The Road Ahead*, Viking, New York

Gilovich, Thomas, Tversky, A and Vallone, R (1985) The hot hand in basketball: on the misperception of random sequences, *Cognitive Psychology*, **17** (3), 295–314

Green, A (2015) *Report into the FSA's Enforcement Actions Following the Failure of HBOS*, Bank of England Prudential Regulation Authority/ Financial Conduct Authority, London

Green, H (2012) How to develop five critical thinking types, *Fortune*, May

Gregory, L (2016) Amazon.com Inc's vision and mission statement (an analysis), *Business, Management* (Panmore Institute), 21 July

Harvey, J B (1974) The Abilene paradox: the management of agreement, *Organizational Dynamics*, **3**, 63–80

Hill, N (1928) *The Laws of Success: Teaching, for the first time in the history of the world, the true philosophy upon which all personal success is built*, Ralston University Press, Meriden, CT

Janis, I L (1971) Groupthink, *Psychology Today*, 5 (6), 43–46, 74–76

Jennings, S and Jones, G (2015) The end of the road: the hard line approach to director disqualification, *DWF, The Lorry Lawyer*, 2 March

Johnson, G et al (2014) *Exploring Strategy: Texts and cases*, 10th edn, Pearson, Harlow

Jones, R (2012) Former Cattles directors fined and banned by FSA for market abuse, *Guardian*, 28 March

Karau, S J and Williams, K D (1993) Social loafing: a meta-analytic review and theoretical integration, *Journal of Personality and Social Psychology*, 65 (4), 681–706

Kean, F (2016) Survey explores directors' emerging D&O liability concerns, Willis Towers Watson, 11 July, www.towerswatson.com

Liedtka, M J (1998) Strategic thinking: can it be taught?, *Long Range Planning*, February

Luchins, A S (1942) Mechanization in problem solving: The effect of Einstellung, *Psychological Monographs*, 54 (6), i–95

Lynn, M (2015) What next for Tesco, the toxic grocer?, *Management Today*, February, 32

MacLean, D and MacIntosh, R (2014) *Strategic Management: Strategists and work*, Palgrave Macmillan, London

Mankins, M C and Steele, R (2013) Stop making plans; start making decisions, in *On Making Smart Decisions, HBR's 10 Must Reads*, 157–76, Harvard Business Review Press, Boston, MA

Maslow, A H (1966) *The Psychology of Science: A renaissance*, Joanna Colter Books, New York

Mintzberg, H (2011) *Managing*, Berrett-Koehler, Oakland, CA

Patterson, A (2013) Dell finally goes private: delisted Tuesday, *Tech Times*, 31 October

Porter, M E (1996) What is strategy?, *Harvard Business Review*, November–December

Sinek, S (2011) *Start with Why: How great leaders inspire everyone to take action*, Penguin, London

Speculand, R (2005) *Bricks to Bridges: Make Your Strategy Come Alive*, Bridges Business Consultancy Int, Singapore

Stasser, G and Titus, W (1985) Pooling of unshared information in group decision making: biased information sampling during discussion, *Journal of Personality and Social Psychology*, 48, 1467–78

Sull, D (2010) Are you ready to rebound?, *Harvard Business Review*, March

Taleb, N N (2007) *The Black Swan: The impact of the highly improbable*, Random House, London

Thorndike, E L (1920) A constant error in psychological ratings, *Journal of Applied Psychology*, **4** (1), 25–29

Webster, M (2010) *The Director's Handbook: Your duties, responsibilities and liabilities*, Kogan Page, London

Wiseman, R (2004) *The Luck Factor: The scientific study of the lucky mind*, Arrow, London

Middle-out decisions

04

An executive is a man who can make quick decisions and is sometimes right. ELBERT HUBBARD

Sooner or later everyone sits down to a banquet of consequences.
ROBERT LOUIS STEVENSON

This chapter examines the characteristics of 'middle-out' decisions and their implications for the strategy process. 'Middle-out' describes the decisions made every day by managers and staff within organizations. The decisions are made from within, rather than descending from the top, and radiate out, shaping the organization and its links with the environment.

In Chapter 3 we looked at the conventional perspective of strategic decision making, according to the top-down approach. Strategy and management texts are likely to cover top-down decision making, where leaders deliberate and choose between options. The same attention has yet to be devoted to middle-out decision making and its impact on strategy. Richard Rumelt (2011) talks about strategy as a cohesive response to an important challenge, his point being that multiple resources are required to be focused on the single objective. Effective strategy is now less likely to be about the prominent 'silver bullet' and more likely to be about the secret sauce with a myriad of ingredients prepared in a unique way. It is unlikely an organization's top tier has the scope to curate directly all that is contained within the secret sauce – as one director put it, 'If the board did everything, it would need to meet every day.'

Strategy is what happens when you're not in the room

The view that 'Strategy is what happens when you're not in the room' was shared with us by a chartered director who is a leader within one of the UK's prominent law firms. He makes the point that, for most of the working week, the leader is not in the same room as those whom he or she is leading. This means it is only for a minority of the time that leaders can provide direct guidance or feedback to their reports. Yet, for the majority of the time, while the leader is elsewhere, his or her team members will be making decisions that impact on the organization's strategy.

This view wraps together several considerations about strategy in practice. Strategy becomes real when the rubber hits the road and actions are taken by the organization. It reminds us that the actual actions to implement strategy are more likely to be carried out by the rank and file of the organization than they are by its senior leaders. It also illustrates that decisions culminating in actions are very much in the hands of those translating thought into action. Middle-out decision making recognizes that actions that effect strategy may result from the interpreting of top-down intent, but they may also result from the seemingly random decisions that everyone in the business makes, day in and day out.

The bulk of middle-out decisions are made by people lower down the organizational hierarchy than those who make top-down decisions. Such decisions have a more intimate connection to local conditions and greater access to local information. This gives organizations a potentially empowering connectedness with the flow of their markets in a way that top-down models might find difficult to emulate.

What middle-out decisions look like

Organizations function in a sea of the decisions made by their people. Small-scale decisions whose presence can be off the radar for the senior leaders can have a potentially massive collective impact.

Human lives are a constant stream of decisions, typically about 35,000 per day for an adult (Hoomans, 2015). Big decisions are comparatively few, but the cumulative impact of smaller decisions also has consequences. While some of these decisions are the result of deliberate thought, most human decision making is unconscious, as we've discussed in Chapter 2. The kinds of arguments that people find influential or persuasive are far from universal. They are deeply rooted in the prevailing culture and its philosophical assumptions. Interpretation is personal.

Sixty years ago, the pioneering work of Nobel laureate Herbert Simon raised awareness around the idea of 'bounded rationality' (Gigerenzer and Selten, 2002). Simon pointed out that people making decisions rarely access and utilize the full information open to them in decision making. We tend not to weigh up all the options in the light of a full and frank perusal of all the data and choose the optimum solution. Instead our 'rationality' is bounded by the way that we individually choose to frame things in our mind. We have to cope with potentially an enormous amount of information from round about us, but it is our 'inner world' that gives us the lens through which we gaze at the external world. Our inner world guides our focus on some things at the expense of others.

The basis for the way information is processed and middle-out decisions made also varies. Mintzberg and Westley (2001) drew attention to decisions made by three different mechanisms – 'thinking first' (which is discussion and words as the ordering of thoughts), 'seeing first' (which is about building or seeing a picture and visual artistic representation) and 'doing first' (which is the physical crafting and doing). In 'thinking first', people will build a rational view by ordering their thoughts around the information presented, which shows a disposition to system two thinking. In 'seeing first', the building of a collage of information generates intuitive insight from the resultant visualization, which is very much a system one approach. In 'doing first', the dominant route to understanding is sensemaking through taking action, the fruits of which help generate additional understanding. This means that three different people can have different ways of interpreting the same data. It further illustrates the challenge leaders can have in framing information within their organizations for appropriate effect.

Unconscious decision making and influence

A believed 95–99 per cent of the processing power of the human brain is unconscious (Goleman, 1984), and the subject of unconscious bias is becoming more recognized with respect to its impact within the organization. Research reported in *CDO Insights* estimates that we're exposed to up to 11 million pieces of information at any one time, but our brains can only deal with around 40 (Ross, 2008).

In Chapter 2, we looked at decision making biases that related to how information is processed in our minds. We went further in Chapter 3, when we looked at challenges for people making decisions in groups. In this section we're looking at a further complication, unconscious biases. Unconscious bias is about our impression of the person who is communicating the information. This is not a conscious, considered reaction but an automatic, instinctive one: a reaction that happens in the moment and before our rational consciousness has a chance to intervene.

It is understood that people are more readily influenced by those they like (Cialdini, 2006). People are usually aware of who they like and don't like, so that perspective sits more in the conscious mind than the unconscious. However, psychologists have noticed that, at an unconscious level, people can react positively or negatively towards others according to the type of person. This can be due to gender, age, ethnicity or disability, for example. These are unconscious reactions. They happen before we're able to mobilize a conscious reaction, and they also happen without us being aware. It is to our established patterns of making unconscious decisions that our brains turn. These hard-wired patterns create in us a perceptual lens on the world. While this lens may be malleable, it is also present as a first point of reference.

One action people can take is to become more aware of their personal biases. Tests like an implicit association test (IAT) (Greenwald, McGhee and Schwartz, 1998) can be used to assess the hidden attitudes and beliefs that determine our preferences for certain groups over others. IATs are not perfect and are subject to many of the criticisms levelled at personality testing generally. But, just as the psychometric assessment of personality type can be useful,

IATs can make a positive contribution to managing personal bias (Oxford Learning Institute, 2014).

Research indicates that unconscious biases are present in the way we make business decisions. Here are some examples. We apparently favour CEOs who are taller (Gladwell, 2005), while research conducted by economists at the University of Wisconsin and reported in the *Daily Telegraph* (Titcomb, 2014) has indicated that a CEO's looks have a positive influence on the share price. Work conducted by the University of Melbourne showed that people whose names were easier to pronounce were more likely to succeed in their jobs (Laham, Koval and Alter, 2012), while a survey conducted on behalf of the charity Changing Faces found that 9 out of 10 people implicitly judge those with facial disfigurements negatively (Secker and Nestor, 2013). A study carried out by business psychologists Pearn Kandola looking at the associations between senior and junior positions and women and men found a bias that associated men with senior jobs and women with junior ones (Kandola, 2009). The bias was as true of the women in the research sample as it was for the men. Experiments have also shown that people who believe they've been categorized as higher performers perform to a higher standard than others whose perception of their categorization is lower. On one hand, this creates the opportunity for senior leaders to build on this and position themselves and their colleagues as the 'A team'. On the other hand, such self-assurance can lead to complacency or hubris.

In years of testing around unconscious biases and working with thousands of candidates, psychologist and unconscious bias expert Dr Peter Jones, author of the Implicitly IAT (Hogrefe, 2017), has only found one person who has not exhibited unconscious bias. She is a woman called Emily from Scotland. It is possible that any one of us might be the second, but the odds are stacked against it. 'You need to give up on the idea that it's other people who are biased', said Dr Jones (2014). We can't see our own biases. Somewhere between 3 and 10 times faster than our eyes have seen the picture (ie conscious recognition), our unconscious has made the connections – with very little control of our activation. Our biases develop and are maintained from our upbringing, our experiences and the media we absorb. Our biases offset what we hear, remember and value. Our implicit biases are fundamentally bigger than our explicit ones. There's a great gap between the two – the problem is that we don't see that gap.

Conditions like ambiguity, being under time pressure, being under an emotional load or being physically tired or low in glucose militate against us being successful in conscious thought. We talk about being 'ego depleted' (Baumeister and Tierney, 2012). Ego depletion refers to the idea that self-control or willpower draws on a limited pool of mental resources. Exerting self-control, which is needed to counter instinctive reactions in the way we view people, process information and frame decisions, is a strenuous act.

'Middle-out' decisions rather than 'bottom-up'

The usual contrast to 'top-down' decisions is 'bottom-up'. Middle-out decision making is not the same as bottom-up. Bottom-up decision making describes the garnering of opinion from lower levels of an enterprise and its elevation to more senior tiers, usually prior to formal consideration and choice. In many respects it follows the same axis as top-down method, but the other way around. Organizations that embrace bottom-up approaches tend to have mechanisms in place, connected to their strategy processes, to capitalize on wisdom and energy from within. Middle-out decision making is different. It happens whether the organization encourages it or not. It works irrespective of whether the organization's leaders deliberately connect it with the strategy process or not.

Henry Mintzberg (1978) used the term 'realized strategy' to describe what happened in reality and to recognize the difference between best intentions and the way real life conspires to impact on events. Retrospective understanding is relatively easy here. It is often more straightforward to look back and reflect on why something did or didn't happen. Although 'attribution bias' illustrates how our accounts looking back are conveniently manicured in our memories in our attempts to seek meaning and tidy ambiguity. When scrutiny is applied, organizations can become more aware of subtle internal tempering factors, as well as the way that environmental and market shifts were interpreted by the organization along the way.

The sentiment, often attributed to Peter Drucker, that 'culture eats strategy for breakfast' reminds us that the reference point for strategy in practice is the organization's prevailing culture. The effect is subtle. As a result, organizations tend to have their own strategic DNA, an unwritten code governing what they're predisposed to do readily and also find difficult. This concept, which has its roots in Gareth Morgan's (1998) idea of corporate DNA, is represented in a range of diagnostic products from the consulting industry aimed at helping organizations find out what theirs is. PwC, for example, has an Org DNA Profiler® Survey citing organizational DNA as a metaphor for the underlying factors that together define an organization's personality and help explain its performance. The original work for PwC's organizational DNA approach was carried out by Booz & Co. PwC acquired Booz & Co in 2014. Within this approach, the illumination of the four building blocks of organizational DNA shows the reference points for middle-out decisions. These four building blocks are:

1 the formal mechanics of how decisions are made (and who makes them) and the norms in place (the unwritten rules that govern behaviour);

2 the motivators and career incentives for people and the aspirational commitments that drive and motivate;

3 the prevailing information around how performance is measured and activities coordinated, and the mindsets that outline the beliefs team members deploy when processing information; and

4 the formal structure of the organization and how the people in the organization are informally connected through networks.

These four building blocks relate very closely to what we understand as the levers of strategy (the ways that strategy is enabled in enterprises). For the most part, the implications of organizational DNA are indirect rather than direct. This means an organizational DNA creates the conditions that set the tone for decisions people in the organization will make. Law professor Cass Sunstein applied the label 'second-order decisions' to decisions that follow rules such as those inferred by organization standards, culture and presumptions (Sunstein and Ullmann-Margalit, 1998).

In strategy, anything concerned with analysis, issue selling and decision making is a precursor to where the rubber hits the road – implementation. Decisions are the bridge between thought and action. Without implementation as the prosecution of decisions, strategy is just a conceptual exercise. The engine room for the execution of strategy is widely recognized as middle management, for two reasons. First, middle management control local resources, including allocating budgets, agreeing job roles and communicating staff priorities. Second, by their actions and behaviour managers influence the local work climate and the culture that their staff experience. Managers make the weather for their teams. The chairman of a UK-based training firm we know related this story about the time his firm hired an organizational development consultant to conduct an independent assessment of the health of the firm. The firm had grown to become the UK's biggest provider of support for start-ups and small businesses, with eight regional offices, each with a regional manager, a team of advisers and administrative support staff, in addition to its head office. The opening words that the organizational development consultant spoke when she delivered her report to the firm's board of directors were 'Are you one company or six?' Despite the efforts of the consulting firm to work under the umbrella of a single brand with a single service offer across its offices, the firm had unwittingly created a federalized array of different working cultures, which became the guiding lights by which people in the regional offices took action and implemented the strategy.

Middle-out decisions and their challenge to strategic intent

In 2009, two British academics, Robert Chia and Robin Holt, published a book that explored this dimension to strategic decision making. *Strategy without Design: The silent efficacy of indirect action* (Chia and Holt, 2009) sought to explain the strategies realized by organizations. Their account framed implementation not as the result of deliberate strategy well executed but by the 'emergence of a coherent strategy, even though people involved may not have deliberately intended it to be so'.

Chia and Holt point out that organizational success may inadvertently emerge from the everyday coping actions of a multitude of individuals. These would be the actions of people in the organization but also those of people around its periphery, none of whom necessarily intended to contribute to any preconceived design. Why might this happen? It is a consequence of the number and nature of decisions we make and of the actions we take in our working days. Here, strategic decision making rests less with a grand plan and more with the melding of a myriad of unconscious acts.

Chia and Holt's work suggests it is the conditions within which people make these multiple decisions that generate the strategy that plays out in reality. Many leaders have been able to look back from an achievement and piece together the steps that led to the accomplishment of the result, and contrast this with their inability to have predicted the steps in advance. Such examples relate to business opportunities secured, star employees recruited and alliances formed. Our own partnership as authors was the result of our publisher Kogan Page's desire to extend a series of business books into new subject areas, one of us coming on the publisher's radar through his having central strategy roles in two organizations the publisher had looked into and the two of us liking the cut of each other's jib, having been brought together by a mutual client who had asked us to help facilitate its annual global conference. That's a simplified account, but the fact that each part of the foregoing was itself the product of a prior series of events, each of which involved more than the two of us, our client and Kogan Page's commissioning editor of the time, should help illustrate the point. People use terms like 'fate', 'luck', 'serendipity' and even 'planned serendipity' to describe the apparent good fortune present within a sea of randomness (Muller and Becker, 2012). Management researcher Ralph Stacey suggested that the idea of planned achievement is fraught with challenges. He points out that the sheer volume of variables that need to be considered, together with their interconnectivity, challenges the very idea that organizations can 'manage' change and the pathway to their goals.

In his words, 'Any organization at a moment in time is a result of its history and what it will become can only be known if one knows every detail of future development, and the only way one can do that is to let the development occur. The future of such a system is open and hence unknowable until it occurs' (Senior and Swales, 2010).

Chia and Holt (2009) go further. They posit that the more a single-minded goal is sought, the more likely that what they call 'calculated instrumental action' eventually works to undermine its own initial success. Consider this example, where a deliberately chosen metric drove an unintended behaviour, resulting in a perverse outcome.

> This organization is not KFC, but it does what KFC does, namely fried chicken-based fast food. The business is based in Asia and, similar to many multi-sited fast food ventures, has a central head office that supports a series of stand-alone retail outlets, each located in an area of strong passing trade. Every week there is a phone call from head office to each of the outlets. The purpose of the phone call is to gather the management information necessary to run the business. One of the questions that head office asks each outlet each week is 'How much fried chicken did you dispose of last week?' The question is focused on waste and efficiency. Many of the managers within these outlets formed the view that the ideal answer to the question was zero. In an effort to give the perfect answer to head office and be truthful at the same time, some local managers changed their cooking practices in the outlets, especially in the last two hours of the shift, to cooking the chicken to order rather than having a stock cooked and ready to sell. We might reflect on whether people would be prepared to wait any more than five minutes in a fast food outlet for their order before leaving. Fast food – the clue is in the sector's name. Here's a business heading towards zero waste, but also towards zero customers.

The phrase 'What gets measured gets done' is recognized by many managers. In the above example, the single blunt indicator (measuring the wastage of cooked food) drove behaviour in a direction that was contrary to the organization's requirements of success.

A bigger-scale example of the same characteristic comes from the US-based bank Wells Fargo. John Stumpf joined the organization in 2007. By 2011 the bank was following an aspirant strategy, as articulated in its vision statement in its annual report to stockholders: 'Our vision is to satisfy all our customers' financial needs, help them succeed financially, be recognized as the premier financial services company in our markets and be one of America's great companies' (Wells Fargo, 2011). This vision was underpinned by a top-down strategy that made direct reference to growth, cross-selling of products to existing segments, and opening up new segments. The goal for cross-selling was set out as follows:

> Our cross-sell strategy, diversified business model and the breadth
> of our geographic reach facilitate growth in both strong and weak
> economic cycles, as we can grow by expanding the number of products our current customers have with us, gain new customers in our
> extended markets, and increase market share in many businesses. Our
> retail bank household cross-sell increased each quarter during 2011 to
> 5.92 products per household in fourth quarter 2011, up from 5.70 in
> fourth quarter 2010. We believe there is more opportunity for cross-sell
> as we continue to earn more business from our customers. Our goal is
> eight products per customer, which is approximately half of our estimate of potential demand for an average US household.
>
> (Wells Fargo, 2011)

But then the wheels fell off, spectacularly. In the 2016 US Justice Department's investigation into the conduct of Wells Fargo it was revealed that Wells Fargo employees had secretly created around 2 million bogus accounts in order to meet internal sales targets and receive performance bonuses. Employees went as far as creating phoney PIN numbers and email accounts to enrol customers in online banking services, and creating over half a million credit card accounts without their customers' knowledge and consent. The bank was so driven in its aspiration that those who rebelled, feeling uncomfortable about executing instructions tantamount to fraud, were fired. The internal whistle-blowing line for Wells Fargo employees seemed to be supporting the institutional machine too, according to former

Wells Fargo employees whose employment was terminated after they used the line to voice concerns. An after-the-event investigation by Wells Fargo saw the dismissal of over 5,000 members of staff. As well as taking a 20 per cent hit on its stock price, Wells Fargo's contamination extended to commercial partners. Prudential Insurance of America was accused of covering up fraudulent sales of insurance products through Wells Fargo to low-income customers.

Guiding middle-out decision making

We don't see middle-out decision making as disempowering strategic leadership. It provides a richer perspective on how strategy happens. Leaders would probably be delinquent in their duty if they didn't use this insight to help their organizations. Over-restrictive and hyper-rationalistic strategies may well set themselves up to fail through the presence of routine and unconscious activity, unplanned opportunities and unexpected outcomes. But this doesn't mean that strategy should be entirely middle-oriented and laissez-faire. As Ikujiro Nonaka and Zhichang Zhu (2012: 147) point out, 'if strategy is all non-intentional, non-purposeful, mindless and effortless, then what is not strategy?'

If middle-out decision making is to be guided, organizations are unlikely to prosper unless those in the middle ranks recognize and promote the need for change. The management consulting industry has focused on this in recent times, supporting projects centred on helping the client's employees become ready and able to change. A potentially empowering aspect for leaders is the mobilization of nudges: subtle guides of behaviour as distinct from direct control, which seek to influence decision making by working with the nature of human behaviour. This means using indirect influence by controlling environmental conditions to encourage certain types of decisions or behaviour. The term 'nudge' has come to be associated with this form of decision making. According to Richard Thaler and Cass Sunstein a nudge is any feature of a person's context that influences the person to behave in a predictable way (Thaler and Sunstein, 2008). Nudges are signals to encourage people to make decisions, albeit usually small ones, in particular ways. Choice architecture and nudges can help subconscious decision making lead to the 'right' choice. Here's an example from our consulting work.

The organization in question is a prominent financial services business in the Republic of Ireland. The organization is seeking to modify its working practices towards a more contemporary approach with the prime drivers of environmental considerations and cost efficiency. This particular example relates to the reduction of printing, which was one of the initiatives being pursued. The organization communicates its intent around print reduction to all staff and explains the rationale. It invests in notebook computers and tablets for all its executives and provides training in how to use them. The senior executives know they need to lead by example, and senior meetings become paperless affairs. True to good strategy, implementation is multifaceted, and cohesive actions all point in the same direction. The organization then moved its printers to points of inconvenience in the offices. What used to be for most people an easy trip of a few metres to pick up a document they had printed out now became a deliberate journey. The organization also removed waste paper baskets from people's work areas and created 'recycling pods' for waste. One pod served several teams of people but wasn't located close to any of them. The business then issued everyone with their own printer code, which was necessary to get any of the printers to work. To print a document, the code needed to be entered twice – initially into the computer to enable the print command and later in the process when the person arrived at the printer to pick the documents up. Instead of printing out documents when people hit the print instruction on their keyboard, the printers were now programmed to wait until the people in question had walked to the printer and re-entered their print code before a document printed. Finally, at the end of each month, data on the amount of printing across the business, compared to its aspiration, were shared across the organization. The business has never reported data against each individual printer code as part of the sharing of the management information, but it is not lost on any member of staff that the business is capable of interrogating this level of detail.

We've seen examples where blunt approaches to changing behaviour in organizations failed to deliver the hoped-for result. Blunt, direct approaches are the opposite of nudging. Here's an example. One business that, some years ago, attempted to direct its staff to use the new coffee stations sent a memo around that the local tea and coffee making that had pervaded the business through the use of personal kettles and coffee makers was to stop. Many senior managers chose not to follow the instruction, on the basis that the important meetings they hosted weren't best supported by the new coffee stations. The personal assistants to these senior managers continued to make and serve tea and coffee as they had always done. Within the rank and file of the organization, tea and coffee making went 'underground'. Certainly, the personal kettles and coffee makers disappeared from view, but only as far as under people's desks and behind cupboard doors. The point here is that, if middle-out decisions are going to favour the intentions of the organization and its strategy, they are typically the culmination of subtle influence and shifts.

Middle-out decisions can lead to a step-change

In Chapter 3 we offer the argument that step-change in strategic direction requires a top-down approach to decision making. However, there are instances when a more democratized approach to decision making (closer to middle-out) has been able to alter substantially the direction of travel. CAMRA (the Campaign for Real Ale) was established in the UK in 1971, as an independent third sector body promoting traditionally brewed cask beers, opposing the mass production of (perceived poor-quality) beer by large corporations. CAMRA has grown to over 180,000 members and, with shifts in consumer tastes and the brewing sector, reached the stage where real ales and ciders are in a substantially stronger position than they were 40 years ago. In 2016 CAMRA embarked on a revitalization project, recognizing it had achieved its core purpose. The revitalization project sought formally the views of the members as the main input to guide the organization's future. This was after informal feedback from members highlighted both the shift in CAMRA's market and the recognition of CAMRA's success in the brewing industry (the UK had 1,500 breweries in 2016). The revitalization project has seen CAMRA's attentions directed more towards pubs and bars as the current part of the brewing ecosystem that appears at the greatest threat from corporatization. This was not a top-down decision, but the reflection of CAMRA's rank and file, its members. While large membership organizations, such as CAMRA, have different governance arrangements to private sector counterparts (1,400 of CAMRA's members attended its 2016 AGM in person), CAMRA has demonstrated an alternative to top-down strategy, enabled by an engaged stakeholder community.

Helped by advances in technology, organizations are able to engage with their stakeholder groups in the co-creation of strategic opportunities. 'Crowdsourcing' approaches, a term coined by the co-editors of *Wired* magazine in 2005 (Safire, 2009), are harnessing the perspectives of multiple minds to provide potentially a broader and more immediate contribution to strategy than conventional research techniques. For example, on 29 and 30 May 2013, the University of South Australia staged 'unijam' – a wide-ranging conversation about the University's future direction. Using IBM technology, the University enabled real-time conversations to take place from around the globe and, as its Vice Chancellor and President expressed it, 'capture the ideas and insights that allow us to incorporate them into our medium and long-term strategic planning... open to all members of the University of South Australia community – taking the best and brightest input forward to determine our future actions' (Lloyd, 2013). Other universities around the world are now adopting the technique.

Heading towards agile

We are witnessing a shift in how organizations are beginning to approach strategy. We are seeing a move from strategy as a 'thoughtful multi-stakeholder process... of careful deliberation based on the maximum amount of information' (Leberecht 2016) to a pacier, organic experience. The term 'agile', which is drawn directly from the world of software development, is becoming widely adopted to describe both this new approach to strategy and the configuration of organizations to deliver it.

In agile strategy, there is still the role for the organization's purpose and principles to be the guiding light for what the organization does, although, because of the nature of change in the world, the organization's 'vision' is less likely to be permanent and its mission or purpose less likely to be narrowly defined. We have one client that refers to its organizational purpose as the 'crash barriers' that provide the boundary for each of its business units to operate within – providing the scope for local responses while retaining sufficient unity. The biggest change relates to the execution part of the strategy. In agile approaches the tone is more one of improvisation, with implementation incorporating a higher degree of experimentation than would be the case with more traditional approaches. The improvisation helps keep an organization in motion and encourages the trialling of different ideas that generate experience and learning.

In respect of organizational design, people are beginning to think about what an organization able to anticipate and react to change, to reallocate resources swiftly and respond to customer needs, would look like. Structural changes can include delayering the organization (to speed the flow of information, up and down) and lowering the centre of gravity for decision making (so people at lower levels in the organization are empowered to make bigger decisions), enabling the organization to experience a stream of opportunities and investment in multiple options as routes to learning. However, as Jafarnejad and Shahabi (2006) say, goals and working practices are part of the recipe, but so are softer wiring elements such as attitudes and management approaches.

Understanding of middle-out decisions and their links to strategy is likely to become of increasing importance, as organizations seek greater agility in response to external turbulence. An organization's capability in fostering good middle-out decision making means that it can benefit from a lower centre of gravity. Writers like Michael Raynor (2007) and Donald Sull (2009, 2015) have explored this area and, with others, suggested the organizational qualities in which middle-out decisions can be harnessed. These qualities include:

- Using the top tier of an organization to decide and communicate the parameters within which decisions can be made. This can be in the form of risk appetite or exposure, preferences in terms of market sectors or activities, and thresholds for escalation of investment decisions.

- Strengthening the ability of the organization to work as a supply chain with the ability to move resources and information around more freely.

- Placing greater decision making freedom lower down the organization (including decisions on resources), and supporting this by a no-blame culture that fosters enterprise and experimentation without the expectation that all options pursued will pay dividends.

- Placing more faith in real-time data and in-the-moment insights rather than formal research processes. This typically places more emphasis on the role of 'boundary workers' (those in the organization connected with the external environment or markets) as conduits of information into the organization.

- Promoting the merits of joint endeavour with a preparedness to work with and through other organizations. This involves sharing rewards for the privilege of capitalizing on the capabilities of others, in the knowledge that this enables the organization to move more easily out of an area as well as enter a wider range of opportunities than would be possible under its own auspices.

Whilst agile strategy and organizational design for agility are in their infancy, it is easy to see these ingredients played out in the strategies of businesses like the Virgin Group. Virgin Group's strategic ability centres on functioning as a relatively sector-agnostic investment company, deploying its core capability to great effect in capitalizing on opportunities in conjunction with partner organizations (Feloni, 2015). Agile recipes are not suggested as a panacea, as they are not universally relevant to all industry types, strategic challenges and organization styles. But they seem to bring the qualities of middle-out decisions more to the fore in the pursuit of strategic advantage.

The self-tuning organization

In these days of prolific data and processing power, people are beginning to ask whether strategic decision making can be automated.
Can the collective hearts and minds of the enterprise, and its connection with the flow of markets, be replaced by an algorithm? We have
a client in the payday loans sector whose strategy is based around
digital technology rather than human judgement. The payday loans
sector provides loan finance to people unable to engage with the
conventional sources such as friends, family, banks, building societies
and credit unions. Our client uses an algorithm to provide a lending
recommendation in a matter of seconds, based on the characteristics of the applicant and the assimilation of data from a range of
other sources, including data in the public domain. The algorithm
has to extract information, avoid irrelevant noise and determine the
correctness of what it sees. The business's prosperity in its competitive
market is testament to the approach. On a greater scale, organizations like Amazon, Alibaba and Google use a similar approach to
recalibrate their business models and the allocation of their resources
without deliberative direction from the top. Their ability to reorient
their offerings to each of millions of customers based on the gathering and interpretation of real-time data is central to their strategies. It
is not a major stretch of the imagination to view this as an automated
style of middle-out decisions. The terrain that is yet to be crossed by
the self-tuning enterprise is that of substantial changes to business
models and even overall visions. Just as middle-out decisions have
the organization's prevailing climate and practices as their reference
point, so too does algorithmic-based decision making. The question
worth considering is for how long this will be the case as we progress
along the path towards machine learning and artificial intelligence.

Perpetuating the status quo

Research by McKinsey & Company has suggested that organizations typically devote 90 per cent of their resources to areas in which
prior commitments have been made. Even when freedom exists to
alter strategic focus through the application of resources, the vast

majority of corporate energy appears to support the continuation of the present. This may be partly due to the comfort senior leaders experience in the avenues they are currently guiding the enterprise down. It is also likely to be a result of middle-out decisions, as these are made in the context of the prevailing climate of the organization and the foundation of the here and now. Breaking this mould usually requires firm hands on the tiller.

In the first decade of the third millennium, IBM embarked on a brave transformational strategy. It became, 10 years later, the world's third-largest seller of software applications, which signified its shift from being a hardware business to a services firm. The moves of 'Big Blue' catalysed by the custodianship of Lou Gerstner and Sam Palmisano saw it regenerate after its 1993 position of posting the biggest loss in US corporate history. The business's transformation saw brand unification and the movement of energy towards the world's developing markets. It also included some more radical moves, the likes of which would have been remarkable in a middle-out approach to strategy. Such steps included significant cost cutting to the extent of 40,000 job losses, ceasing the development on the OS/2 operating system (to which IBM had a great emotional attachment), acquiring PwC's consulting business and buying a suite of significant software businesses including Lotus and SPSS, as part of a shift from the hardware that had made IBM's name. In that shift, IBM first sold its PC business, including its ThinkPad branded products to Lenovo in 2005, followed by the sale of its x86 server business to the same customer nine years later.

The IBM example points out that, while there is merit in middle-out approaches to strategy, the limits of its scope need to be recognized. The phrase 'turkeys voting for Christmas' epitomizes the difficulties in seeking perspectives that stray far from being self-serving. Middle-out decisions may help the evolution of business models where the future horizon is a modest step from the first. It is questionable, however, whether middle-out would have catalysed Suzuki's journey from making weaving looms to manufacturing motorcycles and cars, or provided the hand holding for 3M's move from being a mining company to its presence as a global innovator around technology with branded products such as Scotch tape and Post-it notes.

The healthy organization doesn't need to view middle-out approaches as an alternative to top-down decision making. Discontinuity and step-change are likely to need senior-level drive and sponsorship for no other reason than that the scale of the tasks involved is unlikely to be conceived and resourced from the organization's middle. Both top-down and middle-out strategic decisions have their place. Neither is necessarily superior to the other, as they are different in nature. The combination of both, where the best of each can be capitalized upon, is where decision dexterity lies.

As the reference point of middle-out decisions is the prevailing climate within the organization, it is unsurprising that middle-out decisions can temper attempts at step-change rather than promote it. In addition, success in transformational steps needs resources beyond the usual. Ramping up or significantly reorienting resources is usually a top-down effort. The result of this is that middle-out decision making, while likely to be present in every organization, can cope better in a context where change flows rather than steps. The wise leadership team is likely to understand the implications of middle-out decision making and do its best to harness its qualities, at the same time recognizing that a more directed orientation is required.

Summary

This chapter has focused on 'middle-out' decision making in strategy, an area that hasn't benefited from the depth of attention devoted to top-down strategic decision making.

- In a more unpredictable world, it's harder to forecast. If we take this as given, organizations should move to action more quickly in order to create the insight valuable to their strategies.

- To balance top-down and middle-out, organizations are tailoring plans and ideas, respecting the tension between standardization and local conditions.

- The more local conditions change, the more an organization needs to flex away from standard approaches.

However, because the dominant model is top-down, it is difficult for managers schooled in this approach to understand and capitalize on nuances of decisions made by the melding of top-down and middle-out in strategy.

References

Baumeister, R F and Tierney, J (2012) *Willpower: Rediscovering the greatest human strength*, Penguin Books, New York

Chia, R C H and Holt, R (2009) *Strategy without Design: The silent efficacy of indirect action*, Cambridge University Press, Cambridge

Cialdini, R B (2006) *Influence: The psychology of persuasion*, rev edn, Harper Business, New York

Feloni, R (2015) How Richard Branson maintains the Virgin Group, *Business Insider*, 11 February

Gigerenzer, G and Selten, R (2002) *Bounded Rationality: The adaptive toolbox*, MIT Press, Cambridge, MA

Gladwell, M (2005) *Blink*, Back Bay Books, Boston, MA

Goleman, D (1984) New view of the mind gives unconscious an expanded role, *New York Times*, 7 February, http://www.nytimes.com/1984/02/07/science/new-view-of-mind-gives-unconscious-an-expanded-role.html

Greenwald, A G, McGhee, D E and Schwartz, J L K (1998) Measuring individual differences in implicit cognition: the implicit association test, *Journal of Personality and Social Psychology*, **74** (6), 1464–80

Hogrefe (2017) Implicitly, http://www.hogrefe.co.uk/implicitly.html

Hoomans, J (2015) 35,000 decisions: the great choices of strategic leaders, *Leading Edge Journal*, 20 March, https://go.roberts.edu/leadingedge/the-great-choices-of-strategic-leaders

Jafarnejad, M and Shahabi, B (2006) *Organizational Agility and Agile Manufacturing*, Gentle Book Publishing, Tehran

Jones, P (2014) Presentation to the West of Scotland branch of the Institute of Directors

Kandola, B (2009) *The Value of Difference: Eliminating bias in organisations*, Pearn Kandola, Oxford

Laham, S M, Koval, P and Alter, L A (2012) The name-pronunciation effect: why people like Mr Smith more than Mr Colquhoun, *Journal of Experimental Social Psychology*, **48**, 752–56

Leberecht, T (2016) Making strategy more agile, *Harvard Business Review*, October

Lloyd, D (2013) Unijam, *Viewpoint*, 1 May, http://www.unisa.edu.au/About-the-Vice-Chancellor/Viewpoint/unijam

Mintzberg, H (1978) Patterns in strategy formation, *Management Science*, **24** (9), 934–48

Mintzberg, H and Westley, F (2001) Decision making: it's not what you think, *MIT Sloan Management Review*, **42** (3), 89–93

Morgan, G (1998) *Images of Organization*, Berrett-Koehler, Oakland, CA

Muller, T and Becker, L (2012) *Get Lucky: How to put planned serendipity to work for you and your business*, Jossey-Bass, San Francisco, CA

Nonaka, I and Zhu, Z (2012) *Pragmatic Strategy: Eastern wisdom, global success*, Cambridge University Press, Cambridge

Oxford Learning Institute (2014) Understanding the impact of unconscious bias, University of Oxford, http://www.ox.ac.uk/media/global/wwwoxacuk/localsites/uasconference/documents/W19_Developing_an_inclusive_workplace_handout.pdf

Raynor, M (2007) *The Strategy Paradox: Why committing to success leads to failure*, Crown Business, New York

Ross, H (2008) Exploring unconscious bias: proven strategies for dealing with unconscious bias in the workplace, *CDO Insights*, **2** (5)

Rumelt, R (2011) *Good Strategy, Bad Strategy: The difference and why it matters*, Crown, New York

Safire, W (2009) On language, *New York Times Magazine*, 5 February

Secker, J and Nestor, R (2013) Understanding the impact of unconscious bias, Aurora, Leadership Foundation for Higher Education

Senior, B and Swales, S (2010) *Organizational Change*, Pearson Education, Harlow

Sull, D (2009) *The Upside of Turbulence: Seizing opportunity in an uncertain world*, Harper Business, New York

Sull, D (2015) *Simple Rules: How to survive in a complex world*, Houghton Mifflin Harcourt, Boston, MA

Sunstein, C R and Ullmann-Margalit, E (1998) *Second-Order Decisions*, Coase-Sandor Working Paper Series in Law and Economics, Coase-Sandor Institute for Law and Economics, Chicago, IL

Thaler, R H and Sunstein, C R (2008) *Nudge*, Yale University Press, New Haven, CT

Titcomb, J (2014) Study finds 'beautiful' CEOs boost stock price, *Daily Telegraph*, 3 January

Wells Fargo (2011) *Annual Report to Stockholders*, Wells Fargo, San Francisco, CA

Discovery-led decision making 05

It ain't what you don't know that gets you into trouble. It's what you know for sure that just ain't so. MARK TWAIN

We have seen in the preceding chapters that we find ourselves in a world that seems to be getting more confusing and turbulent, as characterized by the term VUCA – volatile, uncertain, complex and ambiguous. However, we have also observed that organizations and individuals are not well placed to cope with – let alone capitalize upon – the resultant disruptions to their environment. We have compared two contrasting ways in which organizations mobilize themselves to adapt: top-down and middle-out. In this chapter, we'll describe how we advocate organizations and their leaders respond to these challenges in terms of strategic decision making, using our discovery-led decision making framework (Shenoy, 2017). The subsequent three chapters explore the different modes of this framework in greater detail.

The turbulent, confusing context we've described presents decision makers with a number of dilemmas to overcome. Some of these are not new; the psychological processes by which we sift and weigh information have evolved over millennia, and the inertial nature of established organizations is well documented. Today we have the benefit of a growing body of research into individual and organizational behaviour. An awareness and understanding of this knowledge can help to highlight and avoid the decision making pitfalls into which we might otherwise stumble.

No process is ever perfect, especially if applied rigidly and without reflection. But are there ways in which the problems already discussed can be minimized or even rectified? The emphasis of contemporary management practice has been on helping businesses deal with a stable and easily quantifiable reality, whereas the challenges outlined earlier demand a more fluid, dynamic approach tailored to addressing the unknown. Here we examine what characteristics such an approach needs to be able to tackle VUCA environments.

What does a more contingent approach to decision making look like?

Tim Lasseter has pointed out that the father of scientific management, Frederick W Taylor, misused the term 'scientific' (Lasseter, 2014). Taylor conflated the concepts of science and arithmetic, desiring to quantify everything in the spirit of reductionism. This approach works well in predictable, well-understood settings such as mature markets and stable, high-volume operational settings. However, there aren't many meaningful indicators to measure the situations we've described in earlier chapters. A further problem with extreme reliance on analytical models is that there may not be sufficient relevant data available if your organization is breaking new ground with a pioneering product, service or business model. Devoting effort to measuring meaningless or immeasurable indicators offers an illusion of comfort but does little to grapple with the unknown or validate critical assumptions.

For many organizations, strategic planning occurs in annual or sometimes biennial cycles. Some organizations take an even longer perspective. The global charity UNICEF operates on a three-year strategic planning cycle. The multinational technology conglomerate Honeywell uses a strategic planning process with a five-year outlook, combined with annual operating planning that provides a road map for the forthcoming year.

One of the criticisms levelled at traditional planning models is that they are slow and cumbersome. Could it be that, in today's dynamic environment, the rhythm of strategy planning needs to change to reflect the fluid and evolving climate? The music seems to have changed from a slow, ceremonial march to a whirling, spinning tarantella dance.

In the 1970s and 1980s, General Electric Company (GE) was seen as the master of corporate strategic planning. But three decades ago, in 1988, Larry Bossidy, then Vice-Chairman of GE, was heard to say – much to the astonishment of his audience – that the company had abandoned strategic planning. He went on to explain that General Electric had not set aside strategic thinking and strategic management. When Jack Welch succeeded Reginald Jones as CEO of GE, he inherited a hierarchical and overly bureaucratic, stilted and formalized process that hindered rather than helped the formulation of insightful thinking. Welch replaced this with a more streamlined and fluid system. Instead of an annual process, Welch created the Corporate Executive Council, which met quarterly and was designed to cut across the mountains of aggregated data and get to the heart of important issues. It provided a forum for an exchange of ideas and critical reflection upon business plans.

Centralized formal strategic planning processes can often act as a brake on business units. The need to seek and wait for approval from a higher authority means that opportunities may be lost. Indeed, US management academic Gary Hamel has called the strategic planning process in *Fortune* 500 companies 'the last bastion of Soviet-style central planning' (Hamel, 1999). Facing a rapidly mutating market and several quarters of declining revenues, IBM recognized this and devolved strategic planning control to the business units, in an attempt to allow the rhythm of decision making to speed up in time with the music.

Johnson & Johnson is a multinational corporation manufacturing medical devices, pharmaceuticals and consumer goods. It too has seen the benefits of decentralized management. Each operating company is responsible for its own strategic plans. The management team meet with board members throughout the year to discuss strategy. As its own website says, 'this interactive, on-going dialogue provides our Directors with insight into the activities and direction of the Company's business'.

In 2007, Nokia had more than 37 per cent of the global mobile phone market. It was by far the dominant player, with a market share over two and a half times that of its nearest rival, Motorola. The story of Nokia's demise is well known and multifaceted. Today the Nokia organization does not have a stand-alone presence in the mobile phone market. A contributory factor was that the company failed to realize that the tempo had changed. When it needed the flexibility and manoeuvrability of a downhill skier, it had the agility of a supertanker.

As we have seen, part of the problem is that management techniques, developed for the more stable, regimented business environment of the 20th century, aren't well suited to the emerging world. For example:

- As Clayton Christensen of Harvard Business School (Christensen, Kaufman and Shih, 2008) and Columbia University's Rita McGrath (McGrath and MacMillan, 1995) argue, financial tools such as net present value calculations systematically undervalue potential innovations.

- Conventional marketing approaches such as survey-based market research are ill suited to predicting consumer responses to novel products and services. For example, the initial survey research for the Sony Walkman in 1975 indicated that customers did not wish to listen to music on the move.

- Classic project management tools don't cope well with situations where objectives are initially poorly understood.

In Chapter 1, we explained why conventional strategy techniques aren't adapted to this brave new world. Martin Reeves and his co-authors, of strategy consulting firm Boston Consulting Group, argue that different approaches to strategy fit well with different environments (Reeves, Haanæs and Sinha, 2015). Specifically, classic strategy evolved for – and is well suited to dealing with – relatively stable shifts in markets, consumer segments and consumers.

Instead of obsessing about just numbers, a *truly* scientific approach to management would apply a hypothesis-driven approach designed to eliminate misguided mental models of the organization. Such an approach would forgo an over-reliance on analysis for a bias towards evidence, through a process that echoes the scientific method by testing and either disproving or validating assumptions about a business model. This tallies with our comments in Chapter 3 about Jeanne Liedtka's work: namely, that a vital quality of strategic thinking is the ability to be hypothesis-driven, meaning the ability to nurture challenge and creativity by considering multiple perspectives (Liedtka, 1998).

Jeanne Liedtka and Tim Ogilvie also argue that there are 'Six things managers know… that are dead wrong' (Liedtka and Ogilvie, 2011). Their maxims – such as 'If the idea is good, then the money will follow' and 'Measure twice, cut once' – are aimed at applying design thinking to product and service development, but are also applicable to strategic decision making. Such principles can give shape to a reformed approach to strategy formulation and execution.

A 'discovery-led' approach to decision making, grounded in the scientific method, needs to draw on principles inferred from design thinking, agile software engineering and the lean start-up movement. The core premise of a discovery-led approach, better suited to a VUCA environment, is that how you make decisions should be based on the balance between what you know, what you *don't* know and what you *think* you know (ie your assumptions).

'Discovery-led' means reducing unknowns and assumptions with a bias to action

Managers, however, don't have the luxury of performing tightly controlled experiments in an obsessive pursuit of the nature of truth. Strategies are the organizational analogues of scientific theories, and strategic decisions are equivalent to specific hypotheses. Managers need to guess what might work in the future to frame an organization's strategic direction. This future can't be created (or even discovered) by simply examining the past. Answers to these tough questions cannot be found just in an analysis of numbers. At the same time, managers can't guide an organization based on a set of wild guesses. A revised approach to strategic decision making requires that 'good enough' analysis is confronted with messy reality through rapid, well-designed experiments.

Experiment: how do we *learn* what we need to know?

So when what we know is eclipsed by what we *don't* know and what we *think* we know (but might not be true), we should *experiment*.

The purpose of this mode of the discovery-led decision making framework is to develop and refine a range of options to reduce the unknowns associated with the situation confronting us, by means of a number of 'tests' to (in)validate key assumptions by means of prototypes, demonstrations or field trials (see Figure 5.1).

During the *experiment* mode the decision making team, either with cross-functional internal partners (such as engineers, developers, programmers and marketing teams) or collaborating with external partners, develops one or more 'tests' that will address the problems or opportunities identified through analysis and experience. The techniques used at this stage involve the development of business experiments designed to validate or refute core assumptions

Figure 5.1   Discovery-led decision making – *experimentation*

UNKNOWNS &
ASSUMPTIONS   KNOWNS

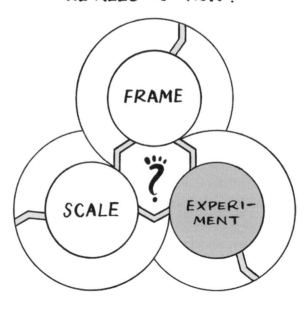

HOW DO WE LEARN WHAT
WE NEED TO KNOW?

FRAME

SCALE

EXPERI-
MENT

in the most resource-efficient way, including consumer observation in the field, surveys and focus groups, role-play and co-creating products and services with partners and consumers.

In the spirit of avoiding paralysis through over-analysis, these 'tests' need to start very simply, with complexity and sophistication emerging through iteration. While each test may be individually simple, a series of tests build upon each other to weave together a rich tapestry of data about what actually happens. Furthermore, to be useful, tests need to be both 'falsifiable' (ie they are designed so that they go wrong if the core assumptions are incorrect) and time-boxed (ie they have clearly defined endpoints). Failed pilots are unusual in most organizational environments for a variety of reasons (eg political). However, breakthrough insights are frequently hidden within failed experiments, which means that reflecting on failure is an essential component of learning from experience.

The 'tests' should be discovery-led: designed to (in)validate decision makers' key assumptions and flush out unknowns. Discovery manifests itself as validated or refuted assumptions, with unknowns converted into knowns. This process of discovery will gradually increase the ratio of knowns to unknowns and assumptions – in other words, *learning*.

Think big, start small, expand what's proven

In established organizations, there's often a hurdle of minimum value and attractiveness that an opportunity has to clear in order to be pursued. However, transformational strategies – especially novel ones – often start small and build momentum incrementally. In reality, the problem is that our strategy frameworks don't recognize the fact that we don't know if new ideas are worth anything – with truly radical ideas that might be beyond the current understanding of even loyal customers. Given the increasingly fragmentary and messy nature of the changes in the environment, it is becoming increasingly rare that a generic strategy can be applied wholesale to an opportunity to generate the scale of returns demanded by incumbent firms. Each context for a given product or service, customer base and societal context is unique.

At an INSEAD conference in 2014 investigating why Nokia lost the smartphone battle, the former Nokia CEO Olli-Pekka Kallasvuo recalled the competitive environment during his tenure from 2006 to 2010. He recounted that nowhere in business history has a competitive environment changed so much as it did with the convergence of several industries – to the point that no one knew what to call the industry any more. Mobile telephony blended with the mobile computer industry, the internet industry, the media industry and the applications industry – to mention a few – and today they're all rolled into one, he reflected.

So while it is commendable to have a grand end vision, it is better to complement it with small initiatives to test whether our assumptions about an opportunity are more than just fantasy. As the discovery process unfolds, and the ratio of knowns to unknowns and assumptions increases, the decision making process can shift emphasis from searching for solutions to scaling those that are proven to resolve the key challenges being confronted.

Scale: how do we do *more* of what works?

When we are content that what we know about a situation comfortably outweighs what we don't know – and that we've validated our most critical assumptions – then we are ready to *scale* what we have proven to work. The purpose of the *scale* mode in the discovery-led decision making framework is to spread proven solutions tested in the *experiment* mode, based on knowns, validated assumptions and tolerable unknowns (see Figure 5.2). What 'scaling' specifically means depends on the context: it might involve increasing the volume of production for a new product that's proven successful in market testing, or spreading a particular organizational practice or mindset from a couple of departments to the whole enterprise.

Defining the right 'exam question'

> *Definition of statistics: The science of producing unreliable facts from reliable figures.* EVAN ESAR

Well-run organizations pride themselves on making data-driven decisions, increasingly seeking to apply 'big data' techniques to their

Figure 5.2   Discovery-led decision making – *scaling*

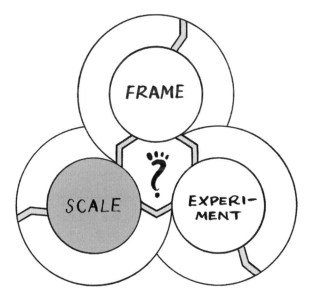

business problems. However, data are not always an organization's best friend. There is a temptation to believe the numbers will tell you all you need to know. But as the quote from US humourist Evan Esar demonstrates, even the most accurate of figures can lead to misrepresentations and misinterpretations. This is in part because it is all too easy for annual strategy reviews to become an exercise in examining financial minutiae. Digging deeper and deeper into statistics can mean that you lose sight of the bigger picture. In other words, you can't see the wood for the trees.

Often, especially in larger organizations, much of the data under consideration will have been pulled together and aggregated by junior staff. As reports get passed from subordinate to boss, they may be aggregated several times until the level of abstraction means that they have lost all useful meaning.

Data tunnel vision can lead an organization to commit what Ian Mitroff terms Type III errors (Mitroff, 1998). Type I errors are commonly termed false positives, or finding an effect that is not actually present. Type II errors are false negatives, or failing to find an effect that is actually present. Mitroff argues that Type III errors occur where we fail to identify the correct problem. Solving the wrong problem, however precisely, is a more fundamental problem than Type I or Type II errors, as it misses the very core of the issue at hand. We are especially vulnerable to Type III errors in VUCA environments.

Mitroff describes five different types of Type III error. Two, in particular, are vulnerable to tunnel vision of the kind already mentioned. First, they may lead to too narrow a set of variables being applied to articulate the problem. Second, the boundaries or scope of the problem may be too tightly drawn, highlighting perhaps only one part of a bigger issue, often a symptom when misdiagnosing wicked problems. Whether the answers you get are meaningful depends entirely on whether or not you ask the right questions, framing the problem appropriately. As Pablo Picasso once said, 'Computers are useless. They can only give you answers.'

The relentless pace of life today does not help. We can often feel as though we are constantly running just to stay still. The ubiquity of mobile devices means that we are always accessible. The most pressing problems, though perhaps not the most important in the overall scheme of things, demand our attention.

In all this mayhem, it can be hard to stop, sit back and ponder, but if we don't pause for thought it's very easy to lose perspective. Taking the time to reflect on the bigger picture can bring valuable insights. A couple of examples of defining the wrong problem precisely relate to industry definition and competitor analysis.

What's your industry?

As discussed in Chapter 1, traditional models incorporate analytical frameworks such as Porter's five forces to analyse the level of competition within an industry. That is all well and good, but what if your product straddles two or more industries?

Defining what industry a given organization is in is a much tougher question now than it was 20 or even 10 years ago. In the last five years, there has been an explosion of products and services that do not fit neatly into an existing sector or industry.

In her book *The End of Competitive Advantage*, Rita McGrath (2013) introduces the concept of an 'arena', which she defines as a combination of a customer segment, an offer and a place in which that offer is delivered.

For example, wearable technology is evolving from small wristband devices to ordinary clothing made from textiles with microsensors woven into the very fabric of the garment. Top sports professionals have already adopted this technology, which not only measures the wearer's current biological state but also is able to predict what it's likely to be days ahead of an important match.

Smartlife, a UK wearable tech company, has already collaborated with several pharmaceutical companies to produce clothing to monitor the effect of new medications during clinical drug trials. Scientists are able to receive accurate data 24 hours a day without the need for expensive laboratory or hospital monitoring. Volunteers can go about their normal daily lives, causing them less inconvenience. This novel collection mechanism helps to reduce the astronomical costs of testing new drugs.

Dr John Coates, a senior research fellow at the University of Cambridge, is exploring the hypothesis that people employed in high-stress environments, such as stock market traders, experience physiological changes during stressful events. As they make or lose money during market fluctuations, traders experience changing levels of endogenous steroids, which can affect behaviour, especially in risk-taking environments. Coates hypothesizes that these measurable physiological changes can push traders between the extremes of irrational exuberance and pessimism, thus altering their risk preferences (Coates, 2013). Many financial institutions are extremely interested in this work. If proven and combined with wearable technology, it might potentially warn traders to slow down or take time out if they are not performing at their optimum. Employers of those in other high-pressure jobs, such as surgeons, airline pilots, firefighters and military personnel, are showing a similar interest.

BioBeats is another British company that uses biometric information, collected via a smartphone touch screen or wearable technology, to assess the well-being of individuals. The app then generates custom music in any genre chosen by the user, based on the user's heart rate. While the user enjoys the music, the software collates relevant information. Used regularly, the app can show when the user is most stressed, allowing action to be taken to reduce this. BioBeats has already partnered with health insurers, the UK National Health Service and employers interested in staff well-being.

The above examples illustrate how the boundaries between established industries are being blurred, leading to the creation of hybrid sectors spanning one or more conventional industries. Strategic decision making needs to devote more effort to defining the arena in which an organization participates rather than just analysing its industry in the classic sense.

Who could destroy you?

In developing its strategy, an organization needs to be mindful of who its competitors are and what they are doing. This relates to the discussion above about the arena in which the organization operates. An already established firm will seek to block new entrants in a number of ways. For example, using economies of scale, product differentiation and customer loyalty, an organization can try to maintain its competitive advantage over newcomers for as long as possible.

Rita McGrath (2013) argues that an existing competitive advantage is now most likely to be disrupted by the emergence of something totally different from outside the company's industry. Using a classic strategy approach, you may not even see a competitor coming.

Nokia, once the biggest mobile phone company in the world, had the vision and creativity to foresee the future of mobile devices in the 1990s. Nokia prototyped a phone with a colour touch screen and no keyboard more than seven years before Apple launched the first iPhone. At the same time, it was also developing a tablet computer with a touch screen and wireless connection. But the vision that was present in the creative departments was sadly lacking in strategic management, who failed to spot the danger of Apple blindsiding them.

A revised strategic decision making approach therefore needs to shift the emphasis towards the front end of the process: understanding exactly what is the nature of the decision to be made. This brings us on to another requirement: broadening our horizons.

Broaden the field of information

Conventional strategic management focuses on quantification, which is well suited to providing the control required to manage organizations operating at scale. This numbers-based search for 'generic strategies' and 'best practices' has reduced managers' horizons in relation to the data they seek, the people with whom they discuss decisions and the options they consider. However, reflecting upon contemporary challenges and looking ahead, a focus exclusively on 'the numbers' is not well suited to the ambiguity arising from shifts in the environment.

Let us consider the problem of not discussing issues with a wide enough variety of people. When people gather together to debate open issues, they overwhelmingly tend to discuss information that is common to them all, a phenomenon known as the common information effect (Stasser and Titus, 1985). There is a tendency not to share unique information that is held by only one member of the team. Even in situations where unique information is shared with the group, it appears to carry less weight in the decision making process. This may be because common information is seen as more credible, coming from a number of sources. Common information is more memorable and more easily recalled after meetings. Again this may be due to the fact that it has been repeated by many voices. Of course, as the Emperor discovered in Hans Christian Andersen's classic children's tale, hearing something from a number of sources does not necessarily make it true.

Very pertinent information may not be shared because it is negative in nature and highlights problems. Most corporate cultures are not overly tolerant of mistakes. Despite the many academics and management books that advise executives to allow experimentation and to encourage a culture of learning from mistakes (eg fail-fast), this counsel is rarely truly implemented. Against this background, it is not surprising that there is an unwillingness to disclose negative information.

Amy Edmondson has spent many years researching factors influencing team learning. With her co-authors, she introduced the concept of psychological safety in teams (Tucker, Nembhard and Edmondson, 2007). This is a belief shared by members of a team that they are in a supportive environment that allows interpersonal risk taking.

In a fascinating study Edmondson and her fellow researchers compared how 16 different surgical teams implemented a difficult new technique for cardiac surgery. Heart surgery is a complex procedure involving a number of specialists who need to work extremely closely. In this study, the teams studied were adopting a keyhole approach to cardiac surgery that was novel at the time. Edmondson and her colleagues were particularly interested in what allowed some surgical teams to master the challenging new technique more quickly than other teams. They found that teams that cultivated a 'free and open environment', where suggestions were welcomed and members felt comfortable pointing out potential problems and mistakes, were more successful in learning.

Although Edmondson's research focused on team learning, creating a psychologically safe atmosphere is equally important in strategic decision making.

Strategic decision making therefore needs to adapt to changing circumstances by broadening the horizons of information being examined, people being consulted and options being considered.

Frame: what's the *right* problem to solve?

The discussion above highlights the need for the final mode of the discovery-led decision making process to take into account a wide array of information to help focus the decision making process on defining the *right* questions to be answered (see Figure 5.3).

In order to broaden their field of information, decision makers need to encounter insights and data that – by design or inadvertently – shake up their thinking about their environment, resulting in fresh

Figure 5.3   Discovery-led decision making – *framing*

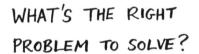

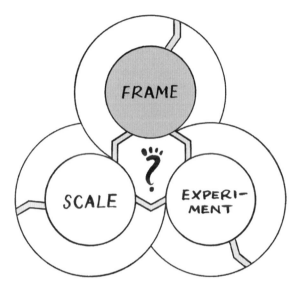

WHAT'S THE RIGHT
PROBLEM TO SOLVE?

FRAME

SCALE

EXPERI-
MENT

?

ideas and inspiration. The initial objective of this phase is to stimulate divergent thought, where decision makers strive to maintain wide horizons to allow for a wide range of provocations and influences. At this point, the organization is asking questions, posing hypotheses or identifying paradoxes by analysing market data, puzzling over observations from the field or focus group results, or examining analogical situations in other industries. The result of this search is enough insight into the available information to have a stab at defining the right challenge to be addressed by the subsequent modes of the process.

The trap of solving the wrong problem precisely is an especial threat when confronting the hard-to-interpret trends thrown up by a turbulent environment. Decision makers therefore need to (re)define clearly the assigned challenge in light of what they've learned about their assumptions and unknowns.

This is why we have labelled this mode *frame*: it can be thought of as figuring out the most appropriate way(s) to perceive a given situation. Insights from the earlier information search are analysed, defined and redefined as challenges. Decision makers should maintain a broad perspective and an open mind to flush out problems – what Michael Roberto (2009) has called 'problem finding'. A combination of the ideas or directions identified earlier are analysed and synthesized into a decision frame with specific questions and possible hypotheses related to strategic options. The *frame* mode ends with a clear definition of the problem or opportunity questions and initial ideas for how to address them.

How the phases of a discovery-led approach fit together

Given the degree of uncertainty and ambiguity confronting us, iteration is integral to the discovery-led decision making framework. We cannot be certain that the strategic choices we make are the correct ones. Instead, 'discovery-led' means that we should focus on maximizing our confidence that we have focused on a worthy problem or opportunity, and we have then focused our energies on validating key assumptions (ie converting them to knowns) and reduced the unknowns to a level we can collectively tolerate. This means that the framework is fluid rather than linear in three ways: there is no predefined sequence of decision making steps, there are different types of iterative 'sprint' and there are multiple points at which to begin and conclude the decision making process.

No predefined sequence

The way to validate the problems we define – and the initially small-scale solutions we develop – is through iterative discovery. Depending on what is discovered during each mode, decision makers can cycle between *frame*, *experiment* and *scale* several times, sifting through knowns, unknowns and assumptions, continually improving their understanding of the strategic decisions and gradually refining their understanding. There might be multiple, interwoven sequences of *frame*, *experiment* and *scale* iterations (the 'α', 'β' and 'γ' cycles

Figure 5.4   *Frame, experiment* and *scale* iterations

in Figure 5.4), creating and testing increasingly well-honed 'experiments,' resulting in a deeper understanding of the problem to be tackled and progressively more viable solutions.

Different types of 'rinse and repeat'

This means we have to conduct different types of 'rinse and repeat': namely, we have to iterate our way from a relevant problem to workable solution over time, adjusting our trajectory in a zigzag fashion, cycling through *frame, experiment* and *scale* depending on what we have learned. The iterative 'sprints' are contrasting in nature: the exploration inherent in considering multiple perspectives when *framing* is not the same as the trials to be conducted during *experiment*, and both differ considerably from the discipline of spreading organizational practices and mindsets when *scaling*. In pursuing this process, it is important to avoid the temptation to equate failures with faulty decision making: indeed, as we shall see in the next three chapters, the concepts of 'failure', 'learning' and 'risk' are subtly different during *frame, experiment* and *scale*.

Multiple entry and exit points

As Figure 5.4 implies, the *frame* mode is not necessarily the start of the decision making process. In practice, discovery can occur at many points in the cycle, whenever leaders notice and choose to act upon new information such as changes in consumer behaviour, competitive contexts or emerging technologies. The initial influence or inspiration for engaging in discovery can be triggered in a variety of ways. It may involve noticing societal trends, the launch of a competitor's service or the launch of a new technology. The idea or challenge may come from many sources: a customer service representative, a marketing manager, a senior executive or even an existing or prospective customer. Wherever the initial idea comes from, the *frame* mode provides a structure within which to make sense of the initial ideas or inspiration. It introduces the frame within which the problem or opportunity can be addressed – in effect the decision making canvas. The discovery-led decision making framework can be used to allow ideas to be captured and developed in this way, and leaders can employ it to foster a creative environment among managers and staff.

Marrying strategy and innovation through an evolutionary approach

As we've discussed, today's business environment is more confusing, more ambiguous and in a greater state of flux than ever before. Conventional strategy approaches can manifest themselves as mechanistic and rigid, leading to a narrow framing of the issues at stake and a consequent limiting of potential options. In addition, there is often an overemphasis and over-reliance on analysis. But, in a fast-moving world, there may be a lack of available data to analyse.

Many management books promise simple step-by-step approaches to achieving decision making success, but the use of a rigid process gives a false sense of security. It can be tempting to allow the process to take over and remove the need for critical reflection. When this happens, strategic planning decisions appear to be a series of disconnected interventions. As Rita McGrath has pointed out, strategy and innovation used to be different disciplines within management science and business administration. But, in the fluid environment confronting us, the two are increasingly inseparable, because innovation is increasingly becoming a required strategic response to rapidly emerging disruptive threats (Kinni, 2014).

There is a place for formal strategic planning models, but they should be used carefully and where appropriate as one of a number of tools. Just as a hammer is not the most appropriate tool for inserting a screw, so a strategic model applied without thought can be a similarly inappropriate device. What we advocate is a more flexible, contingent strategic decision making process that can be tailored to circumstances – but requires considerable reflection and dialogue so that it's applied intelligently.

This more fluid, discovery-led approach echoes the evolutionary model of adaptation advocated by naturalist Charles Darwin. Darwin's model can be characterized as three stages: many random mutations of genes in each generation of a species, which are subjected to severe selective pressure imposed by the need to survive, so that only a tiny proportion of the mutations are propagated as adaptations into subsequent generations. Steven Johnson and others (Johnson, 2011; Hansen and Birkinshaw, 2007) have described the 'natural history' of innovation by using such an evolutionary model as an analogy:

- *Variation*: many ideas are generated through a variety of means.
- *Selection*: most of these ideas do not survive the extremely tough competitive pressure of their environment (which could be a market or an organization).
- *Adaptation*: a small fraction of the ideas survive and become successful.

This evolutionary 'natural history' of ideas is echoed in the discovery-led accumulation of knowns from right to left in Figure 5.5. Once the problem has been suitably defined in the *frame* mode, variation and selection are driven by the *experiment* mode, which generates ideas and validates them through 'tests', before a chosen few ideas are diffused more widely (adaptation) in the *scale* stage.

Figure 5.5   An evolutionary approach to strategy and innovation

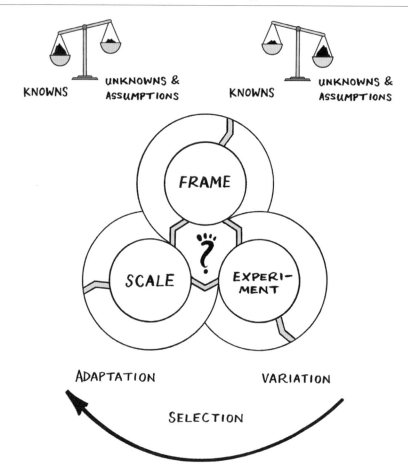

Summary

In this chapter, we've looked at the requirements of a new approach to strategic decision making that is better adapted to the rapid, ambiguous shifts in our increasingly VUCA environment. We introduced the idea of a 'discovery-led' approach focusing on reducing unknowns and assumptions, and with a bias to action.

We introduced the discovery-led decision making framework, the core premise of which is that how you make decisions should be based on the balance between what you know, what you *don't* know and what you *think* you know (ie your assumptions). This framework is composed of three modes:

- *Frame*: what's the *right* problem to solve?
- *Experiment*: how do we *learn* what we need to know?
- *Scale*: how do we do *more* of what works?

This is a fluid not linear approach, characterized by no predefined sequence to progress through the modes, different types of 'rinse and repeat' iterations, and multiple entry and exit points.

In the next three chapters, we'll explain how to go about conducting these modes to help make sense of the confusing world in which we live and to formulate meaningful responses.

References

Christensen, C M, Kaufman, S P and Shih, W C (2008) Innovation killers: how financial tools destroy your capacity to do new things, *Harvard Business Review*, **86** (1), 98–105

Coates, J M (2013) *The Hour between Dog and Wolf: Risk taking, gut feelings and the biology of boom and bust*, Fourth Estate, London

Hamel, G (1999) Bringing Silicon Valley inside, *Harvard Business Review*, **77** (5), 70–84

Hansen, M T and Birkinshaw, J (2007) The innovation value chain, *Harvard Business Review*, **85** (6), 121–30

Johnson, S (2011) *Where Good Ideas Come From: The natural history of innovation*, Penguin, London

Kinni, T (2014) Rita Gunther McGrath on the end of competitive advantage, *strategy + business*, **74** (Spring)

Lasseter, T (2014) Management in the second machine age, *strategy + business*, **75** (Summer)

Liedtka, J M (1998) Strategic thinking: Can it be taught?, *Long Range Planning*, **31** (1), 120–29

Liedtka, J M and Ogilvie, T (2011) *Designing for Growth: A design thinking tool kit for managers*, Columbia University Press, New York

McGrath, R G (2013) *The End of Competitive Advantage: How to keep your strategy moving as fast as your business*, Harvard Business Review Press, Cambridge, MA

McGrath, R G and MacMillan, I C (1995) Discovery-driven planning, *Harvard Business Review*, **73** (4), 44–54

Mitroff, I I (1998) *Smart Thinking for Crazy Times*, Berrett-Koehler, Oakland, CA

Reeves, M, Haanæs, K and Sinha, J (2015) *Your Strategy Needs a Strategy*, Harvard Business Review Press, Cambridge, MA

Roberto, M A (2009) *Know What You Don't Know: How great leaders prevent problems before they happen*, Wharton School Publishing, Philadelphia, PA

Shenoy, B (2017) Discovery-led decision-making, 1 April, http://benshenoy.com/index.php/dilemmas/discovery-led

Stasser, G and Titus, W (1985) Pooling of unshared information in group decision making: Biased information sampling during discussion, *Journal of Personality and Social Psychology*, **48** (6), 1467–78

Tucker, A L, Nembhard, I M and Edmondson, A C (2007) Implementing new practices: an empirical study of organizational learning in hospital intensive care units, *Management Science*, **53** (6), 894–907

Mode I: Framing

A problem well stated is a problem half-solved. JOHN DEWEY

The importance of solving the *right* problem

The previous chapter introduced the discovery-led decision making framework: our way of tackling the perplexing times in which we live and overcoming the obstacles of organizational inertia and individual biases. In this chapter, we'll look at one of the three modes of this framework, namely *framing*, which focuses on problem *finding* rather than problem *solving*.

We have seen that the world is in a greater state of flux than ever before. As a result, there are more unknowns for us to contend with. Even more disconcertingly, many are, as former US Secretary of Defense Donald Rumsfeld famously said, 'unknown unknowns' – which can blindside us.

Our *nescience* – our lack of knowledge – is compounded by the fact that we are blinded by the knowledge that we *do* have. Our knowledge acts like blinkers, keeping us on a linear path without seeing what's happening at the periphery. And, as we have also already seen, it is from the periphery that the biggest threats and opportunities may well arise.

In 1956, Smith's was the largest manufacturer of potato crisps in the UK, producing over 10 million packets of crisps every week. Smith's crisps came in translucent paper bags and so remained fresh for only a few days. Because of their short shelf-life, crisps were not sold in retail outlets but through pubs and hotels. Smith's must have felt confident in its market dominance, as it supplied nearly every pub and hotel in the country.

In 1960, Golden Wonder introduced crisps in a cellophane bag. The new packaging meant that Golden Wonder crisps lasted longer – weeks rather than days – and could be sold through the supermarkets that appeared after the Second World War. Golden Wonder grew the potato snack market by appealing to housewives and children rather than poaching pub and hotel customers from Smith's. As Golden Wonder was not muscling in on the pub and hotel scene, Smith's remained ignorant of the threat posed by Golden Wonder, failing to appreciate the broadening market. By 1966, Golden Wonder had overtaken Smith's, having amassed a market share of 45 per cent against Smith's 34 per cent. The fortunes of Smith's crisps were never quite the same again.

George Day and Paul Schoemaker tell a similar tale regarding a large pet food manufacturer that failed to take into account the rise of scientifically formulated pet foods sold through veterinary practices and speciality outlets (Day and Schoemaker, 2006). Managers in the traditional pet food company relied on their steady sales growth to confirm that all was well. But they missed the fact that the total pet food market was growing while their *share* of the market was actually diminishing.

The pet food market is still evolving, as affluent Western pet owners are now looking for pet foods that more closely resemble their own foods, with ingredients that are perceived to be more natural, healthy and transparently sourced. It is interesting to note that Hill's, which was at the forefront of manufacturing scientifically formulated pet foods, has been slow to respond to the latest evolution in the pet food market.

The above examples show that large multimillion-pound corporations, focusing on running their existing operations well, can be blindsided by new competitors and market changes. Why is it that their efforts to scan the environment failed to alert such established companies to imminent threats?

Solving the wrong problem

As we saw with our discussion of wicked problems in the Introduction, we are confronted by highly complex problems that cannot be encapsulated in a neatly articulated question. If we were to stop and take time to reflect, we might even find that we struggle to arrive at a clear definition of the issue. And yet this is a crucial stage. Much time and money have been wasted as a result of poor problem definition. The quote at the start of this chapter from US psychologist and philosopher John Dewey that 'A problem well stated is a problem half-solved' emphasizes this point.

Our world is fast-paced, and the stakes are often high. In such situations, the pressure to act is immense and time spent on reflection can feel like an unaffordable luxury or, worse, idle procrastination. But, as Frank Partnoy (2013) notes, delaying decision making can be beneficial. This echoes something that Albert Einstein is reputed to have said, namely that if he had only an hour to solve a problem that would save the world then he would spend 55 minutes defining the problem and five minutes solving it. Partnoy notes that humans are hard-wired to react quickly. We have a bias towards action, and modern technology not only facilitates but actually exacerbates this.

We are so focused on the apparent end goal – finding the solution to the problem – that we do not pause to consider whether we have formulated the problem correctly. If we are to give ourselves the best chance of finding solutions, reflecting deeply on how to *define* the problem is crucial. Before we can begin finding solutions, we need to ask ourselves an even more fundamental question: are we solving the *right* problem?

Solving the right problem is not as easy as it sounds. In 1959 the British industrialist Henry Kremer offered a prize of £50,000 to the first person to build and fly a human-powered plane in a figure of eight around two markers placed half a mile apart (Grosser, 2004). This enormous sum, over £800,000 in today's money, attracted a great number of entrants. However, nearly two decades passed, with scores of unsuccessful attempts, until a US aeronautical engineer named Dr Paul MacCready came across the challenge. He reviewed the 50 or so failed attempts and then had a striking insight. The human-powered aspect of the challenge that everyone was focusing on was, in fact, a red herring. In his words, 'The problem is, we don't understand the problem.' He realized that, up until then, people had been too focused on the theoretical side of the problem, investing a huge amount of time, effort and resources into complex theories and intricate designs. MacCready saw that he would only identify critical problems if he tested his assumptions as he went along. MacCready's insight, of which more in the next chapter, allowed him to get to the essence of why all the previous attempts had been unsuccessful.

So why is it that we are seduced into solving the wrong problem? As Mark Twain summed up so neatly in the quote at the start of Chapter 5, in our rush to action we leap to conclusions and assume that we know what we are dealing with. In so doing, we have a tendency to commit what have been called Type III errors.

Type III errors occur when we go about 'solving the wrong problem precisely'. First described by Allyn Kimball (1957) and later elaborated by Ian Mitroff (1998), Type III errors involve trying to solve problems using entrenched assumptions, models and mindsets based on past experience. As the world is constantly changing, doing what we've always done without considering different perspectives is less likely to lead to sound solutions. Or, as Albert Einstein once noted, 'We can't solve problems by using the same kind of thinking we used when we created them.'

Problem solving versus problem finding

We don't often go *hunting* for problems. We usually feel that we have more than enough to deal with without going out of our way to look for trouble. This means that we take the problems confronting us at face value and don't ask more probing questions to establish if we are solving the right problem.

When a charity, whose primary aim was to help make dreams come true for seriously ill children, organized an Alaskan hunting expedition for a teenager with cancer, it was astonished to find itself at the centre of a media storm. The organization had been so focused on *how* to make the boy's dream of shooting a bear a reality that it completely failed to consider the more fundamental problem of *whether* it should do so. The resultant backlash from members of the public and animal rights groups, who felt that the decision was indefensible on moral grounds, nearly resulted in the closure of the charity.

Italian home furnishings manufacturer Alessi didn't exactly go problem hunting when in 1985 it asked architect Michael Graves to design a new kettle for it. But it did go out of its way to look at a commonly used product and ask how it could reconceptualize a utilitarian, everyday product like the humble and ubiquitous kettle. Graves's whimsical whistling bird that sits on top of the spout and cheerfully announces that the water has boiled has, for many people, redefined not only their expectations of a kettle but even the whole early-morning ritual. Graves apparently once received a message from a French poet, who wrote: 'I'm always very grumpy when I get up in the morning. But when I get up now, I put the teakettle on, and when it starts to sing it makes me smile – goddamn you!' (Verganti, 2006).

Alessi reframed the fundamental purpose of the lowly kettle and found a 'problem' to solve that most of us didn't even know existed. But that is not generally the case. So what is it that makes us susceptible to committing Type III errors? Framing turns out to be difficult for three reasons:

1 We overfocus on knowledge, which blinds us to what we don't know.

2 We adopt overly narrow perspectives.

3 We pay attention to the superficial and proximal rather than the essential and distal aspects of the problems confronting us.

As will become apparent, these causes of problem mis-definition frequently coincide.

Obstacles to *framing*

Overfocus on knowledge

Knowledge is seductive. It makes us feel secure, happy and confident. From an early age, we are bombarded with cues that tell us that knowing is good. School tests, exams, job opportunities and promotions are all largely based on what we know. In the workplace, it is our specialist knowledge that distinguishes us from the next person.

Knowing signals that we are smart. This filters into our subconscious and our very identity.

Not knowing, on the other hand, is uncomfortable. No doubt we have all been in situations where we have found our knowledge lacking: perhaps sitting an exam, or fielding awkward questions from our boss. We shy away from situations where we feel our knowledge is deficient, because they make us feel inadequate. The discomfort we feel when we don't know something is in part due to the emphasis the world around us places on knowledge. But there is a deeper, more fundamental reason for our unease. We are so used to equating knowledge with self-worth that, when we find ourselves without our protective cloak of knowledge, we feel naked and vulnerable. It is almost as if something in our very core is disturbed. Psychologists use the term 'cognitive dissonance' for this mental distress. It occurs when our internal model of who we are (people who 'know') is contradicted in some way (situations where we don't know). We all seek to minimize situations of cognitive dissonance.

Leadership coach David Rock (2009) says that even small uncertainties are like a constantly flashing error message in our brain. Something that cannot be easily ignored until resolved makes focusing on other things very difficult. According to Rock, uncertainty can be profoundly debilitating and lead to diminished memory and lowered performance because it requires extra neural energy.

Our beliefs and knowledge can blind us to alternative perspectives. This 'curse of knowledge', a phrase originally coined by Colin Camerer and his colleagues (Camerer, Loewenstein and Weber, 1989), describes the phenomenon of well-informed people – experts – finding it exceptionally hard to think about an issue from the perspective of those who are less knowledgeable. Where they have an advantage due to their greater knowledge, they generally fail to exploit it, acting as if other parties also share their information.

A clever demonstration of this cognitive bias was shown by a Stanford University psychology researcher named Elizabeth Newton (Heath and Heath, 2007). She divided participants into 'tappers' and 'listeners'. Tappers were asked to think of a well-known tune and then to tap out its rhythm to a listener. Before the tappers began, they were asked to estimate how many listeners would correctly guess the tune. The tappers predicted that 50 per cent of listeners would correctly identify the song. The results were surprising. Only 2.5 per cent of listeners succeeded in guessing the tune. This was a success rate of one in every 40 attempts. The tappers estimated that one in two listeners – 50 per cent – would be successful because the task seemed simple to them. What they failed to take into account was that, as they were tapping, they had the benefit of the soundtrack and associated imagery running in their heads – whilst all the listener had to go on was a series of apparently disconnected taps.

The curse of knowledge is a manifestation of narrow framing in terms of discipline. A friend of one of us likes to tell the story of an engineer who was asked to build a tracking device in the 1970s. The engineer duly went ahead and built a state-of-the-art device. The tracker was installed on a collar and fitted on a wild moose. The team tracking the moose were surprised to find it not moving for days. When they went to investigate, they found that the device was so heavy the moose hadn't been able to get back up when it came round from sedation. When they went back to the engineer, he looked at them in surprise and asked 'What moose?' The engineer had only ever considered the tracker from an engineering point of view.

Confirmation bias

Most of us take pride in keeping ourselves up to date with advances in our professional fields and in staying abreast of current affairs. We do this almost automatically by watching the news, reading newspapers and journals, and so forth. Although we feel as though we are actively updating our knowledge, this may be a delusion. In part, this is because the information is largely coming from traditional and familiar sources. We may even have pre-selected what we see by allowing our computers to filter information based on our previous interests.

Not only might we apply an electronic filter (knowingly or not), but more fundamentally we also apply our own inherent cognitive biases. One such bias that acts as a set of mental blinkers is confirmation bias, which we have already come across in Chapter 2. Confirmation bias is our tendency to seek out information that confirms our beliefs and preconceptions rather than looking for evidence that would disprove them. Confirmation bias can cloud our thinking in a number of ways:

- *We interpret new information in a way that fits with our existing beliefs.* Where we have a strong belief about something, we will tend to interpret new information so that it is in line with our beliefs. A study in the late 1970s demonstrated this using students with strong views on capital punishment (Lord, Ross and Lepper, 1979). Supporters and opponents of capital punishment – each making up 50 per cent of the participants – were given two studies, one seemingly supportive of the efficacy of capital punishment and the other apparently providing disconfirming evidence. Unbeknownst to the students both studies were entirely fictional. Both sets of students reported finding the study that confirmed their own views to be the more convincing. The authors found that 'there is considerable evidence that people tend to interpret subsequent evidence so as to maintain their initial beliefs'.

- *We judge disconfirming evidence more harshly.* Lord, Ross and Lepper also found that participants in their study tended 'to judge confirming evidence as relevant and reliable but disconfirming evidence as irrelevant and unreliable, and to accept confirming evidence at face value while scrutinizing disconfirming evidence hypercritically'.

- *We seek confirming evidence and don't seek, or ignore, disconfirming evidence.* According to Matthew Rabin and Joel Schrag (1999), people also tend to 'misread evidence as additional support for initial hypotheses. If a teacher initially believes that one student is smarter than another, she has the propensity to confirm that hypothesis when interpreting later performance.'

- *We cling to our original beliefs even in the face of contradictory evidence.* Rabin and Schrag (1999) have also shown that even an infinite amount of information does not necessarily overcome the effects of confirmation bias. This overwhelming reluctance to change our minds is borne out in an experimental study (Cipriano and Gruca, 2014) that found that, once people had reached a conclusion, they were unlikely to change their mind even in the face of evidence showing their belief was most likely incorrect and liable to cost them money.

As a result of this cognitive information processing bias we are overconfident in the validity of our beliefs. Nearly 400 years ago, Galileo Galilei ([1632] 2001) already knew the truth of this:

> In the long run my observations have convinced me that some men, reasoning preposterously, first establish some conclusion in their minds which, either because of its being their own or because of their having received it from some person who has their entire confidence, impresses them so deeply that one finds it impossible ever to get it out of their heads. Such arguments in support of their fixed idea as they hit upon themselves or hear set forth by others, no matter how simple and stupid these may be, gain their instant acceptance and applause. On the other hand whatever is brought forward against it, however ingenious and conclusive, they receive with disdain or with hot rage.

Overly narrow framing

An obsession with knowledge drives us to frame our thinking too narrowly. We also think too narrowly in terms of stakeholders and time. Our narrow perspectives limit our ability to take all potentially relevant information into account. If we are to avoid Type III errors, we need to make a conscious effort to change perspectives so that we can get a holistic view of the problem.

Narrow stakeholder framing

Stakeholders are a wide and disparate group and include anyone with an interest in the organization. The charity caught up with the desire to fulfil a terminally ill teenager's dream clearly failed to consider the effect of its decision on a wider group of stakeholders.

Type III errors often occur because we assume we know what our stakeholders are thinking. Ron Johnson made this mistake in 2012, as the newly hired CEO for J C Penney. The retailer, which can trace its roots back to the early 1900s, had been losing market share for decades to companies such as Walmart. Johnson sought to move away from the promotions, coupons and frequent price-slashed sales that had been a J C Penney hallmark. He wanted instead to reposition the brand as providing its customers with 'everyday low prices'. J C Penney's tactics had been to apply inflated prices to goods and then to discount them, sometimes by as much as 50 per cent. Knowing the company's methods, Johnson thought that consumers would welcome this fairer and more transparent approach, but he was wrong. He failed to look at the sales from his customers' point of view. They saw a shirt priced at $10 as poor quality, but the same shirt marked down to $10 from $30 was a bargain. Customers complained bitterly, and Johnson was fired after only 17 months and discounting was reinstated.

US clothing retailer Lands' End made a similar mistake when it published an interview with the 81-year-old feminist and political activist Gloria Steinem in its spring 2016 catalogue. The article was part of its legend series featuring those 'who have made a difference in both their respective industries and the world at large'. What Lands' End failed to consider was how polarizing a figure Steinem would be to its customers in the United States. Although the interview made no mention of the abortion debate, Steinem's well-known pro-choice stance outraged many Lands' End customers, who were vociferous in their criticism and threatened to boycott the company. The many Christian schools that buy their uniforms from the company similarly threatened to go elsewhere. It did not take long for Lands' End to remove the article from its website and issue an apology – only to find it had caused a further furore by angering those on the other side of the debate, who saw this as an affront to women's rights. One post on the company's Facebook page read: 'What a terrible message to send to all the women and girls who wear your clothes.' It continued: 'I'm sorry you see equal rights for women as a divisive issue. I see it as a human issue.'

No doubt the legend series was supposed to provide a human-interest angle to the clothing catalogue and, in featuring an octogenarian, the company was perhaps hoping to appeal to an older group of stakeholders. But failing to put itself in the minds of its consumers cost it dearly.

Coke, new and old

Let us consider the story of a new recipe for Coca-Cola that illustrates the pitfalls of failing to see things from a stakeholder perspective.

In April 1985, the Coca-Cola Company announced that it was changing the secret recipe of Coke. Three months later the company was forced to back down and bring back 'old' Coca-Cola in the form of Coke Classic.

What happened? How had such a large corporation got such a big decision so wrong? This decision is often held up to ridicule, but it was not taken lightly. The Coca-Cola Company had done thorough market research and, based on market share figures, had taken an apparently rational decision.

At the time, Coca-Cola was the market-leading cola drink, but it had been slowly losing market share to its rival Pepsi for nearly 15 consecutive years. In addition, the general state of the cola market was lethargic. By introducing a new formulation for its top-selling product, the Coca-Cola Company hoped 'to change the dynamics of sugar colas in the United States', as Roberto Goizueta, then Chairman and CEO, said at a later date. Not only was Coke slipping in market share, but in blind taste tests consumers preferred the sweeter taste of Pepsi – something that PepsiCo exploited fully in its 'Pepsi Challenge' commercials. Coca-Cola fully understood that it would be a huge deal to change its flagship product, and it carried out extensive tests. It found that over 200,000 consumers not only preferred the new formulation to the old but also preferred it to the taste of Pepsi. Based on this solid evidence of what the consumer apparently wanted, the change went ahead.

Unfortunately, what the company had failed to appreciate was the very special relationship that many cola drinkers had with Coke. To them it was more than just a soft drink. It was part of their lives in good times and in bad, and their loyalty to the brand was fierce. The announcement in July 1985 that 'old' Coca-Cola would return to supermarket shelves was front-page news in almost every major US national newspaper, and was the lead story on two US network newscasts. In the two days following the announcement, the company received more than 31,600 telephone calls. This question of identity and stakeholder attachment was the essence of the mistake made by Coca-Cola. It had done its market research and had taken a rational decision. But it underestimated the strength and depth of the emotional attachment that so many people had to the drink. Coca-Cola's decision has been lambasted over the years, and this is rather unfair given the benefit of hindsight.

Coca-Cola is not the only company to have suffered a failed brand relaunch. During Christmas 2010, Gap launched a new logo design and rebranded its company to suit, without warning. The original Gap logo, in existence for more than 20 years, disappeared suddenly to be replaced by the new one. Soon a buzz of online activity indicated that people didn't like the new design. After Gap initially responded that the new design was the first stage of a crowdsourcing process to reinvent the company, it reverted to its original design just six days after the brand relaunch. The difference between New Coke and the Gap logo redesign was that, unlike Coca-Cola, Gap did not consult extensively with customers and other stakeholders.

Narrow temporal framing

A dilemma often faced by executives is how to make their company more innovative while still maintaining performance in the core business. Firms struggle with this because the processes required to foster innovation are often the antithesis of those required for the stability of a mature business. As the former Chief Technology Officer of Microsoft and founder of Microsoft Research, Nathan P Myhrvold, remarked, 'Most large organizations have a mission, and invention often takes you in another direction. When it comes to mission versus invention at most companies, mission wins.'

Eastman Kodak's failure to invest in the digital camera that they invented in 1975 provides a powerful illustration of how executives can see the world in narrow terms and fail to anticipate change even when their own company has pioneered the change.

We tend to take a short-term view, focusing on the here and now in preference to looking to the future. This was certainly the case at Kodak. The debate about whether short-termism is a problem has gone on for decades, with evidence accumulating on both sides of the divide. No doubt there are times when quick decisions and fast action are needed. But equally there are times when a short-term perspective should be put aside. Arguably such was the case when Rupert

Murdoch bought Myspace in 2005. At the time Myspace was ranked the fifth most viewed internet domain in the United States. Having spent $580 million on the purchase of Myspace's parent company, Murdoch was keen to see a return on the investment. He tried to monetize his acquisition too quickly by flooding the site with ads, which, so former Myspace CEO Chris DeWolfe maintains, alienated its users, who ended up flocking to Facebook instead. Myspace was sold in 2011 for a mere $35 million, and Rupert Murdoch admitted on Twitter that they 'had screwed up in every way possible'.

Attraction to superficiality

Sometimes referred to as the 'Oracle of Omaha', Warren Buffett is one of the most successful investors in history. It is said that one of his key investment tenets has been to focus on the fundamentals of how a company operates rather than superficial aspects such as stocks and sector trends. Whether this is true of Buffett's investment strategy or not, it is good advice when it comes to thinking about a problem.

Attending to the proximal and superficial at the expense of deeper problems landed the Co-operative Bank in serious trouble in 2013. The British retail and commercial bank hit the headlines after discovering a £1.5 billion capital shortfall in its books. At least part of the Co-operative's woes can be traced back to its merger with the Britannia Building Society some four years earlier. At that time, the Co-operative was a full-service bank making modest profits as a result of its small branch footprint and relatively high costs. Merging with the Britannia was intended to give it access to a bigger branch network and greater economies of scale. One would think that, when contemplating a £70 billion merger, the Co-operative would want to know exactly what it was taking on. However, according to a report by the Prudential Regulatory Authority, a Bank of England supervisory body, a small in-house team spent only two days doing a cursory inspection of a very limited portion of Britannia's corporate loans. As a result, the merged entity ended up with a loan portfolio that was far outside its risk appetite, which no one took steps to redress.

The management of capital is at the very heart of what a bank is supposed to do. However, in the four years that followed the merger, capital forecasting and planning were poor, to say the least. Instead of focusing on the core essentials of its business, the board was distracted by things such as a costly IT replatforming and so consistently failed in its oversight of the banking executive.

Our tendency to focus on the superficial means that we often do not realize that problems do not exist in isolation, though we tend to act as if they do. We behave as if they are distinct and separate, with stand-alone solutions. As David Kord Murray (2010) states, the reality is that problems and their solutions form an interconnected web. Some problems exist at a high level, with lower-level sub-problems dependent on the answers to problems further up the hierarchy.

Approaching a problem by looking at the interconnection between questions and answers, rather like a logic tree, can help to widen thinking and avoid possible unintended consequences. If the charity we considered earlier in the chapter had viewed the wish to hunt and kill a living creature from a wider perspective, it might have anticipated the furore an affirmative decision was likely to cause. It might then have broadened out its thinking to ask if it was still possible to fulfil the wish in a different way, perhaps by taking the boy on a photographic safari instead.

One reason we focus on a part of the hierarchy rather than the whole pyramid – contributing to our attraction to superficiality – is because our brains have limited information-processing capacity. To prevent information overload, we filter what we pay attention to. This selective attention is useful, as it allows us to focus on a task whilst ignoring background distractions such as phones ringing, people talking and traffic outside.

Perceptual blindness

The downside of selective attention is that it can lead to us missing things that would otherwise seem to be glaringly obvious. Psychologists have termed this 'inattentional blindness' or 'perceptual blindness'. Dan Simons and Christopher Chabris designed an experiment where participants were asked to count how many times a basketball was passed between a team of players in a video clip

(Simons and Chabris, 1999). Most participants failed to notice when a man in a gorilla suit walked across the screen, despite the gorilla being present for several seconds, even pausing to beat his chest.

Perceptual blindness means that we can be so focused on a part of the problem pyramid that we fail to pay attention to other parts. An independent review conducted by Sir Christopher Kelly into the Co-operative Bank's financial crisis showed no fewer than nine factors that caused the crisis. Out of these nine, only two factors were outside the control of the Bank's board and management.

Vigilance is exhausting

One reason for our obsession with superficiality and attentional blindness is that constant, thorough vigilance is exhausting. Our brains consume more energy than any other bodily organ, expending 20 per cent of the body's total energy intake. In an effort to save energy, the brain has evolved to scan for patterns rather than evaluating each and every new sensory input. Familiar patterns allow the brain to take mental short cuts. Rather than having to reassess the situation constantly, it can fall back on previously learned behaviours that were successful in similar situations. This means that we can perform familiar tasks on autopilot without having to engage the energy-hungry higher brain functions in the prefrontal cortex, which are then free to attend to potential threats. While this is useful today because it allows us to multi-task, it was vital in prehistoric times when the rippling of the long grass meant a fearsome predator was about to pounce and eat you for lunch.

These visual cues kept us safe from sabre-toothed tigers. Indeed, according to Nobel Prize winner Daniel Kahneman (2002), we privilege visual stimuli over other types of stimuli for just such evolutionary reasons. This goes towards explaining why we focus on superficial and proximal things – it was evolutionarily adaptive to do so. However, most of the situations and problems confronting us now are multi-causal, with hard-to-discern sources that present potentially misleading symptoms. Our brains are wired to jump to inferences based on superficial data, rather than take the (effortful) time to diagnose underlying causes. Again, this makes sense from an evolutionary perspective. Those of our ancestors who assumed that the rustling was a tiger and ran, survived. Those who pontificated rather than acting turned into an easy meal.

In order to create order and meaning from our surroundings, the brain is constantly scanning and searching for patterns and signals to interpret. Michael Gazzaniga (2000) has conducted extensive research into the functioning of the left and right brain hemispheres. His research has found that the left hemisphere excels at deciphering clues from the world around us. Gazzaniga says the left-brain 'interpreter' is what we use to construct narratives from external cues to make sense of the world around us. So strong is this sense-making drive that the brain will 'see' patterns even where none exist.

So, as we have seen, Type III errors are easily made. How can we avoid falling into the traps of solving the wrong problem precisely? We will examine this topic in the next section.

How to *frame*?

The following suggestions are not meant to be exhaustive or prescriptive, but more of an indicative guide to avoiding Type III errors:

1 Broaden – but bound – the exploration.
2 Recombine elements of the problem to come up with new formulations.
3 Reframe the problem – repeatedly.

Broaden – but bound – the exploration

When gathering information we need to broaden the exploration, to diverge, so that the information collected is seen in context and all relevant details are captured. Once this has been done, the information can be sifted and filtered in a convergent process. In a VUCA environment, if you simply converge without diverging you are more likely to make Type III errors. However, if you just diverge your exploration without subsequently converging, you will never come to conclusions and make sense of the environment.

Broaden the frame of reference

The specific steps in broadening the frame of reference are scanning the environment widely, followed by searching for non-obvious connections in the information gathered.

Scan the environment Decision psychologists George Day and Paul Schoemaker (2006) advocate different types of active scanning of the environment for signals to determine how to frame a problem: *directed* and *undirected*.

With *active directed scanning*, organizations know that they need to monitor a number of different interest zones such as competitors and customers, suppliers and distributors, influences and shapers, governmental and non-governmental bodies. Keeping tabs on many different channels simultaneously is not easy but is nonetheless essential. The rise of social media has added another dimension, and companies neglect this to their detriment. Consumers can be a company's biggest advocates, but they can also wreak devastating damage on a corporate reputation. Whereas it takes many individual positive anecdotes to enhance a company's reputation, unfortunately the opposite is not true. One critical review can be all it takes.

An online retailer in Northern Ireland discovered that it was losing a large proportion of would-be customers after a dissatisfied shopper posted a negative review on an online forum. Similarly, a hotel in Scotland found an entire Facebook page had been set up calling for people to boycott it following negative remarks by a diner on the same social media site.

Fortunately, companies do not need to devote hundreds of hours to combing the web for bad publicity. Technology can digest millions of internet pages to produce manageable nuggets of information. When thinking about scanning the environment, we can learn from the workings of an insect's compound eye.

The eye of an insect (or a crustacean) is built quite differently from a mammalian eye. Instead of a single unit with a lens and retina, the insect eye is built up of multiple repeating units called ommatidia, each of which functions as a visual receptor focused on just one area in space. Each ommatidium provides the insect's brain with one piece of a large jigsaw. The image formed in the insectile brain is a composite one of all the individual jigsaw pieces fitted together. This remarkable structure confers a very large field of view on the insect owner. Bees and dragonflies have a field of vison of more than 300 degrees, which means they are still watching you after they have flown past. But for many insects this comes at the expense of a lower-resolution image (compared to human eyes). This is a useful analogy when considering *framing*: you need a large field of view, at a height 10,000 feet, with low resolution. Then you need to be able to zoom in to promising areas of interest, just as a dragonfly swoops down on a tasty mosquito!

The other kind of active scanning is *active undirected scanning*. Day and Schoemaker (2006) refer to a technique called splatter vision, where one looks to the horizon without focusing on any one thing. This approach has been used by Native Americans and wildlife trackers and is taught to fighter pilots and intelligence agents. This non-selective seeing helps an observer to spot movement, anomalies or unexpected changes – a useful trick for organizations to master. Once again, insects such as bees have this down to a T. They have a far higher flicker fusion threshold than humans (think of one of those cartoon strip books where it looks as though the characters are moving as you flip the pages at speed). This means that they can home in on one individual swaying flower in a meadow and can easily evade that swatting hand!

Organizations need to develop the ability to flip between directed and undirected scanning when *framing* to stand the best chance of spotting opportunities as well as threats.

Organizations also need to consider *outside and in*. Scanning should occur not only externally but within as well. 'Within' refers to within the organization, and within the industry or sector. Sometimes valuable information is held within the organization, but either its value isn't recognized or it doesn't get passed to the right person – perhaps because the individuals holding the insights are 'positive deviants' whose value might not be recognized by colleagues (Sternin, 2002). Once again the compound eye is a useful analogy: many visual input units, one central processor.

Seek non-obvious connections Companies and individuals have limited time and resources, so choices have to be made about how and where they direct their efforts. With too little discrimination, it's hard to see the wood for the trees. Day and Schoemaker (2006) advocate asking a set of what they term 'thought starter' questions aimed at capturing learning from the past, identifying potential trends and anticipating future shocks. These suggestions include examining past blind spots, speaking to mavericks and outliers both within and outside the organization and imagining the unthinkable.

Seeking information from acquaintances, people outside your close circle of contacts, can provide fresh perspectives, amplify weak signals or triangulate ambiguous information. Imagine two acquaintances, Mary and Jane. Mary and Jane each have a set of close friends (strong ties); they also both have a set of people they know less well (weak ties). The weak tie between Mary and Jane acts as a bridge between their two otherwise disconnected networks. These ideas were first proposed by sociologist Mark Granovetter (1973). He surmised that the *most* valuable information often comes from 'weak ties', people who are at the *periphery* of your network of social contacts. Granovetter's views on social networks remain highly influential to this day.

Allied to Granovetter's concept of weak ties are the 'structural holes' in social networks proposed by another sociologist, Ronald Burt (1992). If you were to map all the contacts of a number of people, the resulting diagram would probably reveal several distinct clusters with relatively few connections between them. Structural holes are the gaps *between* disconnected networks. For example, vets and doctors represent two distinct communities that have a great deal of shared medical knowledge. Many commonalities exist between diseases in humans and animals. You would think, therefore, that a constant dialogue between the two professions would benefit both, and yet this doesn't usually happen. In effect, there is a wide structural hole between the two professions.

The One Health One Medicine initiative has attempted to bridge this gap, but it has largely focused on zoonoses (diseases that can be transmitted from animals to humans) such as rabies, West Nile virus and Ebola. After being invited to consult on some of the more difficult cases at the Los Angeles zoo, Barbara Natterson-Horowitz, a human cardiologist at UCLA, was struck by the similarities in the illnesses and treatment of the animals she encountered there to those of her own patients. She realized the enormous benefit that could be garnered from greater collaboration between these two sets of medical professionals. Together with Katherine Bowers, a writer and journalist, she set up Zoobiquity, a species-spanning approach to human and animal healthcare. Their research has revealed animal correlates in almost every human health area, from heart disease, diabetes, cancer and obesity through to dysfunctional behaviours such as obsessive compulsive disorder (OCD), self-injury and eating disorders.

In a similar way, organizations would do well to identify the structural holes in both their internal and their external networks.

Bound the search

How you limit your search has a material influence on the information you find – which is why we should avoid the temptation to rush to formulate the problem.

In our voyage of discovery, we need to cast our net wide enough to make sure we don't miss something important, but not so wide that we are overwhelmed by waves of irrelevant information. So how do we know where to draw the boundaries? Instead of concentrating on bounding the area of search, consider instead how diverse your search is. The more complex the problem you are wrestling with, the broader your sources of discovery will need to be.

As an instructive example, Thomas Edison was a strong advocate of diverse learning (Boynton and Fischer, 2011). All Edison's prospective employees had to take a written test of more than 150 questions. The questions were designed for different positions, but a score of 90 per cent was apparently required to pass. The questions were as wide-ranging as 'Who invented logarithms?', 'Where is the Sargasso Sea?' and 'Who was Leonidas?' Edison himself is said to have found Shakespeare a great source of inspiration.

At this stage, we are still problem *finding*, so curiosity and questions are more important than answers. Looking for answers too early can mean you are unwittingly funnelled down particular paths, and may miss exploring other potentially promising avenues.

Because our brains are prejudiced towards patterns, we automatically pay more attention to repeated information. Have you ever come across a piece of obscure and new information only to encounter it again, perhaps multiple times in a short space of time? Or perhaps you're thinking of buying a new car, and you've read about a particular new model that has just been launched. All of a sudden, you see it everywhere, next to you at traffic lights, parked outside your office, driven by a parent at school pick-up time. This is the Baader–Meinhof phenomenon at work. A commenter on the St Paul *Pioneer Press* online discussion board labelled it so in 1994 after coming across the name of the German terrorist group of the same name twice in 24 hours. It is also known as frequency illusion, the name given to it in 2006 by the Stanford linguistics professor Arnold Zwicky. It occurs because, having been exposed to an unfamiliar term or concept, we are subconsciously on the lookout for it. When it occurs again, the brain's pattern recognition machine goes into overdrive and promotes this information as the start of a pattern. We are now unconsciously looking for it, driven by the brain's coping mechanism of selective attention. The problem with selective attention is that it biases our search towards this pattern and away from all the other 'uninteresting' (from the brain's perspective), but potentially valuable, information.

Recombine

What do Stephen Jay Gould, Albert Einstein, Arthur Koestler and Steve Jobs all have in common? They all had a gift for making connections between seemingly disparate things. In Steve Jobs's words, 'Creativity is just connecting things.' He went on to say that creative people often feel slightly guilty when asked how they came up with something, because to them they didn't actually 'do' anything. They merely saw something that was obvious to them. Stephen Jay Gould, palaeontologist and popular science writer, was similarly modest. Speaking about his 'talent for making connections', he told writer Denise Shekerjian that 'It took me years to realize that was a skill. I could never understand why everybody just didn't do that' (Shekerjian, 1991).

Arthur Koestler, the author and journalist, coined the term *bisociation* to explain how creativity comes from the intersection of two different frames of reference. The very word is a combination of 'bisection' and 'association', implying that the crucial point in creation is the point at which two juxtaposed ideas intersect. He refers to this kind of thinking as occurring on more than one plane.

Taking an idea from one sphere and transplanting it in another domain to see it grow and flourish into something entirely new is akin to what Einstein termed 'combinatorial play'. The great physicist believed that these 'Lego blocks' for the mind were 'the essential feature in productive thought'. He understood that allowing the mind free rein and simply imagining was extraordinarily valuable. In an interview published in the *Saturday Evening Post* in 1929 he is reported to have said: 'Imagination is more important than knowledge. For knowledge is limited, whereas imagination embraces the entire world, stimulating progress, giving birth to evolution' (Viereck, 1929).

Many new ideas come from the recombination of two or more existing ideas or products. The smartphone is a combination of telephone, computer, camera, voice recorder, photo album and many more things besides. Clothes impregnated with insect repellent are another example of recombination.

Another fertile area for recombination is the application of an idea from one domain in a totally different context. An example of this, which may turn out to be enormously important for the human race, is the work of Dr Adin Ross-Gillespie and his colleagues (Ross-Gillespie et al, 2014). Dr Ross-Gillespie is an evolutionary biologist with a particular interest in the evolutionary causes and consequences of cooperative behaviours, wherever they occur in the tree of life. Having studied collaborative behaviours in mammals (naked mole rats and meerkats), he has applied his knowledge to the field of microbiology with surprising results.

Many bacteria need to obtain iron from their surroundings in order to survive. They do this by producing iron-binding compounds (siderophores), which are excreted into the environment. Siderophores bind to iron and are then reabsorbed by bacterial cells. It should be noted that, in these bacterial colonies, a siderophore may be produced by one bacterium and collected by another. They are a common good, if you will, from which all the bacteria in that colony can benefit. Dr Ross-Gillespie reasoned that this cooperative behaviour could be exploited to thwart antibiotic resistance. He and his colleagues have shown that, at least *in vitro*, bacterial growth is inhibited when the metal gallium is introduced into the environment. Gallium, which is structurally similar to iron, binds preferentially to siderophores, thereby rendering them useless to the bacteria. Perhaps best of all, this mechanism of inhibition appears to remain effective over time, in contrast to conventional antibiotics, where resistance is actively selected for in a bacterial population. In translating mammalian cooperative behaviours to the field of microbiology this group of scientists may have given humankind a badly needed new weapon in the fight against antimicrobial resistance.

Recombination requires us to step out of our comfort zone and look across boundaries to many disparate fields. It also requires us to be not only inquisitive but also playful. Developmental psychologists understand the value of play for learning in children. But we can all benefit from seeing the world in a childlike way, where we are not afraid to ask why or to think the unthinkable.

Using analogies to recombine

There are a couple of ways in which analogies can be useful in helping to formulate thinking. You can take an idea from one context and transplant it into a different context, or you can combine two ideas from different contexts.

Giovanni Gavetti and Jan Rivkin note that analogies lie at the root of some of the most compelling and creative business ideas (Gavetti and Rivkin, 2005). They cite the example of how Taiichi Ohno, pioneer of Toyota's ground-breaking production system, came up with the idea of the andon cord (which stops the production line) after seeing bus passengers using a pull cord to signal to the driver that they wanted to get off. Velcro, the ubiquitous fastener found on coats, children's shoes, and bags and even used by astronauts in space, was inspired by the tiny hooks on the burdock plant. Swiss engineer George de Mestral had the idea for Velcro in 1948 when removing the burrs from his dog's coat following a walk.

An example of a two-product mash-up is the Snuggie, which in case you missed it is a wearable blanket that has earned its makers, Allstar Product Group, more than $500 million since it took off as a must-have sensation in the winter of 2008. Despite its runaway success, the Snuggie was not the first of its kind. The Slanket was invented in 1997 by 17-year-old Gary Clegg when, wrapped in a blanket in a cold dorm room, he solved the problem of changing the television channel by cutting a hole in the blanket. He quickly realized he could combine the blanket concept with the idea of a cosy sweater by adding sleeves to his blanket.

By embracing the 'entire world' in imagination, as Einstein said, we are more likely to make unusual connections that could just spark off something unique. Doggles (goggles for dogs) was an idea born when Roni and Ken Di Lullo fitted a pair of sports goggles on their dog Midnight to help her catch a frisbee in strong sunlight. But Doggles are not just cute fashion accessories for pampered pooches. The shatterproof, UV-protected lenses can benefit dogs following eye operations or with conditions making them sensitive to sunlight. Search and rescue dogs and police dogs now wear Doggles to protect their eyes from dust, wind and debris. There are even specialized night-vision Doggles for use by military dogs. Doggles is now a multimillion-dollar business.

Of course, it isn't always about recombination. Nearly all advances in our scientific knowledge have come about by building on the work of predecessors. One of the world's most outstanding scientists, Sir Isaac Newton, acknowledged how he had built on the work of Galileo and Kepler when he said 'If I have seen further, it is by standing on the shoulders of giants.' For a small number of people combinatorial thinking comes quite naturally, but for most of us it is a bigger challenge. Why is it so difficult for the majority of us to unleash our untapped creativity in this way?

At least part of the problem is that the world is now an immensely complex place. David Kord Murray (2010), a former aerospace engineer, entrepreneur and inventor, argues that there will never be another Renaissance man like Leonardo da Vinci (or Renaissance woman like Maria Gaetana Agnesi), because it is no longer possible to completely master one subject – let alone more than one. Our way of coping with so much complexity is to create simplified mental models that help us. Metaphors and analogies help us bridge the gap between disparate mental models through novel recombinations.

Something as enormously complicated as a country's banking system and economy can be thought of in much simpler terms by comparing it to a plumbing system. Imagine you get into the shower, turn on the tap and, instead of your usual jet of hot water, a mere trickle emerges. Clearly something has impeded the flow of water. When the flow of money in the economy drops, investments fall, consumers stop spending and the economy stagnates. Whilst this is no more than a superficial analogy, it demonstrates how analogous thinking can help clarify thinking in complex situations.

Thomas Edison is reported to have found analogous thinking extremely useful when trying to solve problems. He would start by thinking of something that he was intimately acquainted with and then compare it to the problem at hand. So it was that, when he was working on the problem of how to connect together several of his incandescent lightbulbs, he used the analogy of messages flowing through a telegraph system (something he understood well) to work out the flow of electricity through the wires connecting the bulbs (Caldicott, 2013).

The problems we face today, from ambiguous market signals to climate change to increasing microbial resistance, are so complex that increasingly we need to look across disciplines for sources of ideas that can generate potential answers.

However, it is generally the case that what we know, the way we work, the structure of our organizations and even the way we think ensure that we stay cocooned in our silos. We fail to make connections across structural holes because we simply don't see the potential relevance of other disciplines to the problems at hand.

Reframe – multiple times

Having generated a number of ideas through a broad but bounded search, and recombined these ideas in novel ways, the different perspectives gathered should now be re-evaluated. Initially the net was cast wide to try to ensure that the situation was viewed from more than one perspective. Now we need to start sifting and filtering. However, in so doing we need to remain acutely aware of the cognitive biases already discussed in Chapter 2. Albert Einstein said 'One should never impose one's views on a problem.' In reframing and refining our ideas, we should remain aware that our cognitive prejudices will once again try to push us down particular pathways. Design professor Kees Dorst advocates 'frame innovation' as a way not to provide solutions to a well-specified problem but to put these issues in a new light so that unimagined possibilities for desirable change can emerge (Dorst, 2015). Dorst seeks to use design thinking as a suitable way to help us come to grips with the very types of wicked problems that we introduced in the Introduction.

An interesting example of how important framing can be is Granovetter's ground-breaking 1973 paper on the strength of weak ties, discussed earlier. Granovetter originally submitted his manuscript for publication to the *American Sociological Review* in 1969 when he was a graduate student at Harvard University, only to have it firmly rejected. According to a post on the sociology site *Scatterplot*, Granovetter himself said:

> I'd note also that this rejection illustrates the importance of framing. I framed the original draft, which I wrote in grad school, as a treatment of 'alienation', more or less in response to the ideas of Louis Wirth and others that the city was an 'alienating' place. The editor therefore sent the paper to reviewers who seemed to be European-oriented alienation theorists, who rightly saw that I was not talking about alienation as Marx did, but failed to imagine that there might be any other valid way to talk about it, as you can see from their comments. When I later revised the paper for *AJS* [*American Journal of Sociology*], I pulled all references to alienation out, and it obviously fared much better.
>
> (Khan, 2014)

In the previous subsection we advocated the use of metaphors and analogous thinking to inspire creative thinking. Although this can undoubtedly be a very valuable tool, we need to keep in mind that the very metaphor or analogy we have chosen can itself sway our thinking unduly. Whilst we think we are making logical and rational decisions, the language we use to formulate our thoughts subconsciously influences our reasoning and hence the solutions we are likely to favour. For example, a study conducted by psychologists Paul Thibodeau and Lera Boroditsky (2011) showed that the word used to describe crime ('beast' versus 'virus') influenced whether participants advocated an enforcement-based solution or one aimed at addressing the social causes of crime, reflecting the idea that the terminology used shaped how participants framed the problem.

How can we address these mental obstacles as we reflect on the information we have accumulated? One way to thrash out hidden biases is to engage in a Socratic debate with ourselves and others. By questioning our assumptions and the very language we use, we can develop our thinking and break out of mental ruts.

The importance of questions should not be underestimated. French philosopher and writer Voltaire said: 'Judge a man by his questions rather than by his answers.' This is because it is the questions that drive us forward like an engine, whereas answers by contrast act like a brake, bringing our thinking to a stop. Stuart Firestein, Chair of Columbia University's Department of Biological Science, argues that we may be too enthralled by answers these days (Firestein, 2012). He goes on to say: 'Scientists don't concentrate on what they know, which is considerable but minuscule, but rather on what they don't know.' In the confusing, ambiguous world confronting us today, we need to do the same and focus on what we don't know.

McDonald's

An intriguing example of reframing is the transformation of a corporation from capitalist to activist. The idea of one of the biggest global corporations joining forces with an uncompromising environmental organization would seem an unlikely one, but that is exactly what happened in 2006 when US fast food giant McDonald's teamed up with Greenpeace to stop Amazonian rainforest destruction.

The Amazon rainforest contains over 30 per cent of all the world's land-based plants and animals. It is one of the most biodiverse regions on the planet. Deforestation of this precious resource has long been a problem, and soya bean farming is one of the greatest drivers of deforestation. Following a three-year investigation using satellite images and undercover monitoring, Greenpeace had traced the supply chain to meat reared on soya protein. So great was the demand for soya that an area the size of a football field was being destroyed every 10 seconds. Given the size of the market that it commanded, McDonald's seemed an obvious target for the environmentalists.

Greenpeace initially applied public pressure to McDonald's by sending 2-metre-high clucking chickens to stand outside its UK restaurants. But then something unexpected happened. The fast food conglomerate was quick to recognize the scale of the problem and immediately agreed to remove Amazonian soya from its chicken feed. More surprisingly, it formed an alliance with other UK retailers, including Asda, Marks & Spencer and Waitrose, to put pressure on agribusiness operating in Brazil to stop the illegal deforestation. The alliance led to a moratorium on multinational traders buying soya from newly deforested land in the Amazonian rainforest. According to the Greenpeace website, this moratorium is still in place today.

The McDonald's executives should be congratulated for their ability to see the essence of the problem. They also successfully reframed themselves as stakeholders with a conscience in the soya market. From a situation with the potential for huge embarrassment and very bad publicity, McDonald's managed to completely reframe its position.

Summary

This chapter has described the *frame* mode of the discovery-led decision making framework, emphasizing the importance of solving the *right* problem, thus avoiding the risk of committing the Type III errors that are more likely in a VUCA environment. This implies a shift in emphasis from problem *solving* to problem *finding*. At the heart of *framing* is a need to reduce using our over-reliance on existing knowledge as a crutch, instead entertaining the possibility of potential connections to other disciplines, perspectives and analogies in an effort to see a situation through fresh eyes.

The barriers that hinder our ability to frame the problems we face in novel ways are:

- being wedded to and blinded by our existing knowledge, causing us to neglect unknowns and flaws in our assumptions;

- a tendency to frame problems and decisions too narrowly, especially in terms of stakeholders and time horizon; and

- focusing on the immediate, superficial aspects of a situation rather than the deeper, more essential causes.

We can overcome these obstacles, thus framing problems productively, by:

- broadening our frames of reference, by looking for non-obvious connections;

- directed and undirected active scanning externally (ie the environment) and internally (ie the organization and its sector);

- broadening the search and then bounding it once more;

- recombining ideas, across contexts and domains of knowledge; and

- reframing the problem repeatedly until its essence becomes apparent.

The next chapter will consider the stage of the discovery-led decision making framework that marks the shift from thought to action, namely *experiment*.

References

Boynton, A and Fischer, W (2011) *The Idea Hunter: How to find the best ideas and make them happen*, John Wiley & Sons, London

Burt, R S (1992) *Structural Holes: The social structure of competition*, Harvard University Press, Cambridge, MA

Caldicott, S M (2013) *Midnight Lunch: The 4 phases of team collaboration success from Thomas Edison's lab*, John Wiley & Sons, London

Camerer, C, Loewenstein, G and Weber, M (1989) The curse of knowledge in economic settings: an experimental analysis, *Journal of Political Economy*, 97 (5), 1232–54

Cipriano, M and Gruca, T (2014) The power of priors: how confirmation bias impacts market prices, *Journal of Prediction Markets*, 8 (3), 34–56

Day, G and Schoemaker, P J H (2006) *Peripheral Vision: Detecting the weak signals that will make or break your company*, Harvard Business School Press, Cambridge, MA

Dorst, K (2015) *Frame Innovation: Create new thinking by design*, MIT Press, Cambridge, MA

Firestein, S (2012) *Ignorance: How it drives science*, Oxford University Press, Oxford

Galilei, G ([1632] 2001) *Dialogue Concerning the Two Chief World Systems: Ptolemaic and Copernican*, Modern Library, New York

Gavetti, G and Rivkin, J (2005) How strategists really think: tapping the power of analogy, *Harvard Business Review*, 83 (4), 54–63

Gazzaniga, M (2000) Cerebral specialization and interhemispheric communication: does the corpus callosum enable the human condition?, *Brain*, 123 (7), 1293–1326

Granovetter, M S (1973) The strength of weak ties, *American Journal of Sociology*, 78 (6), 1360–80

Grosser, M (2004) *Gossamer Odyssey: The triumph of human-powered flight*, Zenith Press, Minneapolis, MN

Heath, C and Heath, D (2007) *Made to Stick: Why some ideas take hold and others come unstuck*, Random House, New York

Kahneman, D (2002) *Maps of Bounded Rationality: A perspective on intuitive judgment and choice*, Nobel Prize Lecture, The Sveriges Riksbank Prize in Economic Sciences in Memory of Alfred Nobel

Khan, S (2014) Granovetter rejection!, *Scatterplot*, 13 October, https://scatter.wordpress.com/2014/10/13/granovetter-rejection/

Kimball, A W (1957) Errors of the third kind in statistical consulting, *Journal of the American Statistical Association*, 52 (278), 133–42

Lord, C G, Ross, L and Lepper, M (1979) Biased assimilation and attitude polarization: The effect of prior theories on subsequently considered evidence, *Journal of Personality and Social Psychology*, 37, 2098–2109

Mitroff, I I (1998) *Smart Thinking for Crazy Times*, Berrett-Koehler, Oakland, CA

Murray, D K (2010) *Borrowing Brilliance: The six steps to business innovation by building on the ideas of others*, Random House Business, London

Partnoy, F (2013) *Wait: The art and science of delay*, Public Affairs, New York

Rabin, M and Schrag, J L (1999) First impressions matter: a model of confirmatory bias, *Quarterly Journal of Economics*, **114** (1), 37–82

Rock, D (2009) Managing with the brain in mind, *strategy + business*, **56** (Autumn)

Ross-Gillespie, A et al (2014) Gallium-mediated siderophore quenching as an evolutionarily robust antibacterial treatment, *Evolution, Medicine, and Public Health*, **1**, 18–29

Shekerjian, D (1991) *Uncommon Genius: How great ideas are born*, Penguin Books, London

Simons, D J and Chabris, C F (1999) Gorillas in our midst: sustained inattentional blindness for dynamic events, *Perception*, **28**, 1059–74

Sternin, J (2002) Positive deviance: a new paradigm for addressing today's problems today, *Journal of Corporate Citizenship*, **5**, 57–62

Thibodeau, P H and Boroditsky, L (2011) Metaphors we think with: the role of metaphor in reasoning, *PLoS ONE*, **6** (2), e16782, http://journals.plos.org/plosone/article?id=10.1371/journal.pone.0016782

Verganti, R (2006) Innovating through design, *Harvard Business Review*, **84** (12), 114–22

Viereck, G S (1929) What life means to Einstein, *Saturday Evening Post*, 19 October

Mode II: Experimenting

07

There are three principal means of acquiring knowledge...
observation of nature, reflection, and experimentation. Observation
collects facts; reflection combines them; experimentation verifies the
result of that combination. DENIS DIDEROT

Moving from thought to action

We explored *framing* in Chapter 6. We took the time to turn the situation in which we find ourselves over in our minds and consider it from many different angles, getting a feel for its depth and complexity, and seeing how it might fit into a broader hierarchy of interlinked issues. We continue our tour of the discovery-led decision making framework by shifting our focus from problem *finding* to problem *solving* in the *experiment* phase, through a blend of trial and error, experimentation and prototyping.

Experimentation – is it really worth it?

Experimentation inevitably adds time to the decision process. But we are talking about small-scale tests that give results in days or weeks, not months or years. Going full steam ahead with an untested hypothesis can prove enormously costly further down the line in terms of time, money and reputation. Given that, can we really afford not to experiment before embarking on wholesale implementation?

It is not only the added time that has made experimentation underutilized in the past. Until relatively recently, the cost of running experiments was prohibitive for many companies. Multibillion-dollar businesses such as Amazon, General Electric and Google have been able to indulge in experimentation, and their CEOs have, at various times, all commented on the positive value of such a strategy (Gray, 2012):

- 'Size either liberates or paralyzes. We tried every day to remember that the benefit of size was that it allowed us to take more swings' (Jack Welch, former CEO of GE).

- 'Our goal is to have more at-bats per unit of time and effort than anyone else in the world' (Eric Schmidt, Chairman and former CEO of Google).

- 'You need to set up and organize so that you can do as many experiments per unit of time as possible' (Jeff Bezos, CEO of Amazon).

It is interesting to note that the value of experimentation has been recognized both by industrial economy companies like GE and by digital economy companies like Google and Amazon. Although very few organizations have the same scale of financial resources at their disposal as these giants, there is now an array of tools that make business experimentation cheaper, faster and much more accessible.

In 2006, Starwood Hotels and Resorts Worldwide used the virtual world Second Life to debut its newest chain, Aloft. The virtual hotel was opened more than two years before construction of the bricks-and-mortar buildings. Starwood wanted to experiment with the brand concept of its newest venture and, by enlisting the online Second Life community, it was able to get valuable real-life feedback on the in-hotel experience. Comments made by virtual users resulted in a number of design changes to the plans for the final hotels (Gates, 2014). The ability to test out ideas in this relatively low-cost fashion provided Starwood with important insights on how to create the best in-hotel experience before having to commit money to a real physical building. Brian McGuinness, Vice President of Aloft Hotels Worldwide, said: 'Second Life has been a tremendous learning experience for the Aloft brand. Our time spent on the island helped us to create what will surely be the ultimate destination sensation' (*Hotel News Resource*, 2007). Once the company had gathered enough feedback from the experiment it closed its virtual hotel. But, in recognition of the enormous value Aloft Hotels had gained from the experiment, it decided to celebrate the hotel's transition to the real world by donating the virtual land to the international organization TakingItGlobal, which seeks to engage young people all over the world in tackling global challenges from poverty and education to globalization and the environment.

Once we've understood the benefit of experimentation, we need to make sure that we construct our tests wisely. It is an obvious – though surprisingly often overlooked – point that, to be of any use, an experiment must be designed to test the variables in question and give measurable results. All too often people dive into experiments with only a hazy idea of the hypothesis that they are testing and how they are going to measure it.

Sifting out unknowns and assumptions

We can conceptualize our knowledge about any initiative on a spectrum. On the one hand we have known facts, we then progress through to assumptions, and finally we end up with unknowns. Where we find ourselves on this scale will influence the type of experiments we need to conduct.

When entering new markets or launching new products, the unknowns and assumptions far outnumber the things we know for certain. These are inherently risky ventures, and as many as 75 per cent of all start-ups fail (Gage, 2012).

A methodology that combines rapid testing with principles taken from software development is being applied both to risky new ventures and to new ideas in existing businesses. The lean start-up philosophy acknowledges that fledgling businesses and ideas face more unknowns than knowns, and advocates a very different approach from the traditional business plan and product development process (Ries, 2011). The lean start-up movement revolves around rapid experimentation and incremental development. The product or idea is tested with potential customers, revisions are made based on the feedback, and the concept is retested. The emphasis of this iterative cycle is on speed and nimbleness.

The second fundamental building block of the lean start-up methodology is borrowed from agile software development. We need to do just enough to get to the next stage and then reassess. In this way, the product or concept can be developed incrementally and tweaked along the way. This saves time, money and resources, allowing products that actually meet customer needs to come to market, or ideas to be implemented at a much faster rate than has been the norm historically.

Obstacles to *experimenting*

If testing is such an eminently sensible way to tackle the *experiment* mode, why is it so difficult to execute in practice? *Experimenting* turns out to be difficult for two reasons: 1) organizations that have been in existence for any period of time tend to suffer from inertia, because of a bias towards scaling; and 2) organizations – and individuals – are surprisingly poor at learning from experience.

Organizational inertia

As we have already seen in Chapters 2 and 6, confirmation bias means that we can become entrenched in our positions and unwilling to consider alternatives even in the face of overwhelming evidence. A historical anecdote reveals the attitudes of leaders, used to running an organization in a very particular way, to novel and unexpected data from the field.

Gunfire at sea

Elting Morison wrote a famous book and associated case study recounting the story of the introduction of continuous-aim gunfire at sea into the US navy (Morison, 1966). Prior to 1898, a naval gunner had no reliable way of holding a steady aim on his target because of the constant rolling motion of the ship. Firing at a target involved the gunner estimating the target distance and then raising his gun barrel to give sufficient elevation to carry the shell the required distance. With the range fixed, the gunner would wait until the roll of the ship brought his target within his open sights. Only then could he fire. He would not be able to re-aim until the roll of the ship once again brought the target into his sights, meaning that rapid fire was impossible. In addition, there was an inevitable delay between the target coming into view and the gunner depressing the firing button, which would vary from one individual to the next. To hit the target, a gunner would need to take account of his own reaction time and fire just before the target appeared centred in his sights.

It was the one of the gunners in the fleet of British naval officer Admiral Sir Percy Scott who had the notion of mounting the gun on elevating gears so that it could easily be moved up and down with the pitch and roll of the ship, thus keeping the target within the gun sights. Scott also improved the positioning of the telescopic sights. With these simple modifications, the hit rate of British naval gunnery improved 3,000 per cent in six years.

When William S Sims, a US junior naval officer, met Scott by chance on a posting to China, he quickly saw the benefits of Scott's modifications. Sims set about modifying the guns on his own ships. After months of training and monumental improvements in target practice accuracy, Sims wrote to the Bureau of Ordnance and Navigation advocating the adoption of the continuous-fire modifications across the whole navy. One might be forgiven for thinking that this was something of a no-brainer. After all, speed and accuracy of firing had been transformed from a black art to a predictable and precise science. Surely this could only be a good thing?

However, Sims's superiors were unimpressed and unmoved, convinced that continuous-aim fire was an impossibility. Over the course of two years, Sims wrote no fewer than 13 long official reports detailing the case for continuous-aim firing, and supporting each claim with a wealth of factual information, but to no avail. It was only when Sims started sending copies of his reports to other officers that the Bureau of Ordnance could no longer ignore him. They devised a test seeking confirmation, either deliberately or subconsciously, of their belief that Sims was wrong. They set up their experiment at the Washington Navy Yard on the banks of the Anacostia River. However, they did not adjust the gearing of the gun, and by testing on solid ground they changed the physics of the problem, resulting in the inevitable failure to validate Sims's idea (Armstrong, 2015).

Frustrated by his superiors' attitudes and their refusal to listen, Sims, a mere lieutenant, took the extraordinary step of writing directly to the President of the United States, Theodore Roosevelt. Fortunately for Sims, the President took a different view from the Bureau of Ordnance. Roosevelt understood that US naval gunnery was poor and that, if Sims's proposals had even a possibility of working, then they were well worth exploring. Sims was brought home from China, his ideas were validated, and in the space of just a few years he and his team changed naval warfare for ever.

Sims's experience of the entrenched organizational views illustrates how hard it can be to overturn established practices.

Failure to learn

We all know that we should learn from our mistakes. Management literature is full of advice exhorting us to follow the maxim of design and consulting firm IDEO to 'fail often to succeed faster'. But, curiously, we actually seem to be remarkably bad at learning from experience. This appears to hold true across many different settings. A Wharton study found that even catastrophic losses, such as were experienced in New Orleans after Hurricane Katrina in 2005, did not lead to long-term behaviour changes when it came to purchasing insurance protection. The study used a video-game-type simulation to investigate how people calculate risk from hurricane damage and found that people consistently misread past experience (Meyer, 2012). Similarly, a US Homeland Defense and Security study noted that in the field of emergency response the same lessons are identified again and again, incident after incident, suggesting that, whilst we can ably pinpoint failures, we fail to capitalize on our experience (Donahue and Tuohy, 2006).

Amy Edmondson, Novartis Professor of Leadership and Management at the Harvard Business School, has also shown that organizations that learn from failure are rare (Edmondson, 2003, 2011). As with emergency responder organizations, this is generally due neither to a lack of identifying and disseminating lessons learned nor to a lack of commitment to learning. Edmondson sensibly categorizes the reasons behind failures on a spectrum ranging from blameworthy to praiseworthy. On the blameworthy end, she places deviance from prescribed processes and inattention, whilst at the opposite praiseworthy end she places hypothesis testing and exploration. The latter two categories are designed to expand our knowledge in areas where the unknowns are greater than the knowns. If, in such situations, things do not turn out as we had expected and to our detriment, we have nonetheless increased our pool of knowledge.

Jeff Bezos, CEO of Amazon, takes exactly this view on experimentation. He candidly admits to making 'billions of dollars of failures' (D'Onfro, 2014). Speaking at the *Business Insider*'s Ignition conference in 2014, Bezos said, 'If you're going to take bold bets, they're going to be experiments... and if they're experiments you don't know ahead of time if they're going to work. Experiments are by their very nature prone to failure.' Bezos therefore takes a relaxed attitude to the fact that the Fire phone, Amazon's first venture into smartphones, has been less than a runaway success so far. But, rather than accepting the product as a failure, Bezos sees this as the first in a line of iterative experiments for the Fire phone. Each experiment will add to Amazon's knowledge and understanding and ultimately, he believes, it will succeed.

In contrast to conventional legal entities, it is a sad truth that terrorist organizations are often some of the most adept at organizational learning. The high levels of attrition of their members (eg death through suicide bombing) mean they must transfer new knowledge to the group quickly or risk losing it altogether (Gartenstein-Ross, 2017). Furthermore, the challenges to their very existence exerted by state actors mean that militant groups need to constantly evolve and innovate, much in the same way that bacteria and viruses evolve and develop new tactics to evade destruction.

It is the learning from experience and experiments that is the key to this stage of our process. But it is vitally important that we learn the *right* things. Even experienced managers generally fail to incorporate real-world complications into their mental models (Sengupta and Van Wassenhove, 2008). This is often because factors such as time lags between decision making and consequences make connections less salient. But there is also an element of being too set in our ways. The more experience we have, the more likely we are to be trapped in our mental models, which we generally fail to update as we encounter new situations. As we've seen in our discussion of confirmation bias in Chapters 2 and 6, we are surprisingly resistant to anomalous information, because the brain is wired to filter it out (Lehrer, 2009). We see what we want to see: even scientists working in the best labs in the world often disregard anomalous results from experiments. Typically the first thing they do is to assume that they've made a stupid mistake.

How to *experiment*?

How do we overcome the obstacles outlined above to shift from 'problem finding' to 'problem solving'? What do we need to do to move towards designing potential solutions? First, we need to take what we've learned and use it to develop a theory – or mental model – of what is going on. Then we need to generate multiple best guesses at what the answer may look like. These best guesses can be turned into hypotheses and tested. But, in order to generate testable hypotheses, we first need to formulate a theory to provide us with a conceptual 'map' that will guide our search for solutions.

We already have a bank of theories lodged in our minds that we use daily, without much thought (we will use the terms 'theory' and 'mental model' interchangeably). But, when faced with complex decisions and uncertain situations, it helps to bring our decision making theories to the forefront of our minds. Just as we sought to bring to light our hidden biases in the *frame* mode, we now need to surface the models and theories that underpin our thinking in the *experiment* mode. It is only by making our theories – our *beliefs* – explicit and examining them that we can decide whether they are properly formulated and whether they apply to the current circumstances. In other words, we need to validate that they have both internal validity (ie they're true) and external validity (ie they apply to the context of the problem we're trying to solve).

The word 'theory' sometimes has unfortunate overtones, all too often being seen as something abstract and impractical and far removed from the real world. To paraphrase the Nobel Prize-winning physicist Richard Feynman, managers can be inclined to think that theory is as useful to decision makers as ornithology is to birds (Feynman, 2016). This may in part be due to the way in which management theories have sometimes been taken and applied wholesale with little consideration of their relevance to the unique situations of specific industries, companies or problems, leading to the accusation that management theories are faddish and insubstantial.

But by theory, or mental model, we simply mean a generalized prediction that a particular result will follow from a certain action or course of actions. Theories provide a framework that helps us make better sense of what is happening and why. They allow us to take past observations and previous experience and turn them into predictions about future outcomes. If our theories and predictions are sound, then we should be able to make better decisions.

When making strategic decisions there is a tendency to place an over-reliance on quantitative data. After all, it feels as if historical information is all we have to guide us. But unfortunately, as the warnings on investment ads tell us, past performance is no guide to what will happen in the future. This is especially true in volatile business conditions. Does this mean that all we can do is take a leap into the dark, trusting only to luck? Fortunately, it does not. There is a way to generate fresher, context-specific data that can give us deeper and more relevant insight than the analysis of historical data.

So how do we conduct the kind of tests and experiments that will help us test our theories effectively? This arises out of three steps:

1 Formulate intelligent guesses.

2 Test these guesses with 'just enough' experiments.

3 Learn to learn from failure.

Formulate intelligent guesses

By using our theory of what we believe is going on, we can create hypotheses – our best *guesses* – which we can test to see if our understanding of the situation holds water. A hypothesis is simply a logical supposition, a reasonable guess, an educated conjecture (Leedy and Ormrod, 2001). It is an unconfirmed explanation of what is occurring. Given that it is an unconfirmed guess, we need to validate it. We therefore need to break it down into testable components.

By asking a series of questions and formulating multiple hypotheses or best guesses, we will flush out hidden assumptions. We may well find that there are many unanswered questions at this point, so it is helpful to categorize and prioritize those questions that encompass the most critical parts of our hypotheses. The critical elements are those aspects that, if they prove unfounded, cause the whole project or idea to fail. It makes sense to test the validity of these assumptions first, before proceeding down the list to lower-level questions.

Run 'just enough' experiments

How to learn from experiments

Before we embark on any experiments, we need to be clear about exactly what we are testing and how we are going to measure it. It is imperative that we know from the beginning what we will regard as a successful test and, equally importantly, what we would regard as a failure. It is all too easy to dive into testing a hypothesis only to come to the end of the test and find that the results are impossible to interpret or ambiguous because too little thought was given to the variable being tested and its measurement.

Formulating a theory and one or more associated hypotheses, which are then tested for validity, is the essence of the scientific method. Another cornerstone of the scientific method is the fact that causation has to be established – mere correlation (or connection) is not sufficient, as it may be coincidental. We need to understand the causal link between the phenomenon and putative explanations if we are to learn anything of predictive value.

However, a few years ago Chris Anderson, Curator of TED Talks, argued that in this era of big data (which he refers to as the Petabyte Age) the need for theories and the scientific method is now obsolete (Anderson, 2008). As evidence for his assertion that correlation alone is enough, he cites Google's application of statistics and mathematics to create search algorithms that are accurately able to match search terms and advertisements to page contents without 'understanding' that content. Peter Norvig, Research Director at Google, would agree with him, having stated at the O'Reilly Emerging Technology Conference in 2006 that 'All models are wrong, and increasingly you can succeed without them' (Anderson, 2008) – an update on the statistician George Box's maxim that 'All models are wrong, but some are useful.'

Analysing vast amounts of data in the way suggested by Anderson and Norvig may well throw up previously undetected correlations that could provide a jumping-off point for further study. But we would argue that relying entirely on correlation without understanding underlying mechanisms is a dangerous approach, particularly if we are hoping to extrapolate learning to novel situations.

Indeed a no less eminent scientist than Daniel Kahneman has raised concerns that some experiments are poorly founded. He was referring specifically to studies relating to 'priming', where decisions can be influenced by seemingly irrelevant events taking place just prior to decision making. However, a number of scientists are worried that applying number crunching to data can lead to invalid conclusions being drawn (*Economist*, 2013).

The same holds true in business analytics. Applied Predictive Technologies (APT) is a Washington-based company that specializes in helping its clients learn from experimentation by using 'Test & Learn' programs (Bird, 2014). Anthony Bruce, Chief Executive of APT, warns that 'traditional data analytics and data mining often find spurious relationships, and that this can lead to expensive and incorrect business decisions' (*Economist*, 2013).

It is therefore important to know what we are measuring in our experiments rather than going on a generalized fishing expedition. It is equally important that we draw a line in the sand before we start. That is not to say that we should try to predetermine the results but rather that we should have a clear idea of what a successful test outcome looks like and also what it would mean if the experiment failed to validate our hypothesis. If we do not do this at the outset, the subconscious temptation will be to interpret any results positively no matter what they actually are. Here we come back to our old friend confirmation bias. Our brains are far more likely to notice and pay attention to confirming evidence than they are to notice and attend to disconfirming evidence. As Francis Bacon noted as long ago as 1620, 'The human understanding when it has once adopted an opinion (either as being the received opinion or as being agreeable to itself) draws all things else to support and agree with it' (Bacon, [1620] 2012).

To guard against this, we should not design our experiments to look for confirmation that our hypothesis is true, but rather the opposite. We should purposefully set out to falsify our hypothesis and look for disconfirming evidence. If we then succeed in finding that disconfirming evidence, we have to be willing to accept it and let go of any preconceived ideas.

When Kohl's, a US department store chain, wanted to explore the possibility of selling furniture, it set out to run an experiment in three of its stores. In order to create the space needed for the furniture, Kohl's decided to cut back on children's clothing. It realized that it would lose some sales in this area, but thought that the gain from furniture sales would more than make up for it. At the end of the initial test period, the results were surprising. There was the obvious drop in revenue from children's clothes that had been expected, but there was also a significant drop in other product lines. Managers were perplexed. After all, the decision to sell furniture was in response to a market trend. They extended the test period and tried different approaches to product ranges, marketing and pricing, but still the counterintuitive trend continued. The company turned for help to ATP, which specializes in running business experiments, and with the use of the 'Test & Learn' software a complex pattern of interdependencies was revealed. It transpired that, because parents were no longer coming in to buy children's clothes, they were also not buying other things such as toys, shoes and things for themselves. Katy Mackesey, Kohl's Director of Ecommerce Finance, commented that had the company not used ATP's software 'we would have ignored our test results and somebody would have gone with their gut instinct' (Bird, 2014). She added: 'Once you use software like this, you can see that your intuition can be plumb wrong.' This refreshingly honest answer reveals how easily we are prepared to ignore test results that do not fit with our preconceptions.

As the story of Kohl's illustrates, by starting with small manageable experiments we can get quick results and make fast progress.

Retailers can take advantage of a number of different data analytics programs currently available to test what in their stores interests consumers. In this area, online retailers have long had an advantage over their bricks-and-mortar cousins. When shopping online, we are used to (though not always comfortable with) the fact that our browsing is monitored, allowing us to be targeted by ads more precisely. But a number of new companies have sprung up in the domain of onland retail to redress the balance. Companies such as Retail Next, Prism Skylabs, Nomi and Shoppertrak offer services ranging from counting customers entering shops to monitoring where in the shop they go and how long they spend at each location. These systems often work by tracking customer smartphones through their media access code (MAC) addresses (each smartphone has one). The analytics companies are at pains to point out that the codes are scrambled to anonymize the data before they are stored on the retailer's servers.

The US department retailer Nordstrom experimented with just such a system in 2012 in the Dallas–Fort Worth area (van Rijmenam, 2013). However, when it posted up signs about this some months later, customers made their unease very clear, and the experiment had to be halted. Despite this setback, Nordstrom is convinced of the value of running these kinds of experiments, and set up its own innovation lab. One of the apps to be produced by the lab pushes the profiles and buying history of customers who have opted into the service to sales staff, helping them provide a better, more tailored service. Recently, however, Nordstrom has downsized its innovation lab, having discovered along with so many others that innovation is incredibly hard to do within an established business (Berengian, 2017).

There is little doubt that offline retail tracking in the ways just mentioned is becoming big business, even though many people will continue to be concerned about privacy issues and simply unnerved at the thought of being monitored in this way. Euclid Analytics has even made a free version of its tracking technology available, making it even more tempting to retailers and giving Euclid an advantage over its competitors.

For best results, the experiments we run at this stage need to be simple in order to maximize learning in a short space of time. We need to do just enough to give us the information we need. 'Minimum viable product' is a phrase that has been popularized by Steve Blank (2013) and Eric Ries (2011) in the lean start-up movement and concisely captures what is required.

This brings us back to the story of Paul MacCready and the Kremer prize for human-powered flight that we began in Chapter 6 (Grosser, 2004). Seventeen years had gone by since the prize was first offered and more than 50 attempts had been made. MacCready decided to apply himself to the problem in 1977. He quickly realized that each failed attempt had invested too much time and energy in its particular idea – spending months building an intricate plane based on theories and assumptions that, when the plane was finally tested, crashed and shattered not only dreams but the aircraft itself.

MacCready applied the 'minimum viable product' idea nearly a quarter of a century before Frank Robinson of SyncDev coined the phrase. Rather than focusing exhaustively on the design and theories of mechanics, MacCready realized that the best way of collecting information on what worked was through build-and-test experiments. He also realized that he needed a plane that could be built and rebuilt (after the inevitable crashes) in days rather than months. His plane, the *Gossamer Condor*, was built out of plastic sheeting, wire and aluminium tubing and successfully completed Kremer's one-mile figure of eight course on 23 August 1977.

Different types of experiment

Not all experiments will be equally useful or applicable. The kind of test we choose will largely depend on what we are investigating. Some experiments may be technology-based, such as using web forums like Quora to see whether an idea has potential, or use a crowdfunding platform like Kickstarter or Indiegogo to gauge market demand for a new product or service. Airbnb, the room-letting website, has built its own framework for testing single variable changes (Overgoor, 2014). But small companies do not need the same capabilities to run controlled tests. A number of companies already provide out-of-the-box solutions to run these kinds of studies. There are even open source systems available, such as PlanOut, a framework for online field experiments developed by Facebook.

Interviewing potential customers or using surveys can also provide a wealth of valuable information. Even turning anthropologist for a few days and observing people in the real world can provide valuable insight into how potential customers actually behave. E-commerce is a fast-growing area, but bricks-and-mortar shopping visits still account for the majority of all purchases (Tam, 2013). Will Young, director of Zappos Labs, regularly takes his team out to San Francisco malls to observe how shoppers behave in that environment. In working out how to shift more sales to online, he has been trying to figure out how to make online shopping feel more social – in other words, more like a trip to the mall.

Learn to learn from failure

We go back to the United States in the late 1950s for a story about snatching victory from the jaws of apparent failure. It also concerns employees out in the field encountering information at variance with received wisdom from headquarters.

Honda attempts to enter the US motorbike market

The story of how Honda entered the US motorbike market in 1959 with its small 50 cc Super Cub is also a well-known tale of business strategy, and it too is the subject of a business school case study. The original consultancy report (Boston Consulting Group, 1975) recounted a deliberate strategy by Honda to use the large economies of scale it had developed in its domestic market and exploit them in the US market. But a very different account emerges from Richard Pascale, who went to Tokyo to interview the Honda executives who made the first forays into the US market in California (Pascale, 1984). According to these Honda employees, Honda had never anticipated selling many small motorbikes in this new market where bikes were big and macho and ridden by equally macho, leather-clad men. Its initial stock inventory was weighted towards the larger 250 cc and 305 cc models. But things did not go according to plan; it sold only a few of its bigger models. Worse yet, the ones it did sell came back with clutch and oil problems after being ridden more aggressively than they had been designed for. The executives were dispirited and short of money. They began to use some of their stock of small Super Cub bikes for running errands around Los Angeles. It was not long before these bikes started attracting a lot of attention. At first, the US-based Honda executives were reluctant to push these small-engine models, fearing that it might hurt the brand of their bigger counter-parts. But the interest in the Super Cub was gaining momentum, and they decided to go with it. Five years later Honda was making one in two bikes sold in the United States, with the Super Cub as its top-selling model.

It is interesting to note from Honda's early pioneers in the US market that the company's ultimate success had less to do with a brilliant strategy and rather more with 'planned serendipity', aided by vigilance. But our reason for retelling this story here is because the employees' forays into Los Angeles on the Super Cubs can be viewed as a series of inadvertent experiments. Of course, that is not what they were doing consciously. However, the Honda team nonetheless learned from the feedback they received and convinced their bosses to pursue a different line of thinking. It is also worth pointing out that the Japanese bosses were humble enough to listen and learn, which contrasts starkly with Sims's superior officers not being willing to entertain his wild ideas about continuous-aim gunfire.

To paraphrase the famous quote of German Field Marshal Helmuth von Moltke the Elder, no plan survives contact with reality.

Summary

This chapter has outlined the *experiment* mode of the discovery-led decision making framework. It discussed the rationale for designing experiments as tests to convert critical unknowns (what we *don't* know) and assumptions (what we *think* we know) into validated hypotheses (what we can say we know, with an increasing degree of confidence). In describing the design of experiments, we discussed some of the ways in which we fail to learn from experience. Central to effective *experimenting* is the need not to dwell on analysis, instead shifting to action through 'just enough' experiments, and the unique role of failure as a source of insight and learning.

The key principles of designing experiments are:

- separating knowns from unknowns and assumptions;
- designing small, simple experiments that are 'just enough' to vali-date key assumptions; and

- selecting the right type of experiment that can increase our learning as quickly as possible.

The next chapter will consider the *scale* stage of the discovery-led decision making framework.

References

Anderson, C (2008) The end of theory: The data deluge makes the scientific method obsolete, *Wired*, 23 June, http://www.wired.com/2008/06/pb-theory

Armstrong, B F (2015) Armaments and innovations – continuous-aim gunfire: learning how to shoot, *Naval History Magazine*, **29** (2)

Bacon, F ([1620] 2012) *Novum Organum Scientarium*, Forgotten Books, Charleston, SC

Berengian, A (2017) It's time to ditch your innovation lab, *Venture Beat*, 22 March, https://venturebeat.com/2017/03/22/its-time-to-ditch-your-innovation-lab

Bird, J (2014) Experimental analytics helps bosses look beyond the obvious, *Financial Times*, 2 September, https://next.ft.com/content/5d3d28ba-31bb-11e4-a19b-00144feabdc0

Blank, S (2013) An MVP is not a cheaper product, it's about smart learning, 13 July, https://steveblank.com/2013/07/22/an-mvp-is-not-a-cheaper-product-its-about-smart-learning

Boston Consulting Group (1975) *Strategy Alternatives for the British Motorcycle Industry*, Her Majesty's Stationery Office, London

Donahue, A and Tuohy, R (2006) Lessons we don't learn: a study of the lessons of disasters, why we repeat them, and how we can learn them, *Homeland Security Affairs*, **2** (2)

D'Onfro, J (2014) Jeff Bezos: why it won't matter if the Fire phone flops, *Business Insider UK*, 2 December, http://uk.businessinsider.com/jeff-bezos-on-big-bets-risks-fire-phone-2014-12

Economist (2013) Trouble at the lab, *Economist*, 19 October, http://www.economist.com/news/briefing/21588057-scientists-think-science-self-correcting-alarming-degree-it-not-trouble

Edmondson, A C (2003) Framing for learning: lessons in successful technology implementation, *California Management Review*, **45** (2), 34–54

Edmondson, A C (2011) Strategies for learning from failure, *Harvard Business Review*, **89** (4), 48–55

Feynman, R (2016) Richard Feynman quotable quotes, *Goodreads*, http://www.goodreads.com/quotes/132077-philosophy-of-science-is-about-as-useful-to-scientists-as

Gage, D (2012) The venture capital secret: 3 out of 4 start-ups fail, *Wall Street Journal*, 20 September, http://www.wsj.com/articles/SB100008723 96390443720204578004980476429190

Gartenstein-Ross, D (2017) The Manchester attack shows how terrorists learn, *Atlantic*, 23 May, https://www.theatlantic.com/international/archive/2017/05/manchester-terrorism-isis-attack-al-qaeda/527748/

Gates, S (2014) Aloft Hotels in Second Life, http://stephengates.com/portfolio/aloft-hotels-second-life

Gray, D (2012) Experimentation is the new planning, *Fast Company*, 14 September, http://www.fastcompany.com/3001275/experimentation-new-planning

Grosser, M (2004) *Gossamer Odyssey: The triumph of human-powered flight*, Zenith Press, Minneapolis, MN

Hotel News Resource (2007) Aloft donates virtual land in Second Life to TakingITGlobal.org, *Hotel News Resource*, http://www.hotelnewsresource.com/article28475.htm

Leedy, P D and Ormrod, J E (2001) *Practical Research: Planning and design*, 7th edn, Merrill Prentice Hall, Upper Saddle River, NJ

Lehrer, J (2009) Accept defeat: the neuroscience of screwing up, *Wired*, 21 December, http://www.wired.com/2009/12/fail_accept_defeat

Meyer, R J (2012) Failing to learn from experience about catastrophes: the case of hurricane preparedness, *Journal of Risk and Uncertainty*, **45** (1), 25–50

Morison, E (1966) *Men, Machines and Modern Times*, MIT Press, Cambridge, MA

Overgoor, J (2014) Experiments at Airbnb, *Airbnb*, 27 May, http://nerds.airbnb.com/experiments-at-airbnb

Pascale, R T (1984) Perspectives on strategy: the real story behind Honda's success, *California Management Review*, **26** (3), 47–72

Ries, E (2011) *The Lean Startup: How constant innovation creates radically successful businesses*, Portfolio Penguin, London

Sengupta, K and Van Wassenhove, L (2008) The experience trap, *Harvard Business Review*, **86** (2), 94–101

Tam, D (2013) Can e-tailer Zappos demolish the brick-and-mortar model?, *CNET*, 18 August, http://www.cnet.com/news/can-e-tailer-zappos-demolish-the-brick-and-mortar-model

van Rijmenam, M (2013) How fashion retailer Nordstrom drives innovation with big data experiments, *Datafloq*, 22 August, https://datafloq.com/read/how-fashion-retailer-nordstrom-drives-with-innovat/398

Mode III: Scaling

08

Repetition is the mother of learning, the father of action, which makes it the architect of accomplishment. ZIG ZIGLAR

Doing more of what works

Having 'found' the problem during the *frame* mode and 'solved' it during the *experiment* mode, you now need to disseminate it and spread the insights you have discovered to a wider audience. How you diffuse your strategic decisions across the organization – in other words, how you *scale* what works – is the topic of this chapter.

When we talk about scaling up in this context, we are referring to the scaling of business or management models, rather than increasing the production volume of a product or service, which lies in the domain of operations and manufacturing research. Business or management model scaling, by contrast, focuses on replicating a *way* of doing things. This requires a broader perspective than just attending to the product or service being delivered. In this type of scaling, mindsets and behaviours must be addressed and customer needs must be understood. An understanding of how value is created and captured is also imperative when looking to scale a business or management model.

What do we mean by the term 'business model'? Magretta (2002) explains that a business model is a story that explains how an enterprise works, and in doing so answers the questions 'Who is the customer, and what do they value?' and 'How do we make money in this business?' A business model answers the questions 'What business are you in?' and 'Why are you in that business?'

We mentioned Osterwalder and Pigneur's (2010) *Business Model Generation* in Chapter 2 as a useful tool for clarifying an organization's strategy. A management model, by contrast, answers the question 'How are you going to operate?' As such, a management model reflects the choices that managers make about how they define their strategic objectives, allocate resources, coordinate activities and shape employees' behaviour (Birkinshaw and Goddard, 2009). The key factor in developing an effective business model and accompanying management model is to understand and validate the *assumptions* underpinning them, which is what we do in the *experiment* mode.

Scale, on the other hand, is about the dissemination and adoption of proven assumptions, mindsets and behaviours across the organization. The more this dissemination can be replicated across the enterprise, not just once, but time and again, the more likely the organization is to succeed and grow.

Sustainable growth is the aim of every organization, but achieving it is not easy. Most companies state that they expect to attain a growth rate in revenues and earnings of around 5 per cent. However, according to a study of more than 2,000 companies by Chris Zook and James Allen of strategy consultancy Bain & Company, over 90 per cent of them failed to achieve that relatively modest goal over a 10-year period (Zook and Allen, 2012).

Obstacles to *scaling*

Young enterprises that succeed do so because, at some point in their early life, they found an opportunity to serve a need with one or more products or services (ie *frame* and *experiment*). As they figure out how to scale what works, they grow (their first *scale*). They survive and become established organizations because they improve their ability to operate at scale. However, as a particular business model and management model become embedded, it becomes ever more difficult to *change* at scale. As markets, customers and the environment change, the ability to adapt to changing circumstances becomes thwarted by organizational inertia.

Scaling is about replication, about finding what works and then repeating that recipe over and over again. This sounds deceptively simple, but in reality it's tricky. In order to achieve repeatability, an organizational 'recipe' is needed that will reliably shape the behaviour of employees. How do McDonald's employees in Tokyo get a Big Mac to look, smell and taste the same as a Big Mac in Chicago, Copenhagen or Cardiff?

As with any large, established enterprise, they repeat the 'recipe' by designing and spreading certain organizational arrangements consistently across all their restaurants around the world. These arrangements echo our earlier discussion of an organization's hard and soft wiring. In an organizational context, we can think of hard wiring as being the formal 'written' rules, and the soft wiring as being the informal 'unwritten' rules. Hard wiring is composed of standard operating procedures, organizational charts, role definitions, metrics, incentives and the design of physical space. These 'written rules' – hard wiring – are combined with more difficult to identify but just as important unwritten rules. Organizational soft wiring is composed of patterns of expectations and norms of behaviour (often termed 'culture'), informal social networks (who knows whom), the distribution of power, and organizational habits and rituals. As we noted in Chapter 2, Edgar Schein (1999) considers an organization's culture to be a 'residue of success': in other words, the culture is a solution to historical problems. The organization's hard and soft wiring is what makes employees' behaviours (and consequently their outputs) consistent, repeatable and scalable. Just as with computing devices such as laptops, tablets and mobile phones, organizations need *both* 'hardware' and 'software' to work together in order to function properly. And, if we are going to change how an organization operates at scale, we need to realign its hard *and* soft wiring.

Organizational inertia

We now return once again to the topic of organizational inertia, which we first explored in Chapter 2 and more recently in Chapter 7. The organizational architecture in successful, established organizations is geared towards the initial scaling and no longer towards *framing* or *experimenting*. It is the factors that have evolved within this architecture that powerfully shape consistent behaviour, and that ultimately make it hard to change behaviour *at scale*. This is why organizational change initiatives typically have such a high failure rate.

Marks & Spencer (M&S), a retailer that was the undisputed clothing and food king of the British high street during the 1970s, 1980s and 1990s, provides a good illustration of how difficult it is to adapt. M&S prided itself on a number of core capabilities. It owned the land on which many of its high street shops were situated. It prided itself on selling British-made goods, supplied by a network of British family-run companies, often small and medium-sized enterprises, for which M&S was their sole customer. These capabilities supported its value proposition centred on value for money, British quality and innovation (for example, M&S pioneered chilled meals, and was a dominant player in UK women's underwear). In 1998 it was the first British retailer to post a £1 billion pre-tax profit.

But then the world changed and so did the fortunes of M&S. The move towards out-of-town shopping centres in the 1990s robbed the high street of many consumers. Owning its shops meant that it was harder for M&S to respond and follow the out-of-town traffic. The arrival of fast fashion retailers such as H&M and Primark, which sourced their clothes from cheaper foreign suppliers and sold at lower price points, led to a marked fall in profits and an erosion of customer loyalty for M&S. Suddenly it was seen as staid and unfashionable. The decline in the retailer's fortunes was rapid. By 2001 profits had fallen to a mere £145 million (Saunders, 2013).

Ironically, it was the very things that made it strong in the first place that made it hard for it to adapt to changing conditions. The processes that had been embedded and codified into the corporate psyche were the very things that had allowed M&S to operate so successfully at scale. A number of ways of working had formed an 'interlocking activity system' that had been the source of great strength in the company's heyday but was now acting more like a millstone around its neck.

Marks & Spencer is just one of many examples of once great corporations that have struggled to adapt to a changing environment. Zook and Allen (2012) have found that the two most common reasons for this are a loss of focus leading to a dilution of the organization's core capabilities, and an inability to respond to change fast enough.

Dilution of core capabilities

It may be that the core purpose of the organization remains as viable as before, but that the scaled process that allowed it to grow and prosper has become complex and convoluted. Additions are made in response to new situations, until the implementation of the process becomes cumbersome, much in the same way as a ship's hull becomes covered with barnacles over time. The barnacles don't fundamentally alter the ability of the ship to sail through the water, but they do make it less streamlined.

Just as the scaled-up implementation of a business model (and complementary management model) can become bogged down with unnecessary complications, so too can the whole corporate operation. As companies grow from a small number of employees to much larger entities with hundreds or even thousands of workers, it's easy for the original core principles to become lost and for communication to be distorted. This may be related to the concept of Dunbar's number: a limit devised by evolutionary anthropologist Robin Dunbar of the number of meaningful relationships that our minds are capable of handling simultaneously (Dunbar, 2010). In time, there is a danger that complacency sets in and organizations lose their focus by forgetting what it was that made them special in the first place.

Of course, the problem may not lie within the organization itself. As Zook and Allen (2012) point out, the other main reason for successful companies faltering is that the world around them changes and the company either fails to notice or fails to respond with sufficient speed.

Inability to respond fast enough

The story of how Lego, a world-renowned company that until 1998 had never made a loss, came to the brink of bankruptcy and takeover illustrates both these scenarios well. Lego's bright, colourful interlocking bricks have become the most popular toy in history since they were first launched in 1949. Seven new boxes of Lego are sold every second, and Lego mini-figures are, according to some calculations, set to outnumber humans by 2019 (Griffiths, 2013).

Lego's profits started to decline in the early 1990s, and by 2004 its losses had reached £174 million and it was close to bankruptcy. How had this been allowed to happen? Executive Vice-President of Marketing Mads Nipper was to reflect later that Lego had failed to heed warning signs of market change, saying 'we continued to invest as if the company were growing strongly. We failed to realise that we were on a slippery path… children were getting less and less time to play. Some of the western markets had fewer and fewer children. So play trends changed, and we failed to change… We failed to innovate enough' (Tufts Center for Engineering Education and Outreach, 2015).

Jørgen Vid Knudstorp took over as CEO of Lego in 2004 at the depth of its troubles. He ascribed the company's downward plummet to complacency and the fact that it had tried to make itself more modern by becoming a lifestyle brand. Lego had diversified into theme parks, clothing, watches and video games, and in so doing had lost sight of what made the plastic brick an iconic toy. In an interview in 2009, Knudstorp remarked: 'What we realised is that the more we're true to ourselves, the better we are.' Quoting T S Eliot's 'Little Gidding', he added: 'The end of all our exploring will be to arrive where we started and know the place for the first time' (Delingpole, 2009).

Knudstorp's insight about the company's core strengths brought Lego back from the brink of disaster to become the world's most powerful brand in 2015, overtaking Ferrari.

How to *scale?*

The obstacles that we have discussed so far, and the potential ways in which to address them, relate not to the initial scaling of a new enterprise but to the subsequent scaling of an incumbent. This subsequent scaling is hard because it is not just about changing the business model but about changing the *management* model. The conundrum of how to implement organizational change successfully has proved to be enduringly difficult to solve. Studies dating from the 1970s to the present day are surprisingly consistent in the failure rate of change initiatives, putting it as high as 60–70 per cent (Kitching and Roy, 2013; Gilbert, Lorthois and Vas, 2014).

Having found in *experiment* a seed of something good, how do you go about growing and spreading it beyond the small flowerbed in which it currently flourishes to the whole garden of the organization? How can you manage the organizational change required to scale it effectively and successfully? How do you avoid the myriad traps into which the majority of change initiatives fall?

Scaling is about executing a strategy – embodied in a business model and a management model – that you know works. (You know that it works because you have already tested it in *experiment*.) So let us return to the topic of strategy and remind ourselves exactly what it is.

Strategy is about finding true insights into the direction the company should take. These insights are not, as some might imagine, necessarily about finding solutions to problems facing the corporation. Instead they are about analysing the interaction between the idiosyncratic characteristics of an enterprise and its external environment, in search of a unique 'fit' that confers a competitive advantage. The eminent strategist Richard Rumelt has a simple recipe for strategy, based on avoiding common traps in strategic decision making (Rumelt, 2012). First, analyse the enterprise and its environment to identify the critical challenges confronting it. Second, formulate an appropriate and coherent portfolio of goals to address those challenges. Third, translate the plan into action. In other words, diagnose the illness, formulate a treatment plan and then administer it.

Identify the essence: 'what' and 'why'

Let us take IKEA as an example. The radical insight that Ingvar Kamprad, founder of the global furniture chain, originally had was that furniture could be designed in such a way that it could be sold in a flat pack and then assembled by the customer at home. This essentially turned the whole process of buying furniture on its head. If you wanted to buy a sofa from a traditional furniture store, you would generally have to wait several weeks for it to be made, or at the very least a few days for it to be delivered from a central warehouse. Kamprad's flat-pack concept meant that you could go to IKEA, choose your sofa and take it home that very day.

The challenge that Ingvar Kamprad set out to meet was how to design and deliver simple, affordable, stylish furniture. He translated that into action by designing flat-pack units that could all be sold and stocked under one roof – with a huge range of options and accessories – with assembly and delivery outsourced to the customers themselves.

Kamprad had a clear idea of what made IKEA different. This awareness of, and focus on, the essence of what makes a corporation distinctive is what Zook and Allen (2011, 2012) refer to as a 'well-differentiated core'. They call this differentiation 'the essence of strategy and the prime source of competitive advantage'.

However, as we have already seen, all too often the pressures of meeting targets and 'running the shop' mean that the company loses sight of its focus and its distinctiveness. In our conversations with clients, we draw a distinction between working 'in the business' and working 'on the business'. This distinction got blurred in Lego when it lost its way in the early part of this century. It was not until the company returned to its core values, embodied by *leg godt*, which is Danish for 'play well' (and from which the name is derived), that the company's fortunes improved.

For two decades, US multinational conglomerate General Electric (GE) was led by one of the most fêted CEOs in the corporate world, Jack Welch. He was Chairman and CEO between 1981 and 2001, during which time GE's stock rose by 4,000 per cent (Leung, 2005). In the short space of time after Jack Welch announced his retirement, a number of external events conspired to bring about a dramatic decline in the company's share price. The first of these was the terrorist attack of 9/11, followed in quick succession by the Enron scandal, Hurricane Katrina, the collapse of Lehman Brothers and the subsequent global financial crisis. GE had to be bailed out by Warren Buffett (*Economist*, 2014), and Jeff Immelt, who had succeeded Welch as CEO, realized that the company needed a radical rethink. Immelt wanted to get back to the essence of what GE was about and so found himself asking: 'Who are we, as a company?' In other words, what is GE's differentiated core? To find an answer to this, Immelt went right back to the company's beginnings, when it was founded by Thomas Edison. The answer Immelt and his team arrived at was that GE was a company of innovative thinkers that used technology to solve the world's biggest problems. With that in mind, the 'Imagination at work' campaign was born with a play on Thomas Edison's head as a lightbulb from which modern innovations were emanating.

Both Lego and GE found their way back to their core strengths. They managed to return to the essence of what made them unique, whilst changing the outward manifestations of this in order to adapt to new circumstances. Marks & Spencer, on the other hand, always had a well-defined core, but the way in which those strengths were translated into *how* the company did things eventually became a hindrance and it was not able to change the *how* fast enough.

Translate the essence into social norms of belief and behaviour: 'how'

Translating high-level strategy into a set of clear, actionable procedures that will enable a large number of employees across many locations – possibly in different countries – to act with appropriate consistency: this is what Zook and Allen (2012) refer to as 'non-negotiables'. They are the principles and practices of the organization that influence and guide behaviour, shape and reinforce corporate culture and promote the corporate identity both internally and externally.

Such principles and practices need to be clear, concise and meaningful. They provide a framework that allows employees to understand how they should behave, and what is expected of them. They should translate and embody the organization's distinctiveness.

In 1996 – over 20 years ago – John Kotter (2012) set out what became the classic change management method. His eight-step method provided a rational process to institute organizational change. And yet, as we have already seen, the failure rate for change initiatives remains high. Part of what makes change hard – not just in organizations – is that habits, once formed, are difficult to alter. However, in the intervening years since Kotter first published his approach, we have learned a great deal about the brain and behavioural science. We can use this to help influence behavioural change.

Most change initiatives are unsuccessful because they fail to take sufficient account of human behaviour. Ultimately, if we want to change organizational behaviour (in an effort to scale a business or management model, or otherwise), we will need to change the behaviour of individual employees. So let us look at this topic in more depth.

Cognition – and the behaviour associated with it – can be categorized into two types: controlled and automatic. Controlled cognition originates in the frontal cortex of the brain. The brain cortex has evolved from the back to the front, so from an evolutionary standpoint this is the youngest part of our brain. Automatic cognition arises from the more primitive part of the brain cortex, and this is where habits reside. To institute any kind of major change, we need to overcome and replace existing habits with new desired behaviours. Once the new behaviours have been adopted, we need to embed them by reinforcement and repetition. Any programme that doesn't change habits at the individual level is unlikely to succeed.

As we have mentioned in Chapter 2, Jonathan Haidt originally put forward a vivid metaphor for how these two brain systems – governing controlled and automatic cognition – interact (Haidt, 2006). He likened the controlled part of our brain to a rider. The rider is sitting on top of an elephant, which represents the automatic aspects of the brain's cognition. The rider can plan and analyse and then instruct the elephant to go in a certain direction, but if the elephant disagrees and digs its metaphorical heels in there is little the rider can do. This analogy makes it very clear that, while the rider may be smart, it is the elephant that is the more powerful of the two.

While we tend to think that our behaviour is determined by the rider, who takes account of rational and logical reasons, behavioural science has shown that we must not underestimate the role of the elephant when trying to change behaviour. So what is it that motivates and influences the elephant?

Over the past few decades, social psychologists have discovered that our inner elephant's behaviour, geared towards instant gratification, is most influenced by: 1) the actions of people around us, and 2) the environment or setting in which we find ourselves.

People around us

Handwashing after using washroom facilities to prevent the spread of germs and diseases is a generally accepted social norm. However, even though most adults know and accept the truth of this, many studies have shown that handwashing is far from universally carried out. Two studies in the 1980s showed that the presence of an observer in a public washroom increased both the frequency and the duration of handwashing (Pedersen, Keithly and Brady, 1986; Munger and Harris, 1989). In one experiment, the presence of another in the washroom resulted in 77 per cent of users washing their hands compared to only 39 per cent in the no-observer condition. These studies show how behaviour is affected by the presence of others.

There is a famous 1962 *Candid Camera* episode entitled 'Face the Rear', which has been viewed on YouTube over 400,000 times. In this video clip, a man (the subject) steps into an elevator, followed by a number of people who are in on the joke. The subject faces the front of the elevator, but everyone else who enters turns to face the rear. The subject looks confused and a little uncomfortable, but after a matter of moments he succumbs and he too turns to face the rear of the elevator. Whilst highly amusing to the audience, this was actually part of social psychologist Solomon Asch's conformity experiments. Once again, it shows how attuned our elephant is to social cues and how easily we can be manipulated into altering our behaviour.

Another interesting conformity experiment studied pedestrians' compliance with a traffic signal when the behaviour of the experimenter's model violated the rules. The experiment used two different models – one where the experimenter dressed as a high-status individual, and in the other as a low-status individual. In both conditions, other pedestrians conformed to the behaviour of the model, and the conformity was especially high with the higher-status model (Lefkowitz, Blake and Mouton, 1955).

These studies demonstrate that our behaviour is powerfully shaped by those around us, often in ways of which we are not aware.

The environment

The second major factor influencing the automatic side of the brain is the environment. Chip Heath and Dan Heath (2011) add to Haidt's beautiful 'elephant and rider' analogy by referring to the environment as the path along which the elephant travels. Many studies have shown that encountering a variety of cues can affect subsequent behaviour. In one study, subjects were asked to undertake a language task. One group were given a scrambled sentence that included words stereotypically associated with old age, such as *old*, *grey*, *wise*, *wrinkle*, *Florida*, *knits*, *bingo* (think of the nudges and indirect influence we discussed earlier). The other group were given a scrambled sentence with neutral words. Later, when they left the building, the subjects were surreptitiously timed walking the length of the corridor. Even though there had been no reference to walking, speed or time either during the experiment or in the priming words, those participants who had been exposed to the elderly priming walked more slowly than those who had been exposed to neutral words. When participants were debriefed, they were asked if they thought the sentence task might have affected them in any way and whether they noticed any age-related words. None of them expressed any knowledge of the relevance of the words used and, furthermore, none of them believed that the words had an impact on their behaviour (Bargh, Chen and Burrows, 1996).

The same effect was shown when a similar experiment was performed at the Science Museum in London as part of the BBC programme *Bang Goes the Theory*. Guests who had been invited to an exhibition entitled 'Who am I?' walked through one of two different security lines. Along the path of one line there were photographs of older people, and in the second line there were photographs of young, active people. The speed at which people walked over a set distance was measured. Those who had been primed with the visual cues for old age took 50 per cent longer to walk the same distance as those who had been primed with the youthful, active pictures.

Now that we've established the kind of things that influence automatic behaviour, how can we use them to drive and sustain change?

In terms of Haidt's rider and elephant metaphor – and the Heath brothers' embellishment of it – the following three steps will help make *scaling* – or any change – easier in terms of guiding individuals' 'riders and elephants' towards certain behaviours:

1 Get the elephant's attention.

2 Focus on the first step of the journey.

3 Signpost the destination clearly.

Get the elephant's attention

Humans are social creatures, and from our earliest childhood we learn by observing and imitating others, who act as behaviour models. If a young child imitates a behaviour she has seen and is rewarded for it, the behaviour is more likely to be reinforced. A child who sees another child crying and tries to comfort the other child may well be praised for being kind and caring. The praise acts as reinforcement of the behaviour.

Children (and adults) also pay attention to the consequences of other people's actions. If the behaviour of another results in that individual being rewarded, an observer is more likely to copy that behaviour at a later stage. This is known as vicarious reinforcement.

In the early 1960s the Stanford psychologist Albert Bandura conducted what became known as the 'Bobo doll' experiments, which showed that aggression could be acquired by observation and imitation. Seventy-two children were divided into three groups. The first group observed an adult model behaving aggressively towards a large self-righting plastic toy – the Bobo doll. The second group observed an adult model playing quietly with other toys, and the third group were a control group with no adult model. After observing the adult, each child was taken to another room that was stocked with a selection of both aggressive toys (eg mallet and pegboard, dartgun) and non-aggressive toys (eg drawing materials, tea set, plastic farm animals) and also a three-foot Bobo doll. Bandura conducted a number of variations of this experiment. Most notably, in one condition, the children observed the adult models being rewarded, punished or receiving no consequences for their aggressive behaviour. The children who witnessed the model being punished were less likely to imitate the behaviour when left alone with the Bobo doll (Bandura, Ross and Ross, 1961).

Vicarious reinforcement can be a useful tool in an organizational setting, especially when *scaling* a business and/or management model. When trying to implement change at scale, you need to find those pockets of people within your organization who are already modelling the behaviour you want to scale. Then you can use them to seed the new behaviour across the organization. This is an infection model of spreading new ideas where the source comes not top-down but rather middle-out. It is important that those in positions of power are seen to acknowledge and reward such behaviour in order to reinforce it for the surrounding observers.

The role of leaders is of particular importance here. They play a key part as 'signal generators'. Jack Welch once said that leadership is 'relentless and boring'. Leaders are under constant observation and need to be consistent in what they say and do. If there is a mismatch between words and deeds, it is the actions that speak louder.

Focus on the first step of the journey

When we think about altering an established pattern of behaviour, we tend to focus first on the ultimate goal, and then almost immediately we think of the multitude of intervening steps between where we are and our ultimate destination. Suddenly the task seems impossibly large and complicated. We might start bravely, but quite quickly we start to feel overwhelmed and demotivated.

Our inner elephant is easily discouraged when faced with too many obstacles. This is because the willpower required to sustain the effort needed for change is not an infinite resource. Self-control can be depleted by overtaxing tasks. This ground-breaking idea was first demonstrated in an ingenious experiment. The study participants were first asked to wait in a room stocked with freshly baked chocolate cookies and other chocolate treats. Some participants were allowed to eat the goodies, but another test group were not only denied the chocolate but were asked to eat radishes instead. Afterwards the participants were given an apparently unrelated tricky problem-solving exercise. The results were unequivocal. The people who had had to exercise self-control in denying themselves the sweet treats made fewer attempts to solve the puzzle task and gave up more quickly than those who had not had to exercise self-restraint (Baumeister et al, 1998).

At this point we would do well to recall the proverb from ancient Chinese philosopher Lao Tzu that even a journey of 1,000 miles begins with a single step. To help motivate our elephant we need to shrink the task, by focusing only on the initial step and forgetting all the subsequent steps required to reach the ultimate goal.

Our limited willpower suggests that we should design the environment to make change as easy as possible. Old habits are hard to break, and we are resistant to changing ingrained behaviours even if we know we should, because of 'activation energy' – the amount of energy required to initiate an action. Overcoming activation energy is what makes it hard to start on a new behaviour. Shawn Achor (2010) advocates the '20-second rule': namely, reducing the activation energy required to trigger a new habit, by making it between 3 and 20 seconds easier to start, considerably increases the likelihood of doing it. The same logic applies to negative habits that you're trying to discourage: creating a 20-second delay improves the chances of disrupting the habit. For example, if you are trying to eat more healthily, you should hide the sweets and chocolates somewhere inaccessible and put the healthy snacks where they're easy to reach. By increasing access to the good stuff and decreasing access to the bad snacks by about 20 seconds respectively, habits have a better chance of being changed.

Signpost the destination clearly

Now that we have addressed how to persuade the emotional side of our brain to engage in change, we need to consider the controlled or rational side – the elephant's rider. This may appear not too difficult, as the logical, reasoned rationale for most change initiatives is generally aimed at the rational rider. But, while leaders typically have a clear picture in their heads of what they want to communicate, they can sometimes forget that the message they want to convey is not so obvious to everyone else. This is another manifestation of the curse of knowledge, which we encountered earlier in Chapters 2 and 6 (Camerer, Loewenstein and Weber, 1989). So, if you are trying to get everyone to sing from the same hymn sheet, you need to be mindful of the fact that, while you have the whole orchestral score before you, everyone else can only see their individual part. Let's examine a couple of ways that can help to overcome the curse of knowledge: 1) *Provide practical, concrete details.* This focuses on the *how* by setting out processes and rules to be followed and leads to a top-down model (see Chapter 3). 2) *Have a clear, inspiring overarching message.* Here you are seeking to communicate an ethos. You want people to understand the *why.* How the *why* is implemented can then be left much more to the people on the ground – this is more of an infection model working from the middle out (see Chapter 4).

We will consider these two contrasting approaches below.

Top-down and middle-out scaling

In any *scaling* operation, choices need to be made between complete standardization where everything is prescribed (which equates to a top-down approach) and in contrast what has been termed 'mutual adjustment' (Mintzberg, 1992), which allows employees a degree of autonomy in how things are done (effectively a more middle-out approach). Robert Sutton and Hayagreeva Rao characterize this distinction as between being 'Catholic' and 'Buddhist', and they recount how their Stanford University colleague and venture capitalist Michael Deering articulated the challenge thus: 'What is our [*scaling*] goal? Is it more like Catholicism, where the aim is to replicate preordained design beliefs and practices? Or is it more like Buddhism, where an underlying mindset guides why people do certain things – but the specifics of what they do can vary wildly from person to person and place to place?' (Sutton and Rao, 2014). Where your organization chooses to strike the balance on this spectrum will depend to some extent on factors such as:

- the complexity of the work;
- the uncertainty faced by the person doing the work; and
- the level of skill of the worker.

Let us look at how a number of companies approach scaling in different ways.

Lindbäcks Bygg is a Swedish construction company that operates extremely successfully at the standardized (top-down) end of the spectrum. This fourth-generation family-owned company designs and builds large-scale modular housing. Using sustainably sourced wood-framed prefabricated sections, it is building apartment buildings at a rate of 20 a week. Every component has been designed and standardized in a highly industrialized and automated fashion. Huge patented machines construct the building frames, which are then assembled on site, to any level of complexity. And these are not cookie-cutter buildings. They are highly customizable, environmentally friendly and economical both to build and to live in. Although the work is complex and the workers are skilled, there is not much uncertainty involved in the execution of the work once the buildings have been designed and planned. This has allowed Lindbäcks to adopt a 'lean production' method of working, where every step of the process has been examined and streamlined, and waste and inefficiency have been minimized. Thus it is an exemplar of a 'Catholic' approach to *scaling*.

Recreational Equipment Inc (REI), by contrast, specializes in selling sporting goods, outdoor equipment and clothing, and camping and travel gear. It has appeared in *Fortune* magazine's list of '100 best companies to work for' every year since the rankings began in 1998. Instead of prescribing a rigid set of rules for employees to follow, the organization looks to recruit like-minded individuals who share a passion for the great outdoors. REI's overarching mission is to 'inspire, educate and outfit for a lifetime of outdoor adventure and stewardship' (REI, 2017). In pursuit of this aim, the organization looks for a particular mindset in its recruits. A past CEO, Dennis Madsen, explained:

> employees can get benefits and incentives anywhere, but it's harder for them to find a place where they can totally immerse themselves in the culture. We attract outdoors-oriented employees who sustain the culture and attract even more like-minded employees. They share the same interests and values; they're committed to the environment, to the community, to work–life balance, and to having fun outside. And that goes for management, too.
>
> (Morse, 2003)

REI epitomizes a more 'Buddhist' approach to *scaling* a business and management model.

In February 2017, British book retailer Waterstones announced its first year in profit since the financial crash of 2008. Launched in 1982, Waterstones had enjoyed a period of rapid growth and expansion. Bought by HMV Group in 1998, the company suffered a number of years of poor results, culminating in its sale to Russian billionaire Alexander Mamut. James Daunt, who was brought in as Managing Director by Mamut to rescue the struggling bookseller, revealed in 2014: 'We came within a millisecond of losing everything. We were dead in a ditch' (Armistead, 2017). In a brave move, Daunt turned his back on publisher paid-for promotions and moved away from the prescriptive plans that HMV had had for each store. Using a small, carefully selected team of buyers, Daunt established the 'book of the month' feature across all stores. But he gave individual managers the autonomy to select and tailor their book offerings according to local customer tastes. Daunt has managed to capitalize upon the love people have for the physical book (Waterstones stopped selling the Amazon Kindle in its stores in 2015). By laying down some common 'handrails' and communicating his vision of the importance of books and bookselling, whilst granting store managers the ability to tailor to local conditions, he has reinvigorated this much loved retailer. This idea of 'handrails' echoes the idea of strategy professors Kathleen Eisenhardt and Don Sull (2001) of embodying strategy in 'simple rules', and echoes Sutton and Rao's (2014) 'Buddhist' approach to *scaling*.

A different type of learning

'Discovery' is another way of saying 'learning'. But the three modes – *frame*, *experiment* and *scale* – demand different types of learning. In *frame* and *experiment*, the focus is on divergence – the equivalent of a small advance scouting party moving forward 1,000 metres. *Scale* requires a type of convergent learning that is qualitatively different in nature, but just as important. It is more like moving the whole army forward by 10 metres. In Chapters 9 and 10, we will discuss the implications for individuals and organizations of applying the three modes of the discovery-led decision making framework.

Summary

This chapter has provided an outline of the *scale* mode of the discovery-led decision making framework. The core thrust of *scaling* is repeatability: doing *more* of what works. This involves spreading a particular *business* and *management* model, with an associated mindset and organizational practices – which is ultimately about changing individual behaviours and *habits*.

The barriers that hinder our ability to *scale*, which are related to organizational inertia, are: a dilution of the organization's core purpose and capabilities; and an inability to adapt quickly enough to changing external conditions.

The steps required for successful scaling are: identify – and, if necessary, recapture – the 'what' and 'why' that embody the essence of an organization; and translate this essential core of the organization into a clear, concrete and comprehensible 'how' through social norms shaping everybody's behaviour. In practice, this involves influencing people's mindsets and habits through their working environment and the people around them. It also involves working at the level of *automatic* as well as *controlled* cognition and behaviour, so that the desired mindsets and behaviours become habituated over time.

Scaling approaches can be characterized as falling along a spectrum between 'Catholic' (ie following prescribed rules and procedure closely) and 'Buddhist' (ie allowing local adaptation of general principles that act as 'handrails'). This spectrum echoes the difference between the top-down and middle-out approaches to decision making that we discussed in Chapters 3 and 4.

The final two chapters will consider the implications of discovery-led decision making for organizations and individual decision makers.

References

Achor, S (2010) *The Happiness Advantage: The seven principles of positive psychology that fuel success and performance at work*, Crown Business, London

Armistead, C (2017) Balancing the books: how Waterstones came back from the dead, *Guardian*, 17 February, https://www.theguardian.com/books/2017/feb/03/balancing-the-books-how-waterstones-returned-to-profit

Bandura, A, Ross, D and Ross, S A (1961) Transmission of aggression through imitation of aggressive models, *Journal of Abnormal and Social Psychology*, **63**, 575–582

Bargh, J A, Chen, M and Burrows, L (1996) Automaticity of social behaviour: direct effects of trait construct and stereotype activation on action, *Journal of Personality and Social Psychology*, **71** (2), 230–44

Baumeister, R F et al (1998) Ego depletion: is the active self a limited resource?, *Journal of Personality and Social Psychology*, **74**, 1252–65

Birkinshaw, J and Goddard, J (2009) What is your management model?, *Sloan Business Review*, **50** (2), 81–90

Camerer, C, Loewenstein, G and Weber, M (1989) The curse of knowledge in economic settings: an experimental analysis, *Journal of Political Economy*, **97** (5), 1232–54

Delingpole, J (2009) When Lego lost its head – and how this toy story got its happy ending, *Daily Mail*, http://www.dailymail.co.uk/home/moslive/article-1234465/When-Lego-lost-head--toy-story-got-happy-ending.html

Dunbar, R (2010) *How Many Friends Does One Person Need? Dunbar's number and other evolutionary quirks*, Faber, London

Economist (2014) A hard act to follow, *Economist*, 27 June, http://www.economist.com/news/business/21605916-it-has-taken-ges-boss-jeffrey-immelt-13-years-escape-legacy-his-predecessor-jack

Eisenhardt, K M and Sull, D (2001) Strategy as simple rules, *Harvard Business Review*, **79** (1), 106–16

Gilbert, F, Lorthois, L and Vas, A (2014) Demystifying change management, *Deloitte Quarterly*, **4**, 35–39

Griffiths, S (2013) Invasion of the tiny plastic people! Lego figures set to outnumber HUMANS by 2019, *Daily Mail*, http://www.dailymail.co.uk/sciencetech/article-2473163/Invasion-tiny-plastic-people-Lego-figures-set-outnumber-HUMANS-2019.html

Haidt, J (2006) *The Happiness Hypothesis: Finding modern truth in ancient wisdom*, Basic Books, New York

Heath, C and Heath, D (2011) *Switch: How to change things when change is hard*, Random House Business, London

Kitching, E and Roy, S (2013) 70% of transformation programs fail, AIPMM Webinar Series, http://www.slideshare.net/aipmm/70-26633757

Kotter, J P (2012) *Leading Change*, Harvard Business Review Press, Boston, MA

Lefkowitz, M, Blake, R R and Mouton, J S (1955) Status factors in pedestrian violation of traffic signals, *Journal of Abnormal and Social Psychology*, **51** (3), 704–06

Leung, R (2005) Jack Welch: 'I fell in love', *60 Minutes*, http://www.cbsnews.com/news/jack-welch-i-fell-in-love

Magretta, J (2002) Why business models matter, *Harvard Business Review*, **80** (5), 86–92

Mintzberg, H (1992) *Structure in Fives: Designing effective organizations*, Prentice Hall, London

Morse, G (2003) Gearing up at REI, *Harvard Business Review*, **81** (5), 20–21

Munger, K and Harris, S J (1989) Effects of an observer on handwashing in a public restroom, *Perceptual and Motor Skills*, **69**, 733–34

Osterwalder, A and Pigneur, Y (2010) *Business Model Generation: A handbook for visionaries, game changers and challengers*, John Wiley & Sons, London

Pedersen, D M, Keithly, S and Brady, K (1986) Effects of an observer on conformity to handwashing norm, *Perceptual and Motor Skills*, **62**, 169–70

REI (2017) About REI, *REI Co-op*, https://www.rei.com/about-rei.html

Rumelt, R (2012) *Good Strategy, Bad Strategy: The difference and why it matters*, Profile Books, London

Saunders, A (2013) The rise and fall of Marks & Spencer, *Management Today*, http://www.managementtoday.co.uk/rise-fall-marks-spencer/article/1212188

Schein, E H (1999) *Corporate Culture Survival Guide*, Jossey-Bass, San Francisco, CA

Sutton, R I and Rao, H (2014) *Scaling Up Excellence: Getting to more without settling for less*, Crown Business, New York

Tufts Center for Engineering Education and Outreach (2015) Lego history, https://sites.tufts.edu/ceeo/2015/02/26/legohistory

Zook, C and Allen, J (2011) The great repeatable business model, *Harvard Business Review*, **89** (11), 106–14

Zook, C and Allen, J (2012) *Repeatability: Build enduring businesses for a world of constant change*, Harvard Business Review Press, Boston, MA

Implications for 09
organizations

Sir, 'tis the devil's own country to find your way in. But a gentleman with a face like your honour's can't miss the road; though, if it was myself that was going to Cincinnati, sure, I wouldn't start from here. TRADITIONAL

We've outlined discovery-led decision making, our framework for tackling wicked problems and the resultant planning dilemma in the previous four chapters. These final two chapters of the book begin to pull together the implications of adopting such an approach. The next chapter looks at what discovery-led decision making may mean for individual leaders. This chapter focuses on some of the possible consequences for organizations seeking to keep their approach to strategy relevant in a fast-moving environment. We are where we are; that's not the issue. It's how we take it forward from here.

The changing face of strategy

The strategic space model (Figure 9.1) highlights the three essential considerations that bound strategic choice. Strategy remains the simultaneous consideration of *purpose* (what the organization seeks to achieve), *world* (what external stakeholders value and prioritize) and *self* (the capabilities the organization can mobilize in pursuit of its goals). The challenge facing organizations is translating this concept into proficient decision making in an environment that looks and feels very different to what's gone before.

The tone of organizational purpose (as the combination of its intention and motives) has itself shifted. Jennifer Sundberg, in

Figure 9.1   Strategic space

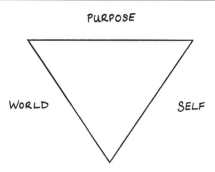

Director magazine (Scott, 2014), reports a survey by Deloitte that asked a sample of millennials whether they agreed with US economist Milton Friedman's statement that the only responsibility of a business is to increase its profits. Of the sample, 92 per cent said no, as did 93 per cent of the 300 directors (Scott, 2014). In her book *The Key*, Lynda Gratton (2014) of London Business School outlines her views on why business goals work best when aligned with a much broader world agenda. Organizational purpose needs to resonate with a broader stakeholder agenda, with corporate responsibility as a central thread rather than a tokenistic pursuit. Organizations are facing up to the importance of the congruence of values between themselves and stakeholders, whether this relates to the competition for talent or the fight for customers. As Simon Sinek succinctly expressed it, 'Start with why' (Sinek, 2011). Businesses can no longer hide behind a veneer of respectability, masking what's really going on inside. External brand and appeal are an extrapolation of internal values and priorities. We spoke with one director in the VW Group who expressed his disappointment and how he felt let down by his organization in light of the 2015 emissions scandal. Enterprises have witnessed a rise in the creation of codes of conduct shared inside and with external stakeholders, and the use of value statements in recruitment and development discussions with staff, as leaders seek more enlightened and transparent practice.

In *No Ordinary Disruption*, Richard Dodds and his colleagues (Dodds et al, 2015) described the four forces of disruption: the rise of emerging markets, the accelerating impact of technology on the forces of market competition, an ageing world population, and accelerating flows of trade, capital and people. A continuing theme of this book has been the changing nature of change and the implications of overlapping domains and simultaneous forces. The main challenge around situational intelligence and decision making relates to interpretation.

When we look at an organization's capabilities (referred to as 'self' in the strategic space model in Figure 9.1), there are two key considerations. The first consideration is the enterprise's trajectory and its related path dependency: in other words, in which direction the organization is heading, how its current situation is a function of what has happened in its past, and how this impacts on its strategic freedom to manoeuvre. The second consideration is the recognition that any step-change in strategy is highly likely to necessitate new capabilities and qualities that most likely are non-existent within the current recipe. The ability to embrace the 'new' while leaving some of the 'old' behind is core to effective strategy.

The question for leaders is: when faced with ambiguity and uncertainty, how do you choose? At what stage do you reach the transition point where you know enough of what you need to know, compared to what you don't know? In such a confusing environment, we need to keep reminding ourselves that much of what purports to be knowledge is actually interpretation or perception. We also need to be mindful of the issue of the 'unknown unknowns' made popular by former US Secretary for Defense Donald Rumsfeld when talking about weapons of mass destruction in 2002. The statement raises a distinction between revelations that are anticipated (known unknowns) and those that are completely unexpected (unknown unknowns). In fact, Jesse Sheidlower, former editor-at-large of the *Oxford English Dictionary*, notes that the first recorded use of the term 'unknown unknowns' was in the US engineering industry in 1969, and it was often abbreviated to 'unk-unk' (BBC, 2007).

The world works in real time, and the strategic advantages of stability are eroding (McGrath, 2013). Life, as John Lennon reminded us, is what happens to you when you're busy making other plans (Lennon, 1980). We move forward on the understanding that decisions are typically made when that which is 'known' exceeds that which is 'unknown' about a situation. In a VUCA environment, this can be a potentially dangerous misapprehension. Organizations can look at the balance between the 'known' and the 'unknown' as the interplay between risk appetite (the propensity to speculate on the ability to derive value from risk) and risk capacity (the ability to absorb the consequences of risks that are detrimental to the well-being of the entity). Leaders are shifting thinking from a clear 'either/or' mindset to one that is more 'both/and' (Smith, Lewis and Tushman, 2016: 65).

In this world, the activities of strategy are not ends in themselves, but staging posts. The only way you can possibly control your destiny is to be more flexible than your environment. In the era of simultaneous strategic thinking, decision making and implementation, the exploration of possibilities through strategic options is probably vital (Stalk and Iyer, 2016: 81). Strategic options are like tomatoes – you're all the time feeding them, figuring out how big each one might grow and when each will ripen. It involves deliberate speculation, and the experience of what Schoemaker and Gunther (2006) called the wisdom of deliberate mistakes. In strategic decision making, reflective execution rather than analysis becomes the modus operandi. Directors need to focus on gazing up at the stars while simultaneously running on the ground.

Getting connected

One of the prevailing trends in management is the reducing emphasis on the insular entity, and the rise in the permeability of organizational boundaries. Connection, rather than independence, is the new order. This has been reflected by changes in strategic thinking over the past few years, including competition between supply chains (rather than individual enterprises) and the recognition of 'complementors' as a sixth force in industry analysis, and the encouragement towards arenas rather than industries. It has also been recognized through what management commentator Charles Handy (2002) has termed the 'shamrock' organizational form (where a professional core is augmented by a flexible workforce, contracted services and temporary enterprises shared with other organizations) and 'hybrid' approaches that mix together the value systems and administrative logics of the private, public and third sectors. The key point is that an enterprise need not 'own' all three modes of discovery-led decision making. For example, some players in the pharmaceutical sector look to specialist laboratories and university research teams for pioneering work around formulation prior to them facilitating scaling up. UK brands Innocent drinks and Green & Black's chocolate benefited from the resources of the corporate sector (Coca-Cola and Mondelez respectively) to commercialize the results of market experiments that led to the creation of great products.

Strategy levers and 'big rocks'

We think there are probably four levers that guide strategy. Decisions made around these four areas affect how strategy unfolds in practice. These four are *resources* (and where these are focused), *organizational 'hard wiring'* (the relatively easy-to-describe 'written rules' relating to structures, processes, systems etc), *goals and metrics* (from the perspective of what gets measured gets done) and *organizational 'soft wiring'* relating to culture and values (recognizing 'the way we do things around here' that guides how decisions are acted upon).

Much has been written about organizational alignment in the translation of strategic decisions to action. Strategy academic Richard Rumelt, for example, talks about strategy being a 'cohesive response to an important challenge' (Rumelt, 2011). Rumelt's inference is that effective strategy is multifaceted and the product of many decisions, all oriented in the same direction. This is what Jean Chitwood, Executive Vice President of Corporate Strategy and Development at INC Research, refers to as the 'secret sauce'. Strategic impact arises out of the assimilation and alignment of the component parts, while strategic resilience is a consequence of the complexity and interrelationships between these ingredients.

Applying these four levers effectively is not easy. Some enterprises use strategic themes to act as focal points to bring together resources, hard wiring, goals and measures, and soft wiring as decisions become reality. The considered choice of a few 'big rocks', to use the term made popular by educator and author Dr Stephen Covey in *The 7*

Habits of Highly Effective People (1989), can help. This enables an organization to select enough strategic themes with which to move forward and make a difference, without diluting the core messages, overstretching capacity and causing confusion. The big rocks provide the ability to communicate strategy and anchor it in a cohesive response.

The tridextrous organization

Our central message around discovery-led decision making has been the requirement for organizations to become *tridextrous*: able to work capably in three arenas simultaneously – *frame, experiment* and *scale*. There are profound implications of the need to be able to operate with such flexibility.

If the overall enterprise needs to be tridextrous, the structure within the enterprise should help each part understand its role in relation to the overall strategy, with the organization's hard and soft wiring enabling the flow of information and resources vital for sustainable purposive activity. At the most senior level, leaders must comprehend tridexterity and shape their strategic decision making based on its principles. Divisional leaders lower down the organization, while understanding the principle of tridexterity, will probably need to skew their focus in accordance with their roles. However, we'd add a note of caution: as we've seen in Chapter 6, an excessive emphasis on focus can narrow one's perspective, effectively acting as a set of blinkers. Should one of the decision making modes become disconnected from the other two, the enterprise ceases to function as an integrated unit and the flows of resources and information that are its lifeblood are restricted.

There is no assertion that every part of an enterprise needs to be equally tridextrous. There may be parts of the enterprise whose focus is more about *scale* than *frame* or *experiment*. We have a client in the south of England that is a wholly owned subsidiary of a multinational enterprise. Our client's factory makes domestic appliances and dances to the tune of its corporate parent. There might come a day when shifting world economics (for example the consequence of the UK's 2017 decision to leave the European Union) or shifts in consumer tastes mean, in the eyes of the corporate parent, that this particular factory has no valuable contribution to make to the multinational's future strategy. There are production facilities like this around the world, unified by one factor. All of them represent the operational arms of the enterprises of which they are a part. They represent the *scale* aspect of the strategy that has been agreed elsewhere within the corporate whole. As such, their main strategic activities relate to the pursuit of efficiency in the provision of products and services to customers. An increasingly valuable consequence of this activity is providing original data to help with the organization's strategic questions. Here, the focus is very much what McKinsey & Company labelled as 'Horizon One' (Baghai, Coley and White, 1999), the current business model. The leadership teams in such centres have a clear understanding of their priorities and where their attention is best devoted in respect of strategic decision making.

Shifting energy

For many incumbent organizations, the strategic recipe sees great emphasis on *scale* (Figure 9.2), the creation of value through the execution of the Horizon One business model.

In business start-up situations, the dominant activity is often *experiment* (Figure 9.3), as the entrepreneur tries out and finesses solutions to unmet needs.

In an established organization, *experiment* relates to 'Horizon Two' and the quest for the business model for the future (Baghai, Coley and White, 1999). In its 2016 strategy Ericsson, the Swedish communications giant, made reference to five commercial opportunities that it sees are part of its future recipe. Its current revenue is dominated by its core activities, including 4G telecommunication technology. Ericsson is guided by its focus on a networked society where everything that benefits from being connected will be connected, and its ambition to lead the market transformation as the new market evolves. Ericsson's 'experimentation' is based on not only a feel for the way the market evolves but also the proactive development of ideas that might shape

Figure 9.2   Discovery-led decision making – *scaling*

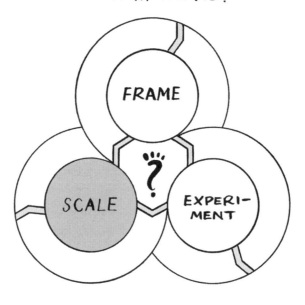

Figure 9.3   Discovery-led decision making – *experimentation*

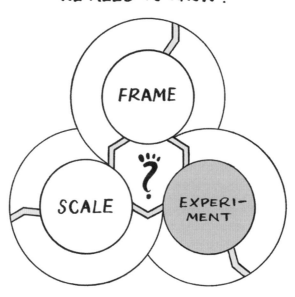

the market. Ericsson owns nearly 40,000 patents (a testament to its investment in research and development), some of which will be the foundation of its progression of such initiatives from Horizon Three (ideas for profitable growth down the road) to Horizon Two (emerging opportunities) and eventually Horizon One (the core business) over time. But Ericsson understands fully that not all of its experiments will bear commercial fruit.

For established organizations, the pathway from *experiment* to *scale* is made easier in some respects and harder in others. Organizations tend to benefit from the brand equity and value chain relationships that can ease the scaling of a recipe. On the other hand, experiences derived under existing *scale* activities can limit the freedom to embrace the fruits of 'experiment' – bear in mind our earlier discussion, in Chapter 2, about organizational inertia. For example, Kodak's entrenchment in film technology, and its assumptions around the business model upon which its success was founded, acted as a barrier to its capable grasp of the digital photographic world. Similarly, one of the globe's most prominent retailers was unable to commercialize the results of a substantial investment in 'Blue Ocean' thinking (Kim and Mauborgne, 2005) owing to the prevailing practices and culture stifling the attempts at re-engineering. The phrase 'turkeys voting for Christmas' is often used when describing the disposition towards self-interest and the maintenance of a status quo. Also, the translation from *experiment* to *scale* for a new value proposition usually necessitates acquiring new capabilities. For example, Coca-Cola's strategy in scaling commercial activity typically involves acquisition (its stake in the energy drink Monster is a case in point). Coca-Cola has learned that it's more viable for it to invest in and capitalize on brand creation by others rather than approach the challenge itself.

In moving from *experiment* to *scale*, there is a balance to be struck between precision and chaos. If intentions are too precise then decisions might be made prematurely that expose the organization to the risk of subsequent changes in the market. Conversely, if *experiment* is too laissez-faire, then there is a danger of incurring the costs of over-speculation and having an organizational ship that appears rudderless. Strategy professors Don Sull and Kathleen Eisenhardt

(2015) see 'simple rules' as a way to tackle this dilemma. Simple rules are intended to provide sufficient guidance in the nurturing and prioritizing of opportunities within the *experiment* mode. Returning to Ericsson, its strategy around prioritizing and elevating ideas from *experiment* to the domain of *scale* is based around the following simple rules: sift for opportunities addressing markets that are expected to grow faster than the core business, have a significant share of software and professional services and have a share of recurring revenues above the norm.

In respect to *frame*, the task facing decision makers is about defining the question that needs to be answered. Strategy is largely an inductive discipline, which means that solutions emerge from the ability to make sense of an array of complex and sometimes contradictory data. It is not as simple as putting data into a formula and running a programmed algorithm. It is a matter of interpretation as to which data are relevant and to what degree. Reiterating the quotation attributed to Albert Einstein that we mentioned in Chapter 6 emphasizes this very view: 'If I had an hour to solve a problem I'd spend 55 minutes thinking about the problem and 5 minutes thinking about solutions.' Faced with a mass of data, and perhaps with the pressure to make a decision that restores some degree of certainty, we can perhaps understand a tendency to bring potentially misleading assumptions and perspectives to the framing process that can work to the detriment of the eventual outcome.

Working five to nine

Some years ago a small legal firm in Scotland that we know faced a commercial difficulty. The area of law in which the firm focused was competitive, and margins were tight. Despite the firm being well established and its reputation being sound, business was hard-going. The firm took advantage of some consultancy support provided by the Law Society. During the consulting assignment, the consultant spoke with each of the people in the firm about ideas for the future. The discussions revealed some interesting angles about moving the firm into a more commercially sustainable position. The consultant convened a meeting with all the firm's partners, at which she shared the ideas she'd gathered. While the partners were receptive, the stumbling block came not from what the firm could possibly do but from its lack of appetite to follow through and implement. It was pointed out to the consultant that there was simply no spare capacity in the firm to pick up the extra tasks associated with new opportunities. Everyone was busy working on client legal matters – and needed to be if the bills were to be paid. It is open to debate about whether the partners' reaction was a genuine reflection of constrained capacity, an issue of employee capability or an expression of self-pity. The point is that the processes of *frame* and *experiment* require investment of time, attention and money. Also, shifting something from *experiment* to *scale* requires extra effort, as it needs to take place against the backdrop of the existing *scale* recipe still in place. The law firm, limited by the demands of its current *scale* activities, chose not to follow up on any of the ideas presented by the consultant. Dr Yanos Michopoulos, a former CEO of Greek Railways and a leadership consultant, uses the expression 'working five to nine' to explain what these shifts across different modes of discovery-led decision making entail when put into practice. The expression, which is a twist on the Dolly Parton song lyric 'Working nine to five', points out that the process of moving the results of experimentation into a scaled solution needs resources beyond the ordinary. There's extra work to be done on either side of the conventional working day in order to make the transition happen. This might be an obvious point, but too often strategic success is curtailed by lack of organizational capacity, as there is insufficient bandwidth to make it happen.

Organizational correctives for collective decision making

Awareness of the presence of personal biases and heuristics can be useful. The shortcoming of awareness as a means of dealing with them is their location in the subconscious. A person knowing about them doesn't necessarily alter how his or her subconscious responds.

It is at the collective, rather than individual, level that these are usually best tackled.

This takes us into the realm of organizational correctives. These are the structural and process steps that can be put into place to help counter the effects of biases and heuristics. How a business is governed and managed can be configured to reduce the potential shortcomings of subconscious effects on decision making. Our clients' examples of organizational correctives in action include the following:

- *Snacking on strategy* – moving away from the annual strategy feasts, where an overwhelming agenda generates weariness, towards more regular, focused discussions helping keep senior leaders participating in the on-going strategy process.

- *Providing a structure for decision making*, for example the use of a 'suitability, acceptability, feasibility' grid coupled with discussion and agreement of what decision is to be made and upon what basis it'll be made.

- *Developing a shared language with the team* (eg *frame*, *experiment*, *scale*) that helps move conversations between the three modes of strategic decision making, while maintaining the ability to focus on the most relevant issues.

- *Multi-modal communication* – having dialogue on the content of the forthcoming decision through more than one mechanism. The matter can be discussed at a meeting in the conventional manner, and briefing papers can be issued in advance to allow all participants to familiarize themselves with and digest the arguments as well as reflect on additional data that might be useful.

- *Diversity of voice* – designing discussion groups to bring in a diversity of perspectives as an antidote to groupthink. The skill here is in enabling the discussion group to accommodate a diverse range of people's styles and views.

- *Ground rules for challenging* – setting the terms of reference to enable people to have challenging discussions without offending colleagues or upsetting relationships. Sometimes all that's required is a reminder from the chairperson that challenging perspectives makes for healthy debate and it's all right both to challenge and to be challenged. We have one client who uses the soccer phrase 'Play the ball not the man' to remind people to avoid challenges being personal.

- *Champion and challenger* – for more important decisions, the voice of challenge can be more deliberately brought into a discussion. One person might be assigned the role of devil's advocate. Alternatively one sub-group of a meeting might be assigned the collective role of advocating why a certain course of action should not be pursued, with another group having the task of explaining why that course of action should be supported. The benefit of 'champion–challenger' approaches is that they help ensure debate happens. The main downside is that, in forcing challenge to happen, they trivialize the challenge. This can result in people gaming the process and playing along with the idea without seriously exploring or considering the content. We have seen one instance where one leader (in this case, a chief financial officer), concerned by the lack of challenge in the board's strategy discussions, took it upon himself to be the challenger. The result was the level of debate in board meetings was raised, but this individual developed the reputation of 'Mr Negative' in the eyes of his colleagues as a result of his typical reaction to propositions (which did his own standing in the organization no favours).

- *Avoiding the first solution* – in direct response to the Einstellung effect we discussed in Chapter 2, a capable chair will encourage discussion and exploration of ideas beyond the first plausible solution.

- *Avoiding unnecessary decisions* – for some leaders, making decisions is a demonstration of their ability to contribute to their organizations. We are aware of one business that makes an acquisition each and every year. These acquisitions aren't driven by a cohesive strategy but by the board's insecurity and the view that they should be doing something. Similarly, decisions are a tangible touchpoint. However, organizations need to remain focused on the purpose of their decisions. The question that should probably be asked more regularly is something along the lines of 'What would be the consequences of us not making this decision today?' The discussion of the issue, the sharing of views and the debating of alternatives should continue, so that the subject is mulled over.

The shift to middle-out decisions

Chapters 3 and 4 made the distinction between top-down and middle-out decisions. Top-down decisions are about direct control, and are conventionally considered the locus for strategic decision making, while middle-out decisions are about intentionality emerging from the distributed activities of the organization. Intentionality is the ability of the mind to form representation; it is the power of minds to be about, to represent or to stand for things, properties or states of affairs. If organizations seek to guide strategy purely top-down, they risk putting on their blinkers. We've spoken about the importance of middle-out decisions in strategy and the reference point for these being the prevailing values and culture. We believe that strategy in VUCA times places greater emphasis on middle-out decision making.

'New power', according to Heimans and Timms (2014: 52), 'gains its force from people's growing capacity and desire to go beyond the passive consumption of ideas and goals.' This way of working values information and a host of other characteristics centred on more overall participation: opt-in decision making; self-organization and networked governance; open source collaboration; crowd wisdom and sharing; and transparency.

Within organizations there are likely to be what change writers Chip Heath and Dan Heath (2010) refer to as 'bright spots'. Organizations don't develop homogeneously, and leaders can use the relative difference as a mechanism to move practice forward. Rather than seek to influence by instruction, influence might be more powerful by peer example, where the bright spot of excellent practice in one location is used to provide encouragement and guidance to others.

The Heath brothers also make the point that social signals are influential. Soft wiring through the combination of culture, values and rewards in place nudges the everyday decisions that people make. This is to say that, although the conventional strategy levers of resource allocation (which is about the energy assigned to the task) and measures (which are about the clarity of focus for this energy) are influential, when it comes to middle-out decisions, organizational architecture and the perceived incentives that relate to the prevailing values and climate powerfully shape what actually happens.

Often organizations are thought about in 'hour glass' form, with many beavering away at the bottom and a few high performers at the top setting the tone and leading by example, but in the absence of a productive middle. In some quarters, middle management is viewed as the most intractable part – or, as learning and development expert Octavius Black (2016) expressed it, the barrier between 'the CEO's ingenious vision and its swift implementation by the noble worker'. Labels like 'permafrost' (Abrahamson, 2000) are used disparagingly to describe the impenetrable layer of middle management. Senior leaders' signals to the rest of the enterprise just bounce straight back from it and don't get through to where real activity takes place. The hearts and minds of this cohort in the middle of the enterprise are key. If a characteristic of leaders is that 'We make the weather for our teams', middle management set the tone for local climate.

In this book we looked at some of the main biases and heuristics that impact on personal decision making. We've looked at how stress, for example from the anxiety of change, uncertainty in the decision-making process and the pressure of workload lead us to exhibit our dominant response more strongly. We also recognize that collaborative endeavour is subject to distortions and nuance in the way that information is processed and opinions formed.

The wisdom of crowds advocated by journalist James Surowiecki (2005) suggests that the aggregation of information in groups leads to decisions that are typically better than could have been made by any single member of the group. However, the wisdom of crowds approach is based on the premise that each person's contribution is independent of those of others. In the working world, this is rarely the case. We've looked at the heuristic of contagion and influence by social signals. In group situations, we realize that collaborative input is skewed, with a few individuals providing a disproportionally high degree of input. We recognize the risk of social loafing, where some don't contribute as much to a collective initiative as they should, trusting others to carry the load of the joint task. We also observe the impact on people of being observed by others in a position to approve or disapprove – performance may be enhanced (we speak about people rising to the occasion) or impaired ('stage fright').

Work by law professor Cass Sunstein and social psychologist Reid Hastie (2014) explored where group endeavour fell short of expectation. The four problems they identified were that groups:

- don't merely fail to correct their members' errors, but amplify them;
- fall victim to cascade effects, following the statements and actions of those who went first;
- become polarized, taking even more extreme positions than originally; and
- focus on what everybody knows, ignoring critical information that only one or two people have.

There is an African proverb that says 'If you want to go fast, go alone. If you want to go far, go together' (Simmons, 2013). When we collaborate, we avoid the myopia that comes from looking through a single lens. However, we've seen that reaping the benefits of joint enterprise is not without difficulty. Former Saatchi Chairman Kevin Roberts, who helped popularize the concept of VUCA (volatile, uncertain, complex, ambiguous) in the business setting, urges leaders to 'replace command and control with collaboration, connectivity and creativity. Turn your world super-VUCA (vibrant, unreal, crazy, astounding), fail fast, fix fast, learn fast' (Roberts, 2016).

Towards an adaptive management model

We encourage organizations to embrace the tenets of discovery-led decision making in their business models, in so doing matching their offers to evolving needs. However, a theme in this book has been our view that VUCA is an existential imperative. In a world so hard to predict and fathom, the ability to control the evolution of business models is much challenged. As Rita McGrath (2013) pointed out, businesses need to look beyond the idea of a sustainable competitive advantage in any of their markets.

Perhaps the greatest strategic capability an enterprise can possess relates more to itself than any market position in which it participates. The idea of a 'learning organization', which became prominent through the writing of Peter Senge (1990), took us partly down this path. Such an entity sought to 'facilitate the learning of all its members and continually transform itself' (Pedler, Burgoyne and Boydell, 1991). In Darwinian terms, the organization was doing the best it could to remain relevant – survival being bestowed on adapting to a changing environment.

Gary Hamel, in *What Matters Now* (2012), cites present-day issues such as once innovative companies losing their glow, entry barriers to industries falling, and business models being rendered redundant overnight, echoing the list of wicked problems that we looked at in the Introduction. Coupled with the sense of protest against the transgressions of the 'corporate' in the eyes of the rank and file, these issues led Hamel to recommend that leadership bandwidth is devoted to five issues he considers paramount in order to build businesses capable of outrunning change and being fit for the future. These five issues are values, innovation, adaptability, passion and ideology. Effective evolution doesn't demand the hand of deliberate design. In organizations, the idea of the survival of the fittest and the structural coupling view (where changes in other systems impact on the system in question) don't necessitate conscious strategy (Stacey, 2010). As Arie de Geus (in Senge, 1990: 4) said, the ability to learn faster than your competitors may be the only sustainable competitive advantage.

Leadership academic Professor Keith Grint (2010) suggests that tackling wicked problems necessitates unconventional organizational recipes. 'Elegant solutions', ie internally cohesive approaches, serve tame and critical problems well. Tame problems respond to the cohesion that comes from management thinking, while critical problems are typically served best by the order than comes from command. Grint feels that wicked problems need 'clumsy' solutions that go beyond internally coherent approaches. Clumsy solutions call for leadership rather than management, and the activity of 'bricoleurs' – people who can create using whatever materials are available. In our final chapter, we discuss the implications of discovery-led decision making on individual leaders.

References

Abrahamson, E (2000) Change without pain, *Harvard Business Review*, July–August

Baghai, M, Coley, S and White, D (1999) *The Alchemy of Growth*, Perseus, New York

BBC (2007) What we know about 'unknown unknowns', *BBC News*, 30 November, http://news.bbc.co.uk/1/hi/magazine/7121136.stm

Black, O (2016) Why middle managers matter, *Management Today*, June

Covey, S R (1989) *The 7 Habits of Highly Effective People: Powerful lessons in personal change*, Free Press, New York

Dodds, R, Manyika, J and Woetzel, J (2015) *No Ordinary Disruption: The four global forces breaking all trends*, Public Affairs, New York

Gratton, L (2014) *The Key*, McGraw-Hill Education, New York

Grint, K (2010) Wicked problems and clumsy solutions: the role of leadership, in *The New Public Leadership Challenge*, ed S Brookes and K Grint, 169–86, Palgrave Macmillan, London

Hamel, G (2012) *What Matters Now: How to win in a world of relentless change, ferocious competition and unstoppable innovation*, Jossey-Bass, San Francisco, CA

Handy, C (2002) *The Age of Unreason*, Arrow, London

Heath, C and Heath, D (2010) *Switch: How to change things when change is hard*, Random House Business, London

Heimans, J and Timms, H (2014) Understanding 'new power', *Harvard Business Review*, December

Kim, W C and Mauborgne, R (2005) *Blue Ocean Strategy*, Harvard Business School Press, Boston, MA

Lennon, J (1980) *Beautiful Boy* [although not an original quote]

McGrath, R G (2013) The end of competitive advantage, *European Business Review*, 7 November

Pedler, M, Burgoyne, J and Boydell, T (1991) *The Learning Company: A strategy for sustainable development*, McGraw-Hill, Maidenhead

Roberts, K (2016) Keynote address at the 2016 Institute of Directors' Convention.

Rumelt, R (2011) *Good Strategy, Bad Strategy: The difference and why it matters*, Crown, New York

Schoemaker, P and Gunther, R (2006) The wisdom of deliberate mistakes, *Harvard Business Review*, June

Scott, N (2014) Boardroom revolution, *Director*, 1 November

Senge, P (1990) *The Fifth Discipline: The art and practice of the learning organization*, Doubleday, London

Simmons, M (2013) If you want to go fast, go alone. If you want to go far, go together, *Forbes*, 22 July

Sinek, S (2011) *Start with Why: How great leaders inspire everyone to talk action*, Penguin, London

Smith, W K, Lewis, M W and Tushman, M L (2016) 'Both/and' leadership, *Harvard Business Review*, May

Stacey, R D (2010) *Strategic Management and Organisational Dynamics: The challenge of complexity (to ways of thinking about organisations)*, 6th edn, Financial Times/Prentice Hall, London

Stalk Jr, G and Iyer, A (2016) How to hedge your strategic bets: Make short-term investments to test opportunities, *Harvard Business Review*, May

Sull, D and Eisenhardt, K M (2015) *Simple Rules: How to survive in a complex world*, Houghton Mifflin Harcourt, Boston, MA

Sunstein, C R and Hastie, R (2014) Making dumb groups smarter: how can you avoid collective bias that may harm team dynamic?, *Harvard Business Review*, December

Surowiecki, J (2005) *The Wisdom of Crowds: Why the many are smarter than the few*, Abacus, London

The force that is you

10

O wad some Power the giftie gie us. To see oursels as ithers see us!
ROBERT BURNS

The achievements of an organization are the results of the combined effort of each individual. VINCE LOMBARDI

This concluding chapter seeks to bring together the implications of discovery-led decision making for individuals, extending the idea of leaders and their teams as bricoleurs tackling wicked problems (Grint, 2010). The term 'the force that is you' is a reminder of the power leaders have in relation to their organization's strategy. This is a power that can be wielded deliberately and sometimes unwittingly, but always with consequences.

Discovery-led decision making and tridexterity

The theme of this book is the interplay between the three modes – *frame*, *experiment* and *scale*. For leaders, this should mean an understanding of all three modes, how they relate to each other and how they differ. Hopefully, this can lead to tridextrous managers: people with not only the comprehension but also the skills to operate in all three modes. Whereas an individual leader's own area of responsibility might steer towards one of the three as a priority (eg the chief operations officer might pay closest attention to *scale*, or the intersection between *experiment* and *scale*), any lack of feel for the other modes (eg the lack of *frame* in the chief operating officer's repertoire) would limit the individual's value to the overall enterprise.

Frame

The essence of *frame* is arriving at the key question that is deserving of an answer. As eminent strategy professor Richard Rumelt pointed out, strategic issues are problems of induction, which means there is no formula into which to slot the numbers and derive the answer (Ricks, 2011). There are just data, and teams of people to make sense of those data.

We are seeing advances in technology leading to some decisions being automated, which has given rise to the concept of the self-tuning enterprise. Boston Consulting Group strategy consultant Martin Reeves and colleagues explain that decisions that once were the preserve of managers now belong to algorithms (Reeves, Zeng and Venjara, 2015: 121). Citing Google, Netflix, Amazon and Alibaba as examples, they noticed the emergence of 'a way for organizations to apply algorithmic principles to make frequent, calibrated adjustment to their business models – without direction from the top'. Computing power is eclipsing the value of people in routine decision making, but the need has perhaps never been greater for ample capability in non-routine decisions.

In Chapter 6 we saw how Kodak so nearly got it right. Harsh critics could say it managed to snatch defeat from the jaws of victory, presiding over the failure of the enterprise after it had accomplished pioneering work in the field of digital photography and taken a strong stake in online photo sharing before the market took off. The limiting factors were not Kodak's sense of enterprise but the assumptions the organization made when surveying the landscape. The belief that digital cameras required an equivalent resource and development base to film cameras made Kodak vulnerable to competitors that tacitly demonstrated this wasn't the case. The confidence that people would still want to have physical prints of their photos in a digital world limited the firm's ability to develop its investment in the photo-sharing website Ofoto. In neither situation was Kodak casual, but it is worth reflecting that in both cases the limiting assumptions are readily traced back to Kodak's cultural DNA. Two of the very qualities that enabled the firm to build a strong market and commercial position in film photography during pre-internet days became the blinkers that obscured an appropriate framing of the problem that Kodak faced. In business, as in business school, there is little reward for the correct answer to the wrong question.

As we've highlighted, we live in an era where the pace of technological development is probably eclipsing the pace at which enterprises can assimilate information and act. It's a moot point whether the last time the human race was subject to such insecurity was at the time of the Industrial Revolution or not; for most leaders the issue is the current situation. Over the past 40 years, strategists have encouraged business practitioners to contemplate and address the question 'What business are we in?' However, the current context has changed how that question ought to be addressed. In a VUCA environment, a voice of reason might point out that the better question is 'What business do we need to be in?'

Experiment

Following the framing of the question, the task moves to one of concocting and testing potential solutions. *Experiment* is about the ability to design and validate recipes relevant to a changing world. There is no single best way to experiment. Some invest heavily in research and development, while others prefer either to license or to acquire technologies and products developed by others. The common ground though is the organizational mindset to be applied when experiments are conducted. There is a degree of speculation, the absence of which would leave the enterprise ceding future market positions to its more intrepid competitors and playing catch-up. This point has been emphasized by several strategy commentators over recent years, including Chan Kim and Renée Mauborgne (2005) and Michael Raynor (2007), who have spoken of the value of businesses investing in and speculating with strategic options. While it is not a casual act, the search for what comes next is very difficult in a culture of operational efficiency, austerity or even blame.

The *experiment* mode of discovery-led decision making typically looks beyond the current business model: Horizon One in McKinsey's 'Three Horizons' model, which we introduced in Chapter 9 (Baghai, Coley and White, 1999). Our reflection, based on having worked with a variety of leadership teams in a range of sectors, is that the greatest challenge is in encouraging leaders to have a critical discussion that links Horizon Three (the future vision) to Horizon One (the current business model) through Horizon Two (the quest for the business model to succeed the current one). This challenge is so substantial because leaders a) are immersed in the current business model, b) see change and uncertainty relating to any new model, c) recognize that there can be significant structural and resource implications in moving the organization to this new horizon and d) see personal threat to their own positions in the move to a new world order. Deeper and more reflective conversations around long-term vision, Horizon Three, are typically well embraced by leaders. Incumbent leaders perceive Horizon Three ideas as low-threat. They can shoot the breeze and speculate as to what might happen, including pitching in with some off-the-wall ideas in the relative comfort that such events are unlikely to become real during their tenure. However, if leaders' strategic dialogue does not couple a visionary future with today's reality through a possibly uncomfortable consideration of Horizon Two and the search for the next business model, they may be condemning their enterprises to complacency and immobility.

Scale

For leaders, decisions around *scale* span the choice of what to take forward, how to move this from experimentation to operation, and then how to continue to develop a new business and management model as the market continues to evolve and the competitive landscape changes.

As Michael Raynor (2007) pointed out, it is difficult for an incumbent to change its business model successfully. Markets can shift so rapidly that evolutionary change is too slow and, as can be seen with the likes of HMV and Blockbuster, both of which failed from seemingly strong market positions, success in the current horizon can reduce the preparedness to change. 'Complacency' is probably too strong a word, but the leadership pitfall is a misplaced belief that good financial performance in the present is an indicator of a sound future strategy.

The second potential pitfall for a leader around the *scale* aspect of strategic decision making relates to organizational capabilities. While it is true that success in Horizon One with its current business model is likely to have generated valuable additions to its armoury in terms of money, market position and competencies, these are unlikely to be the full set of capabilities required to industrialize a new approach successfully. The enterprise, under the custodianship of its leaders, needs to be candid about what additional capabilities it needs in order to take a fledgling idea to full fruition.

Awareness and beyond

It would be easy to see the application of discovery-led decision making as a passive form of categorization, with leaders reflecting upon how their own activities fit with the three modes in the framework. To do this demands the skill of accurate diagnosis, the result of which may help leaders guide their teams' endeavours well in the short run. Once the 'Where does this fit?' muscle is toned and developed, the more important consideration is how to move beyond awareness, such that there is individual influence on the pacing of the strategy process. This may involve accelerating the move to action, in order to generate experience and data. It might mean the prudent choice of measures, such that the shift from data to understanding is a quick one. It may also involve increasing the intensity by which the levers of strategy are pulled, thus incentivizing the enterprise to make the most of scalable opportunities.

Personal bias

In Chapter 2, we showed how part of the human condition was the presence of biases in decision making. The potential magnitude of this issue is well recognized. For example, Paul Schoemaker and Philip Tetlock (2016: 75) suggest that understanding cognitive biases is one of four considerations to improve forecasting ability.

While it is easy to see cognitive biases as a personal shortcoming, our main message is that such biases are a natural consequence of our evolution. A lot of biases and heuristics that present themselves in decision making are brilliant solutions to old problems, but not necessarily oriented to the current tasks in hand. For example, we are typically more readily disposed to bad news than good. Historically this has helped us learn and in some cases survive through the ability to sense danger quickly. But this characteristic can limit our ability to see opportunities rather than threats in change.

We usually make ourselves known to others through our behaviour. This 'tip of the iceberg' is the visible manifestation of our mindsets. Personality and attitude sit below the waterline and out of direct sight, along with unconscious bias. Biases can mean we systematically veer off in the wrong direction. We can make wrong decisions without even realizing.

We looked at cognitive biases in relation to how we process information automatically. These include: being drawn to the familiar; taking instinctive short cuts when needing to analyse objectively; an overconfidence in our estimates; a disposition to confirming what we currently believe; an aversion to risk when in a position of apparent strength; and inflated risk appetite when under pressure. We also commented on people's unconscious biases in relation to other people. For example, this may be due to perceptions around gender, ethnicity, age and disability. Other predilections are also present. These have the impact of making us prize or discredit information according to its source. While people might see themselves as immune from such susceptibilities, a multitude of research studies show otherwise. The point about these heuristics and biases is that we're not necessarily aware of them.

Leaders can approach the management of bias in several ways. In some cases, it can be helpful to be aware of the bias, raising it to a conscious level. The problem here is twofold. First, how do we know whether we're susceptible to a particular bias or not? Second, even when we're aware of the bias, it's still likely to remain as part of our automatic response to a situation.

Beyond awareness, leaders can work on approaches that slow decision making down to counter the dominance of instinctive reactions. Our clients who have achieved this have used tactics like:

- Single-item discussions – giving decisions the time and attention they need by avoiding cramped agendas and instead having focused single-item discussions.

- Timing for decisions – avoiding seeking decisions when energy is low and distractions are high. The times when this is most likely include right at the end of the working day and at the end of the working week.

- Avoiding unfettered decisions by limiting the scope any individual has to make a decision (for example by spending limits, or a 'four eyes' policy).

- Stimulating the exploration of options, to counter the tendency to settle on the first practical way forward considered.

- Avoiding being bounded by false deadlines in decision making. Deadlines are known to help drive an issue forward, but acceleration can be a flawed concept, as it can truncate deliberation. All too often, deadlines are arbitrary points in time without real grounding on a timeline that is truly critical to the enterprise.

- Making recommendations for ratification – treating conversations as leading not to decisions to be implemented but towards recommendations to be decided upon, either at a later date or by a different group.

- Seeking diversity of perspectives through the use of colleagues as sounding boards, critical friends or devil's advocates. The vocalization of a thought process and associated intended decision is more likely to engage the rational part of the brain than the auto-pilot unconscious, helping avoid ideas being glossed over, much in the same way that proofreading out loud works better than proofreading silently.

- Expecting to have a period of reflection – often sleeping on it overnight – after a major decision is made, and to consider not just the decision made but also the process by which the decision was made.

- Giving attention to the environment in which decisions are to be made, recognizing the subtle impact the setting can have on the way that people view information and assign priorities.

Chapter 9 looked at organizational correctives: the steps the enterprise can put in place to help strategic decisions be made more capably. The ideas above though are very much in the gift of the individual leader, and how she or he can interrupt the unconscious default approach.

Leaders as situational architects

One of the themes we've pursued is the difference between two types of strategic decision – top-down and middle-out. The former type is usually what people refer to when they think about strategic decision making (senior people weighing up options and making a choice). The latter however may be even more powerful. As strategic execution is an assimilation of the actions that an organization takes, so much of strategy is a consequence of the seemingly small decisions that each person makes every day, in the moment. While these may not be seen as strategic decisions per se, their cumulative impact on strategy is potentially immense. Strategy, as we've said earlier, is what happens when you're not in the room.

The role of the leader here is to create the environment in which good decision making can take place. Leaders, through their own actions, create the weather for their teams. The actions of leaders give organizational permission for certain courses of action and prevent others. The behaviour of the Wells Fargo bank in the United States and the cross-selling scandal that led to the dismissal of 1 per cent of its work force, after the bank's community banking division was found guilty of exploiting relationships with vulnerable people in an attempt to hit strategic targets (see Chapter 4), is a case in point. The question leaders should continually ask themselves is: 'What have I done or not done to cause this?' While not making the decision directly, the leader is indirectly influential and responsible for the decision taken.

The reality distortion field

So far, we've encouraged readers along a path where the minimization of bias in decision making is a good thing. The 'reality distortion field' relates to the deliberate use of heuristics in decision making to influence a preferred course of action. Co-creator of the original Macintosh computer Andy Hertzfeld remembers the term being used at Apple. Its origin is attributed to the *Star Trek* science fiction television show, and described how aliens created their own new world through mental force (Hertzfeld, 1981).

Our assumption here is that this preferred course is the most advantageous for the organization, and leaders see their main duty as galvanizing support for it. This is akin to the symbolic leadership of Admiral Nelson at the Battle of Copenhagen, which we discussed in Chapter 2. In full view of his crew, he raised his telescope to his blind eye and reported he couldn't see the signal that was calling on him to end the action and retreat.

Here the leader becomes a situational architect and uses an understanding of influencing skills to help muster support. In many respects, the cognitive biases – specifically those we've looked at earlier – could well be part of the mix. Throughout this book we've spoken about the value of being aware of biases and the use of organizational correctives to mitigate their effects. But in situations where leaders have to resort to improvisational bricolage, where people are being encouraged to produce extraordinary results from the materials to hand and imperfect information, cognitive biases can provide the basis for the 'delusions' that might be helpful in giving people, for example, the (over)confidence to remain buoyant as they repeatedly 'fail fast'. Overconfidence can be used to help get people to try crazy experiments and pick themselves up when the experiments don't go to plan. The vividness of representativeness bias can be used to help communicate a vision through 'unrepresentative' – but vivid and engaging – story telling. Powerful organizational visions are stories and pictures painted, rather than a solely rational assessment of probability.

Work in the field of influence and persuasion also demonstrates that 'riffing' on human quirks might contribute to the creation of reality distortion fields. Psychology professor Robert Cialdini's research (2006, 2016) brings together the typical short cuts that people make in their decision making when they deviate from the path of a logical and conscious processing of data. Understanding these short cuts can help the leader frame information advantageously:

- *Reciprocity* – quite simply, we seek to repay those we owe. If someone does something for us that we consider valuable, it creates a credit in the bank of goodwill, which disposes us towards the reciprocal action. For the leader to take advantage of reciprocity, he or she should have first made the valuable gesture. Valuable doesn't mean expensive, but rather seen as valuable by the other party.

- *Social proof* – people are readily influenced by those they see as like themselves. People are pack animals, and those we see as members of our own tribe hold sway over the actions that we take. A leader may well draw attention to 'others out there' who faced a similar situation, and the course of action they took.

- *Commitment and consistency* – people typically act in a way consistent with their values and beliefs, and people also prefer to act in line with commitments they have chosen to make. These commitments may be modest, but they can also be seen as the first step along a trajectory where the first step almost predetermines the next. Organizations have seen this in the way that one initial decision sets in motion a pathway for activity that escalates. A leader may choose not to seek commitment on the endpoint, but aim for a more measured first step, seeing this as a disposition towards more substantial commitments as a result.

- *Liking* – people are more readily influenced by people they like. As well as the credentials of source bestowed on the influencer, part of the way in which this form of influencing works is the motivation to want to be liked in return and therefore a warmer disposition towards what the influencer is suggesting. Leaders may or may not be liked by those people they are seeking to influence, but they can focus energy on particular relationships to help accelerate the seeding of ideas.

- *Authority* – people can respond more positively to those with authority than those without. Leaders might have positional authority, but they might consider how authoritative they appear to those they are seeking to influence. Leaders might bolster the authority they are able to present by positioning themselves not as the source of the authority but the conduit by which the authority is communicated, using a 'higher authority' (real or constructed) as the weight behind an argument.

- *Scarcity* – people are disposed towards things they perceive as being in short supply. The subtext here is that whatever is in short supply is seen as valuable in the eyes of others (social proof) from whence the demand comes, and its scarcity is able to bestow privilege on those who move quickly and capably enough to secure it. Probably the most common forms of this are the use of deadlines or cut-off dates to drive behaviour and a 'first come, first served' approach.

- *Instant influence* – people typically favour that which gratifies immediately. The leader might craft an idea to present a modest but immediate reward, avoiding what might be seen as 'jam tomorrow', where the reward though attractive is around a future promise. We are also assisted by that which is easier to do. Here a leader might work on simplifying a course of action to make it easy for someone to follow. The phrase 'jumping through hoops' serves as a reminder to leaders that task difficulty deters application.

Approaching the subject of influence from a slightly different angle, neuroscientist David Rock explored the potential stress raisers that conspire against effective influence (Rock and Ringleb, 2013). Like Cialdini's work before him, Rock's research looked beyond the idea of a consciously rational approach to processing data, and much of what he found linked well with what we're reported above. Additional perspectives from Rock that leaders may find helpful as situational architects include the dangers of diminishing someone's perceived status when encouraging the person towards a particular course of action, and the value in presenting choice to people such that they feel they have autonomy. Rock also emphasized the importance of a sense of certainty in the field of influence. Our exploration of the psychology of change throughout this book has looked at people's general craving for certainty and how that can discriminate against moves beyond the familiar, even if the familiar is under threat. As family therapist Virginia Satir is reputed to have said, 'Most people prefer the certainty of misery to the misery of uncertainty.' A strident leader may boldly claim certainty of outcome as a means of mustering support. Where a leader is more circumspect, she or he may choose to base the certainty on the process (the steps to be taken) rather than the result. A leader might also invest in 'socializing' ideas well ahead of whenever a decision or a movement to action is sought, in order to reduce the effect of the 'new'. Familiarity breeds content.

Twenty-first-century attributes

The decisions that leaders take typically fall into two categories. The first is routine decisions where the process is guided by rules and procedures. The second is non-routine decisions that are made at the discretion of relevant decision makers. We've spoken about how routine decisions are increasingly the preserve of programs and algorithms where technology can apply sequence and logic more efficiently than is humanly possible. The implications of this are a shift in the way that leaders are valuable to their enterprises.

In her exploration of critical thinking, Holly Green (2012) described five critical thinking types. These are: critical thinking (objective analysis); implementation thinking (ability to organize ideas, plans and resources); conceptual thinking (seeing connections between abstract ideas); innovative thinking (generating new ideas and possibilities); and intuitive thinking (the ability to take what you sense to be true and, in the absence of evidence and knowledge, appropriately factor it into the decision). Leaders may already sense a shift in focus. The future looks to favour an increased capability in more abstract critical thinking styles. With software replacing our left brains in carrying out logical and sequential work, the more valuable critical thinking is probably the non-linear, simultaneous, contextually sensitive and big-picture types. As Daniel Pink (2006) put it, right-brainers will rule the future. Metacognition, whereby leaders are self-aware and possess higher-order skills in which they can think about their thinking, is a valuable attribute in self-reflection and learning. Susan Sobbott, President of Global Payments at American Express, in *Director* magazine said: 'As managers and leaders we always want to have good data, good information and we want to think about things. When you're in a crisis you have to go with what you feel is the right thing to do, and hope you've made a good step in your navigation and correct if you don't' (Dunnett, 2014: 74).

Flexing mental muscles in this way should probably be seen as a useful personal development pathway for leaders. For example, we have one client who instigates what he refers to as a 'potato call' with his team. He brings his team together and invites them to 'throw potatoes' at an idea or proposition as a means of stress-testing or challenging it.

Hand in hand with the recalibration of what an effective contribution to decision making looks like, the qualities deemed particularly useful to someone seeking to flourish in a contemporary work environment need to be similarly redefined. Leadership expert Claudio Fernández-Aráoz, writing in *Harvard Business Review*, draws attention to the core issue:

> What makes someone successful in a particular role today might not tomorrow if the competitive environment shifts, the company's strategy changes, or he or she must collaborate with or manage a different group of colleagues. So the question is not whether your company's employees and leaders have the right skills; it's whether they have the potential to learn new ones.
>
> (Fernández-Aráoz, 2014)

According to Fernández-Aráoz, the key qualities deemed to equip people better for the future are:

- *motivation*: a commitment to excel in pursuing unselfish goals;
- *curiosity*: a tendency to seek out new experiences and knowledge;
- *insight*: a knack for making sense of new information and assimilating it with existing knowledge;
- *engagement*: an ability to blend logic and emotion to communicate ideas richly; and
- *determination*: resilience in the face of setbacks.

These are offered as the foundation of future talent. These qualities seem to resonate with what might be useful in the contemporary context of uncertainty and complexity.

Within the UK Institute of Directors we see other valuable qualities for contemporary talent. These include humility, adaptability and connections with other people (Mark Granovetter's 1973 'strength of weak ties' idea, which we discussed in Chapter 6). The overall picture is that of a shift from what might be seen as traditional attributes such as personal motivation, drive and resilience towards less 'channelled' qualities that lend themselves more to shifting contexts. This is encouraging leaders to develop 'adaptive capacity' with the resilience to adapt as the environment and circumstances change. In an era when the experts' knowledge has less relevance, personal qualities such as curiosity, adaptability, humility and connections help equip the leader with the skills to engage better with the changing world and figure out possible solutions first-hand. The implications for leaders are twofold. First, do leaders see these qualities in themselves? Second, how do leaders create the experiences where these qualities can be nurtured in themselves and those with whom they work?

Shifting towards distributed leadership: throwing down the challenge

In an era when strategic success is shifting away from dominance at the level of the individual organization, and towards more collaborative approaches where strategic success sits more readily with enterprises working together (for example as parts of a supply chain), so too is the tone of leadership. In a world that favours joint initiative, leadership approaches that embrace the importance of relationships and have a focus extending beyond the boundaries of the enterprise are emerging as fitter for purpose. Individual supremacy is replaced by a more distributed approach to leadership under which collaboration can flourish. As history demonstrates, it is difficult for humans voluntarily to relinquish power and place it in the hands of others. So, while the idea of distributed leadership might be readily understood, its translation to practice is more hampered by human traits than supported by them.

This final implication is a challenge thrown down. In a VUCA world beset by wicked problems, as decision making shifts from top-down towards middle-out, the final question is: what can each individual leader do to positively influence her or his organization's ability not only to respond but to thrive? For this approach to be transformed from intriguing ideas to compelling reality, leaders will need to think differently and act differently on a repeated basis. This, like strategy, is a journey. As strategy explorers ourselves, we find it is a journey we're able, like you, to travel and experience first-hand.

Figure 10.1   Strategic decision making – enjoy the journey

References

Baghai, M, Coley, S and White, D (1999) *The Alchemy of Growth*, Perseus, New York

Burns, R (1786) To a louse: on seeing one on a lady's bonnet, at church [poem]

Cialdini, R B (2006) *Influence: The psychology of persuasion*, rev edn, Harper Business, New York

Cialdini, R B (2016) *Pre-Suasion: A revolutionary way to influence and persuade*, Simon & Schuster, New York

Dunnett, R (2014) Susan Sobbott, American Express, *Director*, 1 November

Fernández-Aráoz, C (2014) The future of talent is potential, *Harvard Business Review*, June

Granovetter, M S (1973) The strength of weak ties, *American Journal of Sociology*, **76** (3), 1360–80

Green, H (2012) How to develop five critical thinking types, *Fortune*, May

Grint, K (2010) Wicked problems and clumsy solutions: The role of leadership, in *The New Public Leadership Challenge*, ed S Brookes and K Grint, 169–86, Palgrave Macmillan, London

Hertzfeld, A (1981) Reality distortion field, https://www.folklore.org/StoryView.py?story=Reality_Distortion_Field.txt

Kim, W C and Mauborgne, R (2005) *Blue Ocean Strategy*, Harvard Business School Press, Boston, MA

Pink, D (2006) *A Whole New Mind: Why right-brainers will rule the world*, Riverhead Books, New York

Raynor, M (2007) *The Strategy Paradox*, Doubleday, New York

Reeves, M, Zeng, M and Venjara, A (2015) The self-tuning enterprise, *Harvard Business Review*, June

Ricks, T (2011) Rumelt on enterprise (VI): a real strategy is made more by induction than deduction, *Foreign Policy*, 25 October

Rock, D and Ringleb, A (2013) *Handbook of NeuroLeadership*, CreateSpace Independent Publishing Platform

Schoemaker, P J H and Tetlock, P E (2016) Superforecasting: how to upgrade your company's judgment, *Harvard Business Review*, May

INDEX

Note: bold page numbers indicate figures.